GLOBALIZATION AND SOVEREIGNTY

GLOBALIZATION

Series Editors

Manfred B. Steger

Royal Melbourne Institute of Technology and University of Hawai'i–Mānoa

and

Terrell Carver

University of Bristol

"Globalization" has become *the* buzzword of our time. But what does it mean? Rather than forcing a complicated social phenomenon into a single analytical framework, this series seeks to present globalization as a multidimensional process constituted by complex, often contradictory interactions of global, regional, and local aspects of social life. Since conventional disciplinary borders and lines of demarcation are losing their old rationales in a globalizing world, authors in this series apply an interdisciplinary framework to the study of globalization. In short, the main purpose and objective of this series is to support subject-specific inquiries into the dynamics and effects of contemporary globalization and its varying impacts across, between, and within societies.

Globalization and Sovereignty
John Agnew

Globalization and War
Tarak Barkawi

Globalization and Human Security
Paul Battersby and Joseph M. Siracusa

Globalization and American Popular Culture
Lane Crothers

Globalization and Militarism
Cynthia Enloe

Globalization and Law
Adam Gearey

Globalization and Feminist Activism
Mary E. Hawkesworth

Globalization and Postcolonialism
Sankaran Krishna

Globalization and Social Movements
Valentine Moghadam

Globalization and Terrorism
Jamal R. Nassar

Globalization and Culture, Second Edition
Jan Nederveen Pieterse

Globalization and International Political Economy
Mark Rupert and M. Scott Solomon

Globalisms, Third Edition
Manfred B. Steger

Rethinking Globalism
Edited by Manfred B. Steger

Globalization and Labor
Dimitris Stevis and Terry Boswell

Globaloney
Michael Veseth

 Supported by the Globalization Research Center at the University of Hawai'i, Mānoa

GLOBALIZATION AND SOVEREIGNTY

JOHN AGNEW

ROWMAN & LITTLEFIELD PUBLISHERS, INC.
Lanham • Boulder • New York • Toronto • Plymouth, UK

ROWMAN & LITTLEFIELD PUBLISHERS, INC.

Published in the United States of America
by Rowman & Littlefield Publishers, Inc.
A wholly owned subsidary of The Rowman & Littlefield Publishing Group, Inc.
4501 Forbes Boulevard, Suite 200, Lanham, Maryland 20706
www.rowmanlittlefield.com

Estover Road, Plymouth PL6 7PY, United Kingdom

British Library Cataloguing in Publication Information Available

Library of Congress Cataloging-in-Publication Data

Agnew, John A.
    Globalization and sovereignty / John Agnew.
      p.   cm.— (Globalization)
    Includes bibliographical references and index.
    ISBN-13: 978-0-7425-5677-5 (cloth : alk. paper)
    ISBN-10: 0-7425-5677-8 (cloth : alk. paper)
    ISBN-13: 978-0-7425-5678-2 (pbk. : alk. paper)
    ISBN-10: 0-7425-5678-6 (pbk. : alk. paper)
    [etc.]
      1. Sovereignty.   2. Globalization—Political aspects.   I. Title.
JC327.A485   2009
320.1′5—dc22
                                     2009000699

Printed in the United States of America

♾ ™ The paper used in this publication meets the minimum requirements of American National Standard for Information Sciences—Permanence of Paper for Printed Library Materials, ANSI/NISO Z39.48-1992.

CONTENTS

PREFACE

A popular story today is that state sovereignty is in worldwide eclipse in the face of an overwhelming process of globalization. The central argument of this book is that this story relies on ideas about sovereignty and globalization that are both overstated and misleading. In the first place, sovereignty, the electromagnetic-like charge of state control and authority across an operational zone, is not necessarily neatly contained territorially state-by-state in the way it is usually thought. Nor has it ever been so. Yet, the dominant image of globalization is the replacement of a presumably territorialized world by one of networks and flows that know no borders other than those that define the earth as such. So, in challenging this image, I must trace the ways in which it has become commonplace. Beyond that, however, I also try to develop a way of thinking about the geography of sovereignty, the various forms in which sovereignty actually operates in the world, to offer an intellectual framework that breaks with the either/or thinking of state sovereignty versus globalization.

The term *sovereignty* emerged out of a Western religious context in which sovereignty was first vested in the Roman polis and then the Roman Emperor and later in a monotheistic God represented on the earth by the Pope and the Church. The intellectual descent of sovereignty has been central to European political debate from the Middle Ages to the present. In one sense it is intimately connected to the moralizing of the universe characteristic of all of the three great monotheistic religions. As I hope to show, it has long had a defining role in designating those inside and those outside of various political projects. But it has also been a powerful underpinning of thinking about the limits and potentials of statehood, even when it loses its more obvious religious connotation.

The first chapter lays out some of the main elements of the argument of the book, paying particular attention to what I term the "myths" of globalization that underwrite the transformative view of the present and to the alternative geographies of control and authority that are at work in the world beyond just the state-territorial one that has tended to dominate modern thinking about statehood. Much writing about globalization seems based on the premise that one rarely achieves fame by virtue of understatement. The second chapter discusses the three sovereignty "myths"—the body-politic metaphor, the nation-hyphen-state, and the sovereignty "game"—that buttress the territorialized vision of state sovereignty. In a third chapter I lay out an alternative way of thinking about sovereignty, based on identifying a set of four "sovereignty regimes" (what I call the classic, integrative, globalist, and imperialist) that portray the actual relationships of authority and control; what I term, when they are considered together, "effective sovereignty" and how the various combinations of regimes have worked historically over the past two hundred years. The fourth chapter uses the examples of exchange-rate arrangements between currencies and immigration and citizenship policies to illustrate the workings of the sovereignty regimes in the contemporary world. A final chapter briefly surveys the ways in which state territories do and do not matter for politics today and suggests that globalization, rather than producing a homogenized world, is in fact deeply differentiating in its effects on different places and, hence, cannot be expected anytime soon to give rise to a single worldwide model of sovereignty.

The argument of this book has benefited from the contributions of a number of people other than the author. I would particularly like to thank Merje Kuus, who provided much of the impetus and many of the ideas for the first part of chapter 3 when we were collaborating on a book chapter. More generally, and perhaps unbeknownst to them, Heriberto Cairo, Mathew Coleman, Monica Varsanyi, Emilio Piazzini, Kal Raustiala, Wes Reisser, Henry Sivak, Iñigo Errejón Galván, and Benno Teschke have helped me in various ways, explicitly and implicitly, to sharpen some of the specific ideas and clarify my overall perspective. I am also grateful to my partner, Felicity, and to my daughters, Katie and Christine, for their long-standing moral and intellectual support. Finally, my mother, Anne MacPhail Agnew, died as I was working on the final stages of this book. I dedicate it to her memory.

CHAPTER 1

GLOBALIZATION AND STATE SOVEREIGNTY

Sovereignty is a word with an ambiguous legacy. On one side it can stand for a claim to popular democratic legitimacy vested in a territorial state, while on the other it can represent the often violent origins of such statehood and the masking of its genesis in the necessity to defend a state and its territory against enemies both internal and external. Today it is often said to face a challenge from a globalization that is allegedly undercutting the very territorial base upon which its ambiguous legacy has presumably always rested. But for many scholars and more popularly, *sovereignty* has a primal status as a term that underpins and gives permanence to the flitting everyday politics that they see around them and in which they are involved. Claims to sovereignty provide the linguistic coin in which both domestic and international politics are transacted. Without sovereignty bonded to territory, everything else—meaningful politics; effective administration; a way of dividing up, representing, and mapping the world politically—seems to "melt into air."[1]

This book attempts to tell a rather different story about sovereignty. While accepting the reality of a recent upturn in globalization and its potential to undermine the presumed political monopoly exercised by states over their territories, it questions the ready association between sovereignty and territory. States have never exercised either total political or economic-regulatory monopolies over their territories. Sovereignty talk is also often simply that. Indeed, some states, perhaps a majority, may have aspired to exert sovereignty in some respect or other but have never entirely succeeded in doing so. Thus, rather than a linear story about recent globalization undermining a long-established state territorial sovereignty, I want to emphasize how globalization has merely further complicated an already complex relationship between sovereignty and territory. Rather than the "victory" of Adam Smith's vision of an open world over Thomas Hobbes's conception of Leviathan (the state) and a patchwork of sovereign spaces, these prophets are still competing for whose trumpet will sound the final note in the struggle between each worldview and its associated modus operandi.

The problem is that until recently, with the rise of talk about globalization, the typical debate has been between imperialistic and anarchistic readings of world order that "either place too much control over events in a dominant power or reduce the world to a quasi-autonomous system exerting restraints on sovereign states."[2] Although both sides can agree that sovereignty is the extension and institutionalization of control and authority within a spatial field, they differ profoundly on the nature of this field; specifically, a larger space versus a set of mutually exclusive territories. However, while the uneven distribution of power is undoubtedly a feature of the world (today and previously) and some states do obviously exert authority in various domains within specific territories, there is also evidence for a changing global context in which "sovereignty is migrating from states—where it was never entirely anchored—to a loosely assembled global system."[3] Neither imperialistic nor anarchistic readings of world order offer the purchase on it, either separately or together, that they once seemed to.

Four specific examples illustrate the historically based and thus by no means novel complexity of sovereignty that I will emphasize in this book. The first concerns a London court case about charges of asset stripping in a metals smelter in the Central Asian country of Tajikistan. Remember the case of Jarndyce versus Jarndyce in Dickens's great novel *Bleak House*, a court case that went on interminably in London's High Court of Chancery? That concerned the simple disposition of an English legal estate. This case also seems destined to last for some time (as of summer 2008), not least because, as Dickens was keen to suggest in his time, the lawyers have a financial stake in interminability. Talco, the state-owned aluminum smelter, is suing both its former director and its supplier of alumina for defrauding it through a profit-skimming arrangement. None of the parties seemingly disputes the jurisdiction of the English court; an obscure English business consultancy is also one of the defendants and provides the prima facie grounds for why an English court has jurisdiction. The case has now become one of the most expensive in English legal history. The suit is projected to generate as much as 85 million pounds sterling ($170 million) in legal fees, about 4.6 percent of Tajikistan's 2007 gross domestic product. If Talco loses, under the English "loser pays" system the business will be stuck with all of the legal costs, including those of all of the defendants.

So, three thousand miles away from the site in question and under a foreign jurisdiction, a legal case of major importance to Tajikistan—the smelter is one of the country's only major industrial assets—will be eventually determined. This example indicates several features of contemporary sovereignty and globalization. One is that London is a global center in litigation because of its specialized law firms and the reputation of its courts. This reflects the prior history of London as the seat of both the British Empire and the hegemony that Britain once exercised over the world economy and still does as an "offshore" center of banking and finance under contemporary globalization. But it also suggests, of course, that Tajikistan, "independent" from the former Soviet Union since 1992, has only a nominal sovereignty in many respects over its own territory. Other actors have varying degrees of effective control over its territory. Even authority can be outsourced. Indeed, the decision of a London court can have greater legitimacy, because it is plausibly based on greater transparency, than more local ones.

The second example involves the mobility of the headquarters of big multinational corporations searching out the best tax regime for their activities. It is a commonplace that multinational companies now move their headquarters (and sometimes their plants and offices) to exploit lighter tax regimes and avoid harsher ones. Thus, in recent years Kraft, Google, and Yahoo have all switched their European headquarters from Britain to Switzerland. This tax avoidance example is a more novel case than that of the court suit (foreigners have been suing one another in English courts for many years), not simply because multinational and global companies as non-state actors have acquired increased powers to distribute capital and challenge government policies over the past half century. It also represents a trend in which bigger, presumably "more" sovereign states are now just as vulnerable to decisions by other actors as smaller but presumably weaker states. They may be even more so because they have bigger budgets that they must finance to pay for services to larger dependent populations and for military competition with other large states. As a result, this trend has increased global economic competitiveness between state territories of all types. At one and the same time, therefore, this makes territorial jurisdictions both more important (in setting tax regimes, for instance) and less so (in opening them up to more competition than when businesses are less transnational) and initiates a sort of portable sovereignty on the part of multinational companies. They become the "deciders."

The third example concerns the breakdown of law and order in Mexico over the past ten years because of the struggle for territory between the country's three major drug cartels. These cartels are in effective control of large parts of the country from the Pacific Coast through the industrial heartland to the tourist centers of the Gulf Coast. It is no exaggeration to say that in many places they are more powerful than the government itself. Given the performance of the state on behalf of the interests of most Mexicans its absence may not be that great of a loss. With staggering incomes from drug smuggling to the United States, estimated anywhere between $8 billion and $23 billion, the gangs have better weapons than the police, can corrupt whomever they want, and do not hesitate to kill those who stand in their way. Between 2006 and 2008 close to four thousand people, including many innocent bystanders, were killed in inter-gang wars, with thousands more injured. Yet, the drug cartels are undoubtedly popular with many poor Mexicans; pop songs that celebrate their exploits, known as *narcocorridos*, are wildly successful, even as some of their singers have themselves become victims of the gangs. This weird form of "sovereignty" owes much to the changing nature of the drug business. The growth of the Mexican gangs is a direct result of the U.S. focus on eliminating the Colombian drug cartels. Since the 1990s, the U.S. government has focused on disrupting Colombian drug smuggling operations through the Caribbean and Central America. This created an opening for Mexican gangsters, who have enthusiastically filled the gap in supplying U.S. addicts. Though relatively few drugs are produced in Mexico, fully 90 percent of the cocaine and much of the heroin and marijuana consumed in the U.S. as of 2008 are shipped through Mexico. The gangs buy their weapons in the U.S. and recruit heavily among the ranks of Mexico's elite Special Forces. As with drug cartels in so many countries, they are a veritable "state within the state." They have corrupted every level of government, from local policemen to army generals to presidential aides. The U.S. War on Drugs, in giving priority to restricting the supply rather than demand for illicit drugs, has literally been complicit in undermining the territorial sovereignty (once again!) of its southern neighbor. If the film director Sergio Leone is correct (in *A Fistful of Dollars* and other films, all starring Clint Eastwood), before the drug business it was guns moving south and booze moving north that provided the incentives.

My final example is the story of a Palestinian businessman living in the West Bank town of al-Bireh who was informed by the government of Israel in early September 2006, through the medium of an employee of the Palestinian National Authority, the nominal government of the area, that he had a month to leave.[4] This Palestinian had been born in the United States but had moved back to the town from which his ancestors had come in the aftermath of the Oslo peace process in the early 1990s, but he had no right of return. This town was part of the territory captured by Israel during the 1967 War and has been occupied ever since by the Israel Defense Forces. Fortunately, because his wife was born on the West Bank, he could apply for residence on grounds of family unification. The application has been in course since 1994. In the interim, the businessman had to use his U.S. passport and temporary visas granted by Israel to enter and leave the West Bank. Finally, in summer 2006, he was given a final one-month extension to his visa. Though he was able to get a new visa after the extension of September 2006, he had to go to the Israeli embassy in Amman, Jordan, to receive it. The family unification process is still not resolved.

This is a far-from-unusual story from the present day or previous history and not just in the tortuous relationship between Israel and Palestine. Sovereignty, in this case relating to rights of residence in particular places, is contingent. Effectively Israel is sovereign in al-Bireh but its government now operates in tandem with the Palestinian National Authority, which itself has only nominal control over a small part of the West Bank, and none currently in Jerusalem or Gaza. Millions of economic migrants and refugees face similar situations wherever they happen to end up. This case is all the more poignant in that the people in question have long-standing ties to their current place of residence, which is usually thought of in conventional understanding of sovereignty as the guarantee not only of right of residence but of citizenship more broadly.

The complexities of these examples suggest that the trick in understanding globalization and sovereignty is to develop a way of thinking that moves away from the either/or framework—either absolute state territorial sovereignty or a globalized world without sovereignty—in which most opinion has been trapped. If Thomas Friedman (*The World Is Flat*) is perhaps the best known recent prophet of the latter, then much of what goes for analysis of world politics from the Council on Foreign Relations (as in the magazine *Foreign Affairs*) or in political science journals such as *International Security* is locked into the former. Moving beyond this opposition is the task of this book.

THINKING ABOUT EFFECTIVE SOVEREIGNTY

The sovereignty of states has long been viewed as both a source of inter- and intra-state conflict and a response to it. Among political theorists, most attention has been given to the relationship between sovereignty and political authority: in particular, that state sovereignty has arisen to legitimately enforce internal order and to protect against external threat. Recently, the grounding of this claim in relation to assumptions of international anarchy and equality between states has been subject to examination.[5] Indeed, across a number of fields—from law to sociology—there is a shared sense that the conventional understanding of sovereignty as unlimited and indivisible rule by a state over a territory and the people in it is in need of serious critical scrutiny.[6] But the conceptual connection between sovereignty and state territoriality has enjoyed limited systematic analysis. Implicit in all claims about state sovereignty as the quintessential form taken by political authority are associated claims about distinguishing a strictly bounded territory from an external world and thus fixing the territorial scope of sovereignty. Territoriality, the use of territory for political, social, and economic ends, is widely seen as a largely successful strategy for establishing the exclusive jurisdiction implied by state sovereignty.

But *effective* sovereignty is not necessarily so neatly territorialized. In a landmark essay on sovereignty and territoriality, Murphy distinguishes between de jure (legal) and de facto sovereignty to make this point.[7] This distinction, however, necessarily implies that there actually is a pure de jure sovereignty from which de facto sovereignty is a lapse or anomaly. My claim is that de facto sovereignty is all there is when power is seen as circulating and available rather than locked into a single centralized site such as "the state." The U.S. government, for example, has long refused to recognize a denial of rights to so-called enemy combatants from Afghanistan and elsewhere held at the U.S. base in Guantánamo Bay, Cuba, since 2001. The government claims that the base is not within its formal jurisdiction and thus not subject to judicial review by U.S. courts as to the constitutionality of holding people indefinitely without charge. But Guantánamo Bay is just one of a large chain of detention centers, an American gulag, which the CIA and U.S. military operate worldwide with scarcely a nod to local claims of territorial sovereignty. Indeed, local sovereignty is a mask that allows prisoners to be treated in ways that would be potentially subject to judicial review in the United States proper.

Remarkably, and subject to scarce commentary at the time or since, under a Military Order of 13 November 2001, President George W. Bush gave himself the right to detain any non-U.S. citizen anywhere in the world for as long as he chose if there was suspicion of involvement in anti-U.S. "terrorist activity." In the wake of so-called humanitarian crises, as in Somalia, Bosnia, and Kosovo, the U.S. and other governments (sometimes under the mantle of the United Nations) have also intervened militarily across the globe even when the states facing intervention have defended themselves against such "violations" of territorial sovereignty.[8] Invoking various imminent threats and dangers led to repeated military interventions and implantation of bases by the United States and the Soviet Union governments in states within their putative respective spheres of influence during the Cold War. More recently, the supposed threat to the territorial United States from "weapons of mass destruction" allegedly held by Iraq's government was the prima face reason for the U.S.-led invasion in 2003. But it was clear when the U.S. "handed back" sovereignty to an Iraqi-staffed government on 28 June 2004 that effective sovereignty remained up for grabs.[9] The possibility as of 2008 that the U.S. military will have sixty or so bases in Iraq for many years suggests that the government of Iraq will at best share sovereignty with an ostensibly foreign and occupying power for the indefinite future. The U.S. proposal in May 2008 to build a big prison in Afghanistan that would be under direct American control in perpetuity suggests that this process of decoupling chunks of territory from local state sovereignty is not simply specific to Iraq but part of the wider geographical logic of the so-called War on Terror. But it is not just Great Powers such as the United States that have an extended geographical reach. For example, through its heavy troop presence the Syrian government exercised tremendous leverage over the government of Lebanon for many years and even with its troops now withdrawn still exerts tremendous pressure over its weaker neighbor. Australia has intervened militarily in the face of political instability in various Pacific island states such as the Solomon Islands and Papua New Guinea.

Of potentially longer-term significance, the impact of globalization on states is felt not only in the challenge it poses to their overall or issue-specific authority but also in its consequences for the territorialization of sovereignty at all.[10] For example, to list just a few: the worldwide explosion in negative environmental externalities relating to pollution and global warming does not respect international boundaries; currencies, long seen as the badges of state sovereignty, are increasingly denationalized; many people hold citizenship in multiple states; borders are increasingly porous to flows of migrants and refugees without much costly state regulation well beyond and within the borders themselves; knowledge and innovation networks no longer honor national boundaries but are within firms and between universities that are no longer exclusively networked on a national basis; it is increasingly difficult to establish state origin for a large number of commodities in world trade as transnational corporations coordinate their production activities (supply chains) across multiple locations in different countries; a large number of public and private organizations (particularly NGOs) intervene, mediate, and engage in the provision of public goods (food aid, travel and health infrastructure, credit, etc.) across state boundaries; a supranational organization such as the European Union has the ability to enforce legislative and other changes in countries that aspire to join it; perhaps one of the most important political innovations of recent times, the al Qaeda terrorist network, works across state boundaries while exploiting the lack of territorial sovereignty exercised by some of its host states (such as Pakistan); privateers (in the form of private military contractors such as Blackwater and Halliburton licensed by powerful states) and pirates on the high seas off the coasts of Indonesia, Somalia, and Nigeria (often popular with local populations) have made serious comebacks that challenge the thesis that all modern states invariably monopolize the use of violence (legitimate or otherwise); organized crime is increasingly transnational even as it also is increasingly brazen in asserting its effective territorial control over large swathes of nominally sovereign states (such as Italy, Colombia, Russia, and Mexico); and judicial regulation within states increasingly involves reference to supranational courts (as with the European Union) or to the decisions of foreign ones (as in some U.S. Supreme Court decisions).

In other words, *effective sovereignty is not necessarily predicated on and defined by the strict and fixed territorial boundaries of individual states.* The negotiation and redefinition of power and authority in geographically complex ways suggest the need to change the terms of debate about sovereignty. The purpose of this book is to do so by (a) critically analyzing the conventional wisdom about sovereignty, paying particular attention to the expansion of sources of control and authority beyond states and the attenuation of territoriality as sovereignty's primary mode of geographical organization; (b) examining the historical and geographical incidence of different "sovereignty regimes" (capacities of states in different global situations to exercise sovereignty internally and externally); and (c) showing through the examples of the "geography of money," or how currencies operate around the world today, and the operation of modes of immigration regulation, how the sovereignty regimes have come to operate in recent years.

This book develops the concept of effective sovereignty to argue that any particular state necessarily participates in one or several sovereignty regimes that exhibit distinctive combinations of central state authority and territoriality.[11] Two basic conclusions, drawing from recent research in political geography and other fields, are that sovereignty is neither inherently territorial nor is it invariably state-based. This matters because so much modern political life has been invested in organizing politics in general and democracy in particular in relation to states. Here the emphasis lies in understanding the analytics of power rather than presuming the operations of an undifferentiated territorial sovereignty. From this perspective, sovereignty is made out of the circulation of power among a range of actors at dispersed sites rather than simply emanating outward from an original and commanding central point such as an abstracted "state." Michel Foucault captures something of this approach when he writes: "The state is nothing more than the mobile effect of a regime of multiple governmentalities," meaning that any given state is a centralized deposit of sovereign (police, military), disciplinary (including surveillance and punishment), and biopolitical (medico-corporeal, citizenship, entitlement) powers that while historically concentrated in governmental institutions are often exercised by and can be completely captured by other actors.[12] Rather than being top-down, therefore, in this understanding sovereignty is the emergent and contingent outcome of a myriad of transactions and governmentalities, only some of which need at any point in time be vested in a single central-ized state authority.[13]

In chapter 2 I provide a detailed review of dominant strands in writing about sovereignty, noting the emphasis typically given to sovereignty as a means of establishing central state authority and the lack of sustained at-tention as to why this should always entail a territorial definition of power and as to why states are its sole proprietors. The chapter is organized in terms of three "myths" of sovereignty, or powerful ideas about the work-ings of sovereignty, that have given it the strong association with territory that the book as a whole is calling into question—the body-politic meta-phor, the national-state ideal, and the presumption that all states exercise equivalent levels of sovereignty and have exclusive jurisdiction within their territories: the sovereignty game.

In chapter 3 I propose an alternative model of sovereignty to the domi-nant one by identifying four "sovereignty regimes" that result from distinc-tive combinations of the impacts of central state authority (despotic power), on the one hand, and state territoriality (the administration of in-frastructural power by states), on the other. By "regime" I mean a system of rule, not merely some sort of international protocol or agreement between putatively "equal" states. In this chapter I also examine the general trajec-tory of the combination of sovereignty regimes over time. A periodization of the historical incidence and geography of sovereignty regimes is used that traces combinations of them from the early nineteenth century to the present.

An empirical illustration of the arguments of the second and third chapters using the contemporary geography of currencies and modes of immigration flow and regulation constitutes the focus of chapter 4. Finally, a brief conclusion relates the story of sovereignty as written here as sug-gesting that the dominant Westphalian model of state sovereignty in politi-cal geography and international relations theory, named after the Treaty of Westphalia of 1648, deficient as it has long been for understanding the re-alities of politics, is even more inadequate today, not only for ignoring both the hierarchy of states and sources of control and authority other than states, but also because of its mistaken emphasis on the geographical ex-pression of that control and authority (under the ambiguous sign of "sover-eignty") as invariably and inevitably territorial.

In the rest of this introductory chapter, I first survey some present-day discussion about globalization and its implications for state sovereignty, laying out the dominant either/or mode of thinking that tends to prevail across the intellectual and political spectrum. Just as there are "myths" of sovereignty so there are "myths" of globalization that seem to have taken on a life of their own, not least that we live in a world that is becoming not just smaller and interconnected but also, according to some accounts of globalization, increasingly stateless. I then turn to an overview of how sovereignty has been regarded in the literatures of political geography and political theory. I pay particular attention to how understandings of world politics have tended to view sovereignty as either lodged entirely at the scale of the territorial state or "absent," presumably diffused across the myriad of actors associated with globalization but because no longer territorialized no longer to be named as sovereignty. I then lay out an alternative way of relating political power to geography than that represented by the conventional wisdom. The whole purpose of this book is to dispute the either/or approach to understanding the relationship between globalization and sovereignty by taking a geographical perspective that highlights the crucial but unexamined role of territory in most thinking about globalization and sovereignty. State sovereignty has long taken complex spatial forms involving both territory and space-spanning networks; these forms are made only more complex by the rise to prominence of that bundle of processes we label as globalization.

GLOBALIZATION VERSUS STATE SOVEREIGNTY?

What exactly is meant by "globalization"? For exposition purposes five "myths" or powerful and widely accepted or popular ideas about globalization can be distinguished. Myths are not simply fictions. Fictions are clear symbolic constructs. Myths are fictions that have lost this clarity. But my point is not to portray them as falsehoods but as ideas that are frequently exaggerated in terms of their novelty and/or simplicity about the way the world works. This has happened because globalization has been portrayed as involving a totally new ontology of world order. Lurking behind this claim to a totally new world order is a strong sense of a clean break with the past brought on by processes that have just happened rather than been chosen. That is to say, "Globalization rhetoric has taken on mythical propositions, in Roland Barthes's view of myth as the transformation of the cultural products of history into something apparently natural."[14] The focus here is above all in terms of what globalization is seen as signifying for sovereignty. Usage of the word itself first deserves some attention.

Talk about "globalization" is relatively new, dating back only to the late

1950s and early 1960s in languages such as English and French. But thinking globally is in fact much more deeply rooted in the experience of European imperialism and the associated beginnings of the European state system in the sixteenth century. The period between the sixteenth and eighteenth centuries was the time when the entire earth first became the framing for world politics as we know it today.[15] But this historical framing of the national by the global has been obscured because of its displacement in many academic and popular circles by thinking in terms of an entirely state-centered world. Ipso facto, the new globalization represents the first impact of the global on a previously state-centered world.

At first appearance, usage of *globalization* was relatively straightforward in referring to the global scale at which some transactions, particularly trade, were now taking place. From 1980 to 1995, however, the term was applied increasingly to the entire economic sphere in general and to the activities of multinational companies in particular. If among liberals this trend augured a world of free trade that knows no boundaries and from which all could benefit collectively, for the traditional left it conjured up the world imagined by Karl Marx in the *Communist Manifesto* in which the bourgeoisie was finally taking over the entire globe and capitalism was scaling up to the world as a whole. Not only a change of scale, then, but also a sense of the decomposition of a previous—state-based—order was now entailed by *globalization*. Since the mid-1990s use of the word has exploded. For example, the number of articles in the French daily newspaper *Le Monde* using the term *mondialisation* (the French equivalent of *globalization*) underwent its biggest single-year increases in 1995–1996 and 1998–1999.[16] Though waxing and waning since then, the level of usage still averages five to six times the level before 1995. The meaning has also expanded. Now it refers not only to a change in scale as the world effectively "shrinks" as a result of new transportation and communication technologies but also to an acceleration in the rate of change in scale across a range of transactions, the development of global finance, the changing nature of production (particularly the emergence of global production chains), and the weakening of national and international controls following the demise of the Bretton Woods monetary system in the 1970s. In just a few years globalization has become one of the central "paradigms" in the social sciences.[17]

To oversimplify for the sake of clarification of a hugely complex set of issues, I would say that the recent usage has usually involved reference to one or more of five "myths" of globalization. As I have said previously, I am not contending that these are empirical falsehoods but, rather, that they are systematic exaggerations of the degree to which the world has changed in recent years. As a result, they have contributed to the "either/or" thinking that has affected much contemporary writing about state sovereignty. To one degree or another, however, each does have some insight about what has changed and in what ways. So the discussion is not just simply negative. There is some empirical veracity to many of the claims associated with the myths. This is why they all have a prima facie plausibility.

The first myth is that the world is "flat." Associated above all with the American journalist Thomas Friedman, this perspective sees the world as an increasingly undifferentiated investment surface in which trade and investment flow (or will soon) relatively unhindered from place to place. Certainly, the barriers to trade and investment are much diminished in recent years as compared, say, to the 1940s and 1950s. Much of this is the result of international trade agreements and the rise of global capital markets since the late 1960s. The impressive economic growth of China and other Asian countries in large part because of explosive growth in exports and foreign direct investment is startling evidence for Friedman's claim. The decline in transport costs as an element in the final cost of goods and services, as a result of containerization, rapid telecommunications, and computerized inventories, is central to this globalization of production. Whether this energy-intensive mode of production is indefinitely sustainable in light of dramatic increases in oil prices and measures to mitigate the increases in carbon output responsible for global warming, remains to be seen. Unfortunately, the corollary that Friedman sees as following from this trend in the diffusion of production, the decreased relevance of states to the world order, does not follow. Indeed, China's very economic success has had much to do with its state-organized response to new global opportunities rather than being a simple outcome of increased free trade *tout court*. Relatively weak but poor states have had nothing like the economic success of the relatively strong but poor ones. In addition, not only is much of the world's income still heavily concentrated in the so-called developed world (55 percent of world GDP as of 2005 was accounted for by the G7 countries—the same share as in 1980), there are still very important returns to the spatial concentration of economic activities, particularly creative ones, in places—such as world cities and established industrial districts—with agglomeration economies of one sort or another. Efforts at measuring globalization by country, typically global integration, show that by and large small states tend to rank ahead of larger ones. Much of the world, particularly in Africa, the Middle East, and Latin America, remains effectively unintegrated, in terms of investment by multinational companies, political engagement, and personal contact. Some countries that have "opened up," Argentina most famously, have suffered mainly negative consequences for their efforts (table 1.1; figure 1.1).[18] *The World Is Flat* is a great book title, but it does little justice to how the world still really works.[19]

The second myth is that globalization as we are experiencing it is entirely new. The sense of a largely state-based world such as seems to have prevailed throughout much of the twentieth century has produced a strong contrast with what has been going on, particularly the economic emergence of the global scale, since the 1970s. The fact that most of the major political ideologies of the twentieth century—Communism, Fascism, and Social Democracy—were state-centric has reinforced the image of a whole new world emerging, particularly among those intellectuals raised during the inter-war and the immediate post–Second World War periods. That these ideologies have all run into trouble for a wide array of reasons makes them nevertheless often seem out of kilter with a "globalizing world." As numerous historians and geographers have been quick to point out, however, the world has been somewhere near here before. Since the sixteenth century states have always been part and parcel of an evolving world economy that, if recently becoming more interdependent, has long been global rather than national in many of its essential operations.[20] More particularly, the late nineteenth century was a period of dramatic increases in worldwide trade and of increasingly interdependent capital markets. Such major innovations of the late nineteenth century as the steamship, the telephone, and the submarine cable were perhaps even more revolutionary in their effects on reducing the impact of distance on transactions than recent ones

Table 1.1. The Top Twenty Countries in Globalization Ranked According to the A.T. Kearney/Foreign Policy Magazine Globalization Index (2003)

1. Ireland	7. Canada	13. Norway	19. Israel
2. Switzerland	8. Austria	14. Portugal	20. Spain
3. Sweden	9. United Kingdom	15. Czech Republic	
4. Singapore	10. Finland	16. New Zealand	
5. Netherlands	11. United States	17. Germany	
6. Denmark	12. France	18. Malaysia	

Source: A.T. Kearney Inc./Foreign Policy Magazine Third Annual Globalization Index, 2003. www.foreignpolicy.com.

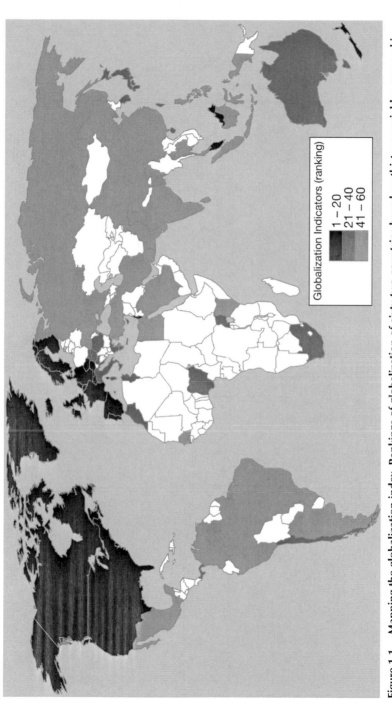

Figure 1.1. Mapping the globalization index. Rankings of globalization of sixty-two countries based on thirteen variables grouped in four categories: economic integration, personal contact, technology, and political engagement, mapped in three groupings: most globalized (1–20 plus Belgium and Iceland not included in original ranking), intermediate (21–40), and least globalized (41–60). Other countries are not included because of insufficient data or total absence of data indicative of globalization.

Source: A.T. Kearney Inc./Foreign Policy Magazine Third Annual Globalization Index, 2003. www.foreignpolicy.com.

Globalization Indicators (ranking)

1 – 20
21 – 40
41 – 60

such as the shipping container and the fax. At the same time, this was also a period of increasingly vibrant internationalist political activity and of growing cosmopolitanism in the arts and culture.

Now, as if we needed reminding, this all ended abruptly and badly in 1914. The point here is that we tend to emphasize what happened next but not what came before. As Saskia Sassen argues, however, the particular "assemblages" of institutional arrangements, technologies, and social logics at work in different periods are not simple replicates of earlier ones. Thus, contemporary globalization, growing out of a previous period that was more state-centered, has depended to a degree on that very state-centrism. States have had to open themselves up just as previously they had closed themselves down. As she puts it: "A good part of globalization consists of an enormous variety of micro-processes that begin to denationalize what had been constructed as national—whether policies, capital, political subjectivities, urban spaces, temporal frames. . . . Much of the writing on globalization has failed to recognize these types of issues and has privileged outcomes that are self-evidently global."[21]

Contemporary globalization is also often merged with the overlapping but hardly analogous idea of liberalization (usually under the label of neoliberalism to distinguish it from classical nineteenth-century liberal thought). This third myth is important because it implies that globalization has at root a singular ideological inspiration: to replace states with markets. From this viewpoint, globalization is a movement rather than a process. Of course, the 1980s did see the emergence in many developed countries, particularly the U.S. and Britain, of a politics committed to reducing taxes, rolling back the influence of the state over domestic economies, privatizing state assets, and replacing state mandates with charitable initiatives. Through their influence in international organizations such as the International Monetary Fund and the World Bank, the governments of these countries also tried to spread the ideas they were busy imposing at home. There is no doubt that these ideological practices have had a serious impact on the course of globalization. They have particularly enhanced the role of financial services within the world economy and reduced the capacity of poor states to use protectionist measures to develop their own industries. Certainly, since the 1980s a sort of "market populism," to use a term of Thomas Frank's, has been used to justify massive disinvestment from some places and equally massive reinvestment elsewhere, all in terms of a twisted logic that "since markets express the will of the people, virtually any criticism of business could be described as an act of despicable contempt for the common man."[22] That this all seems ludicrous looking back from the global financial collapse of 2008–2009, when the financial products of the 1980s and 1990s—derivatives, structured debt instruments, etc.—all finally came home to roost, should not detract from understanding the ideological confusion of democracy (the will of the people) and markets (a mechanism for setting prices) that became commonplace, particularly in the United States and Britain. Because of the ideological association with globalization, said confusion could well write that term's epitaph in the years ahead.

But beyond these influences, it is clear that globalization has several aspects to it that have had nothing much to do with neo-liberalism. For one thing, it is those states that have mobilized their resources in pursuit of economic growth that have been the most successful. The so-called sovereign wealth funds from these countries (e.g. Singapore, China, Kuwait, Abu Dhabi, etc.) now represent major state-based operators within the world economy. But countries that have been successful have also been able to flourish because of the many technological changes that have made possible the out-sourcing and off-shoring endemic to contemporary production. Many of these, such as the shipping container and the Internet, date from before 1970 or have their roots in U.S. military research. Finally, globalization, in the sense of increased reliance on markets and consumer capitalism, is not simply an ideological projection invented in the 1970s (or the victory of a school of economics from Chicago led by Milton Friedman) but the result of U.S. government sponsorship of a "free-world" economy during the Cold War.[23] In its contest with the former Soviet Union, the United States presented itself to the world from the late 1940s on as an agent of an economic rationality based in private ownership and the spread of private consumption that contrasted with the collective conformity and limited personal freedom of Soviet life. Globalization has its ideological roots in this process, not in the neo-liberalism of the 1980s. That was icing on the cake, so to speak.

Whatever its precise ideological provenance, however, from this viewpoint globalization must be antithetical to the welfare state. At least this is the typical story told by both its proponents and by its critics. This is the fourth myth of globalization. The presumption here is that under conditions of globalization states will be disciplined by global "markets" to cut back on their welfare services (pensions, unemployment benefits, etc.) because if other states do so they will be left at a competitive disadvantage when it comes to attracting inward investment interested, inter alia, in lower taxes on repatriated profits. In other words, low tax/low service ju-risdictions will, all other things being equal, both attract bigger external investments and retain higher domestic investments than they would if they continue or increase their taxes and service burdens. In fact, as shown by numerous authors, this is a powerful idea that—though it has attracted considerable support by various political movements, not least the U.S. Re-publican Party, and in various institutions, such as the European Commis-sion—is open to considerable doubt. Dubbed the "race to the bottom" by some pundits, it sees public goods as deadweight in the process of eco-nomic development. Yet, as if we needed reminding, economic develop-ment has always required infrastructure investment and investment in public services to make the private investment pay off at all. Indeed, a case can be made that under conditions of enhanced competition for capital investment states need to increase their spending on education and infra-structure rather than reduce it. Empirical evidence shows that among the developed countries there is little if any systematic relationship between public spending as a percentage of GDP and either growth in GDP or growth in output per hour (a measure of productivity) over the years 1995–2004. Of course, this may still put these countries en masse at a dis-advantage vis-à-vis developing countries such as China. But as China at-tempts to move up the global production chain, from low-wage, low-value to high-wage, high-value manufacturing, it too will need to worry about spending more on public goods.

Finally, the fifth myth of globalization is that There Is No Alternative (TINA) to it. In other words, rather than simply a general trend associated with a certain set of features such as a world of shrinking distances, global-ized production chains, and increasing flows of goods and capital across international borders, globalization is seen as a teleology: a completely new world order that is totally marked off from what came before. Yet, there is all sorts of evidence not only that what has happened so far could go into reverse (remember 1914!) but that many states still have a very important presence within the emergent order that cannot be expected to disappear. There is no destiny to globalization. It has appeared under U.S. geopolitical sponsorship and could be attenuated as the U.S. goes into geopolitical de-cline. Moreover, it could also begin to take on different forms. The emer-gence of sovereign wealth funds mentioned earlier signifies a move toward a direct role for states in economic globalization. The increased competi-tion for raw materials between China and the rest of the world could see the increased importance of long-term inter-state contracts in setting prices relative to market mechanisms. Increased banking regulation in the U.S. and Europe in the aftermath of the 2008–2009 worldwide credit crunch could put limits on the previously free-wheeling activities of hedge funds and other new financial institutions. Neither the globalization we have known nor any of the plausible alternatives to it, therefore, is written in stone. The future is still to be made.

One way of moving beyond the myths of globalization as defining an either/or logic to state sovereignty is to think in terms of some of the ideas of Plato and Aristotle about fixed and mobile communities and the ways these ideas have figured in subsequent thinking and practice about politics in general and statehood in particular. From this viewpoint, the issues raised by globalization for state sovereignty are not really new at all, except and obviously importantly in terms of worldwide scope and impact, but reflect long-standing dilemmas concerning the deployment of power over space. To the geographer Jean Gottmann, for example, who paid careful attention to the thinking of the ancient Greek philosophers about the geography of political organization, the "road to national sovereignty" is best understood in terms of the opposition between two conflicting socio-economic imperatives with different geographical implications: those of what can be termed *security* and *opportunity*.[24] Only when the former trumps the latter does territorial sovereignty finally emerge as the principal geographical form of politics. But the historical record shows that the balance between security and opportunity has *oscillated* over time rather than been in a single direction. Hence, the significance of state territory is not fixed but varies depending upon the contrapuntal pressure from opportunity. This is hardly the stuff of either Whiggish or conservative state-centrism. To the contrary, it is a dynamic theoretical framework for considering the relative significance of territory versus other spatial configurations of power over time and space. In fact it is radically historicist in maintaining that different historical periods have produced distinctive ebbs and flows in the significance of territory.

More specifically, Gottmann designates Plato and Aristotle as the first theorists of political territory, albeit ones with very different emphases. From Plato's *Laws*, he draws an autarkic political imaginary in which Sparta appears as the model polity. Though security is the primary consideration for bounding a polity, the overarching goal is to encourage virtue and happiness. The demand for "stability" discourages more than "modest ambition," however. Thus, opportunity, in the sense of "overseas adventure, speculation, and profit" and extending territory must be strictly limited.[25] The example of Tokugawa Japan (approximately 1640–1858) is used by Gottmann to illustrate an extreme case of Platonic "territorial closure." But the case is made not so much by specific examples as by the general principle of political organization that Plato has provided to posterity: the centrality of security to political organization by territory.

In Aristotle's *Politics* (particularly Books II and VII) Gottmann sees Plato's emphasis on stability and security criticized and the need to balance security with opportunity accentuated. In this way: "The state organizes its territory to be a regular and full participant in the international system and does not seek isolation or seclusion from it."[26] This view, of course, is closer to the practice of the ancient Greeks than was Plato's. It also provided a justification, if any were needed, for a policy of expansion that Aristotle's star pupil, Alexander, was soon to realize. Though not without attention to security, it is to opportunity, therefore, that Aristotle's political imaginary is most devoted. It is Aristotle who thus provides the logic of opportunity, whether territorial or not, with its greatest intellectual boost. Adam Smith was a Johnny-come-lately.

Drawing together the insights of both Plato and his student Aristotle, Gottmann sees the relative *balance* between security and opportunity as determining the relative extent to which territory constitutes the predominant geographical shape of political power, rather than the story simply being that of one versus the other. Indeed, Gottmann interprets the rise of the Roman Empire, the disintegration into feudalism and the overlapping jurisdictions of the medieval period, and the rise of the modern sovereign state as distinctive periods with different equilibria between the two competing principles. The security-opportunity opposition thus provides the structural couplet upon which Gottmann bases his entire approach to understanding the significance of territory.

In turn, this approach leads Gottmann to reflect on the historical situation as he saw it in the early 1970s when he writes:

> The movement toward statehood and national sovereignty, begun in the sixteenth century, seems to have reached its apogee. Is the twentieth century going to stabilize this long sought-after and disputed pattern of territorial appropriation and administration? It would then be necessary and certainly worthwhile to define the present status and significance of territory. The momentum of history has not yet dissipated, however, and in certain respects the twentieth century appears to be only one more stage in an evolutionary process, although perhaps an essential turning point. The sovereign state, based on exclusive territorial jurisdiction, may have been

the evolution's purpose from the sixteenth to the mid-twentieth century. By 1970 [territorial] sovereignty has been by-passed, and a new fluidity has infiltrated the recently shaped map of multiple national states.[27]

Gottmann then goes on to detail some of the ways in which the functions of territorial sovereignty have been fundamentally compromised, from what we now call "weapons of mass destruction" that cannot be defended against territorially and satellite surveillance that cannot be detected to compromised border controls and all manner of fluidities associated with massive urbanization and the vast expansion of world trade and investment. Territorial isolation will not easily be re-imposed even as, Gottmann notes: "one cannot expect the [territorial] partitions in the minds of people to shift quickly."[28] Recent opinion research in the United States, for example, suggests that most Americans have a state-centric understanding of foreign policy.[29] They too inhabit the world of either/or.

WHERE IS SOVEREIGNTY?

I start in this section from the proposition that modern political theory tends to understand geography entirely as territorial: the world is divided up into contiguous spatial units with the territorial state as the basic building block from which other territorial units (such as alliances, spheres of influence, empires, etc.) derive or develop.[30] This is the reason why much of the speculation about "the decline of the state" or "sovereignty at bay" in the face of globalization is posed as the "end of geography." Yet the historical record suggests that there is no necessity for polities to be organized territorially. The conventional academic wisdom, therefore, both of those who continue to adhere to a state-centric world and those who see globalization as washing it away, is based on an either/or logic to state sovereignty. In fact, political power is manifested in a range of different spatialities, not simply territorially. Sovereignty, therefore, operates through a number of spatial modalities: territorial, spatial-interactional, and place-based. After looking at the conventional wisdom, I briefly explore these other spatialities.

THE CONVENTIONAL WISDOM

Fields such as international relations and political geography have long operated very much as if sovereign territorial states and the modern state

system associated with them have not only been around from time immemorial and will continue to be so indefinitely but also exhaust the range of
political actors necessary for understanding the workings of world politics.
Recently, this structural norm has been criticized by those who see a completely new world order without states in the offing. Yet they usually accept
that it was a reasonable facsimile of how the political world was organized
until the recent past. Sovereignty is either expressed entirely territorially
or it ceases to exist.

Most explicit in the case of political geography and the study of international relations, but common throughout the contemporary social sciences, the conventional understanding of the geography of power is
underpinned by three geographical assumptions: first, that states have an
exclusive power within their territories as represented by the concept of
sovereignty; second, that "domestic" and "foreign" affairs are essentially
separate realms in which different rules obtain; and finally, that the boundaries of the state define the boundaries of society such that the latter is
totally contained by the former. These assumptions reinforce one another
to produce a state-centered view of power in which the space occupied by
states is seen as fixed, as if for all time. Thinking about the spatiality of
power is thus put beyond history by assuming an essential state-territorial-
ity to the workings of power. I have called this the "territorial trap."[31]

This perspective did work reasonably well for the state-centered world
that began to develop in Europe in the nineteenth century. It made some
sense in the context of that time to see trajectories of economic and social
change as increasingly characterized in terms of the experiences of the bits
of space delimited by the territorial boundaries of states. Businesses and
trade unions, representative politics, and social life were increasingly organized on a state-by-state basis. But there was also a normative element to
thinking about power largely in terms of states. As a reflection of the burgeoning nationalism in Europe (and increasingly elsewhere) in the nineteenth century, politics was seen as best thought of in terms of national
states. Ideas of distinctive national characters and their reflection in military, sporting, technological, artistic, and educational prowess became
widely accepted.

This process was long seen as largely the prerogative of Europe (and
areas of European settlement). Europe was viewed as having the necessary
prerequisites for statehood, particularly such features as an inheritance
from the European ancients, the Greeks and Romans; racial superiority;
and obvious technological prowess. The rest of the world was available for

European imperialism. Between 1800 and 1914 the major European Powers, Russia, and the United States went from controlling 35 percent to controlling 84 percent of the earth's surface.[32] The world's empires all maintained control by means of acquiescence as much as by force, often operating through local rulers of one sort or another. The example of the United States and the independent republics of Latin America suggested that imperial rule was not destined to last forever. So, in the end, "What had applied to the Roman empire also applied to the British, French, German and, ultimately, Russian empires: subject peoples were only willing to remain in subjection so long as at least a significant number of them could see some benefit in doing so."[33] Once resistance to colonial rule began, the main means of organizing it was, ironically, "the same refashioning of society that had been the driving force behind most modern imperialism, namely nationalism."[34] Modern statehood thus became one of Europe's most popular exports even as the development of the originals themselves had been intimately connected to their competition with one another in creating empires beyond European shores.[35]

At the same time that European nationalism and imperialism were creating circumstances propitious for the development and spread of statehood around the world, the new social sciences (economics, sociology, political science) used the territories of modern statehood to serve as a fixed and reliable template for their investigations into a wide range of phenomena. The modern (European) world was seen as one in which local communities were in eclipse to the rising sun of societies based on the nation-state. *Gesellschaft* (society) was replacing *Gemeinschaft* (community) as the dominant cultural-geographical ordering principle. In this way a largely implicit "methodological nationalism" (a phrase first coined by the sociologist Herminio Martins) came to prevail in political and social thought. Currents of thought allowing for more complex views of the geographical scales at which social, economic, and political processes could take place were effectively marginalized.

The modern territorial state was underpinned, therefore, by the claim that it was the people's "mentor" in the cult of the nation. At its extreme, for the French Revolutionary disciples of Rousseau, the nation-state provided the basis for re-establishing a religious foundation to political authority. Only now, unlike in the person of the emperor-god or divinely appointed monarch, the educating state would give citizens a feeling of moral unity and identification with the father (or mother) land. This sacralization of the nation gave the territorial state an increasingly competitive advantage over other possible types of spatial-political organization such as confederations, loose empires, or city-states.

The drawbacks of a totally state-centered perspective on power have only recently become more obvious. On the one hand, this owes much to perceived changes in the ways in which states relate to one another and to the emergence of a global society in which states must share power with other types of actors. We live in an epoch in which the declining military viability of even the largest states, growing global markets, expanding transnational capitalism, and modes of governance alternative to that of the territorial state (such as the European Union, the various UN agencies, and the World Bank and the International Monetary Fund) have begun to undermine the possibility of seeing power as solely a spatial monopoly exercised by states.

On the other hand, the problem is more profound than one of a mere goodness-of-fit to the changing economic and social conditions of the contemporary world. State-centricity has finally been recognized as the main strategy of modern intellectuals of all sorts of political persuasions in limiting the definition of power to that of a coercive instrument and restricting politics to the domestic realm of the state. Representing space as state territoriality also serves to put statehood outside of time, because of the strong tendency to associate space with stasis or changelessness, and thus to impose an intellectual stability on the world that would otherwise be difficult. As a result, state-centricity has continuing normative attractions for both intellectuals and political activists even as the empirical reach of states to control and regulate recedes. It provides a grounded set of social-geographical units for both longitudinal and cross-sectional data analyses. It offers a set of concrete institutional opportunities (however weakened or compromised in effective performance) for political action.

The importance of the territorial state and the similar roles it performs within different theories can be seen in the writings of such influential contemporary international-relations theorists as Kenneth Waltz and Robert Keohane.[36] They are influential exponents at either end of the continuum stretching from realism to liberalism, the two main conventional positions on state power. This is not to say that these are the only positions available; far from it. But these authors are exemplary in terms of my present purpose. They illustrate the relative dominance of state-centrism in the thinking of international-relations theorists about world politics.

Waltz is concerned with what he calls the "structures of inter-state relations," altogether excluding the domestic character of states from explanatory consideration. To him, the structure of the international system has three features that matter: it is anarchic, without higher authority; states all perform the same functions and are equivalent units; and there is an uneven distribution of resources and capacities among states. From these fundamental features he draws the following inferences: that at any moment the system's shape as a whole is determined by the number and relations between the Great Powers (the ones with most resources and capacities) and that the balance of power between the Great Powers is the key mechanism in world politics. From this point of view, therefore, from 1945 until 1990 the international system was a bipolar balance of power between two Great Powers (the United States and the Soviet Union) in contrast to, for example, the multipolarity of the early nineteenth century in Europe. What drives the system is fear of domination by others. States are thus understood as unitary actors with each state trying to maximize status relative to others. No entities other than states are involved, by definition, in international relations. World politics is entirely about international (i.e., inter-state) relations. The fact that the equivalency of sovereignty gives rise to an inequality of power is put down to the outcome of a competition between states that somehow all started out as "equals."

In seeming contrast, Robert Keohane is interested in how cooperation can take place between states without a dominant Great Power. He argues that there are important incentives for cooperation between states that work against the competitive pursuit of coercive power in an anarchic world, even though he accepts the reality of this world. Treaties, agreements, and formal international institutions do restrict state conduct. This is because states agree to constraints when the benefits that derive from cooperation outweigh the costs. States are thus seen as rational actors pursuing maximum utility rather than maximum status. But states remain the only significant actors in this account. The utility game between states is the only game in play. Despite their differences over status or utility maximizing, therefore, these theorists share the commitment to a state-centered world. This is a conception inherited from a long line of political thinkers and practitioners over the past several hundred years.

More self-consciously empirical in its approaches to statehood and sovereignty, political geography has nevertheless also tended to adopt a territorial understanding of sovereignty. For example, Glassner and de Blij, while observing that the terms "sovereign" and "sovereignty" are often used "too loosely," note that "in a general sense it means power over the people of an area unconstrained by laws originating outside the area, or independence completely free of direct external control."[37] Wisely, they then say that the terms deserve to be used with quotation marks given that "there are so many qualifications and exceptions to the general concept." Unfortunately, they do not say what these are. Later, they write that a state "must have territory" and devote most of the book to showing how such territories vary in size and shape and come into conflict locally and globally over access to resources and in terms of more general geopolitical competition.[38] Indeed, it is the territorial character of states that has consistently attracted the central attention of political geographers. In this respect Glassner and de Blij's book is illustrative of a much more pervasive obsession with state territory on the part of political geographers. In distinction from the international-relations theorists, however, they seem more interested in the particulars of different states and less concerned with making general statements about "the state." This could well be because the wider field they represent, geography, is much less defined in terms of making universal claims about "the state" than is the political science with which much international-relations theory is tightly associated.[39]

In much recent political geography, however, sovereignty operates more as a background assumption than as a central theme of analysis. It is the state as a bureaucracy or apparatus of rule rather than as a territorial polity endowed with popular sovereignty that has been the focus for much of the most innovative theoretical work in the field over the past thirty years.[40] The tendency in this literature has been to see a state in functional terms as performing certain tasks for the accumulation of capital or the reproduction of certain social relations rather than in terms of how a state is constituted or takes on meaning as an effective agent.

In recent years, and largely in response to the perceived impact of globalization, many books and articles have appeared criticizing the "methodological territorialism" of established theoretical positions in political science and other fields and proposing the incipient emergence of a "post-international system." This system is seen as fundamentally different from the previous "Westphalian system" defined in and around a system of sovereign, territorial states. So, for example, to Jan Aart Scholte the world of territorial states is under eclipse in the face of the rise of a "distanceless space" produced by global financial markets, satellite communication, and rapid transportation.[41] From another perspective, it is not that globalization is directly challenging the state; it is that the state itself is in decline, partly because it does not live up to its billing in delivering public goods to people and partly because it is redundant with the rise of other entities (businesses, international organizations, etc.) that can do the same things better.[42] In a more moderate vein, David Held holds that globalization is posing the question as to whether global networks are displacing "notions of sovereignty as an illimitable, indivisible, and exclusive form of public power" such that "sovereignty itself has to be conceived today as already divided among a number of agencies—national, regional, and international—and limited by the very nature of this plurality."[43] In a legal framework, the distinguished Italian jurist Sabino Cassese says: "The crisis in the territoriality of the state and the affirmation of other public agencies, beyond the state, requires the establishment of guarantees in relation to power independent of territory."[44]

Such positions rely on two assumptions that are inherently problematic. One is that there was indeed a "Westphalian system" that monopolized world politics and that is now being undermined/replaced/transformed.[45] Yet, it is historical fact that world political-economic development over the past centuries has hardly been the singular outcome of this idealized state system. All sorts of actors have been involved, and states themselves have taken on quite different roles depending on their standing in the global hierarchy of states. This brings me to the second assumption: sovereignty is uniquely associated by these authors with the territory of the state. Thus, in the absence of a continuing territoriality "the state" is without political footing and we must look to other arrangements to manage public affairs. That sovereignty was perhaps never singularly sited in the territory of the state is not open to discussion.

QUESTIONING THE NEXUS BETWEEN
SOVEREIGNTY AND TERRITORY

Territoriality, the use of territory for political, social, and economic ends, is in fact, as I mentioned previously, a strategy that has developed more in some historical contexts than in others. Thus, the territorial state as it is known to contemporary political theory developed initially in early modern Europe with the retreat of dynastic and non-territorial systems of rule and the transfer of sovereignty from the personhood of monarchs to discrete national populations. That modern state sovereignty as usually construed did not occur suddenly following the Peace of Westphalia in 1648 is now widely accepted. Territorialization of political authority was further enhanced by the development of mercantilist economies and, later, by an industrial capitalism that emphasized capturing powerful contiguous positive externalities from exponential distance-decay declines in transportation costs and from the clustering of external economies (resource mixes, social relations, labor pools, etc.) within national-state boundaries.[46]

Two issues are crucial in this context: that political control and authority are not restricted to states and that such control and authority are thereby not necessarily exclusively territorial. Authority is the legitimate exercise of power and is typically strongly associated with statehood. In no case, however, has the authority of the state ever been complete. There have always been competing sources of political authority, from the church in the medieval context to international organizations, social movements, businesses, and NGOs today. Sovereignty is not the same thing as irresistible power emanating from a single site. Indeed, sovereignty can be seen as the locus for a range of social powers, including many from well beyond the state's nominal borders, attracted by the prospect of influencing state decisions.[47] Thus, even ostensibly private entities and supranational governments are often popularly accorded great or even greater authority in the face of the control that they exercise than are states. Think, for example, of credit rating agencies such as Moody's and Standard and Poor's, charitable organizations such as Human Rights Watch, and supranational entities such as the European Union. Using two countries as examples, within the United States there is widespread popular suspicion of the efficiency and accountability of the federal government, not just since the military debacle in Iraq and the pathetic governmental response to Hurricane Katrina. This often leads to perhaps excessive faith in the virtue of privatization through corporate networks of what are elsewhere seen as "public" services, such as health care. In Italy, much of the popular enthusiasm for the European Union has been driven by the hope that Brussels would increasingly supplant Rome as the seat of power most effective in relation to people's everyday lives, not so much territorially as in relation to the functional effects of Europe-wide initiatives.

In many languages the word *territory* typically refers to a unit of contiguous space that is used, organized, and managed by a social group, individual person, or institution to restrict and control access to people and places. Though sometimes the word is used as synonymous with *place* or *space*, territory has never been a term as primordial or as generic as they are in the canons of geographical terminology.[48] The dominant usage has always been either political, in the sense of necessarily involving the power to limit access to certain places or regions, or ethological, in the sense of the dominance exercised over a space by a given species or an individual organism. Increasingly, territory is coupled with the concept of network to help understand the complex processes through which space is managed and controlled by powerful organizations. In this light, the territory associated with statehood is only one type of *spatiality*, or way in which space is used, rather than the one monopolizing its employment. From this perspective, *territoriality* is the strategic use of territory to attain organizational goals, including actors other than states. But it is only one way of organizing space socially and politically.

MODES OF SPATIALITY

I begin by exploring how territory operates as a mode of spatiality or way in which space figures in human transactions. I then argue that the concept of territory has become fatefully tied to the modern state, particularly in English-language understandings. Finally, I suggest that two further modes of spatiality, spatial interaction and place-making, provide analytically important and complementary ways of thinking about space and society beyond the limitations imposed by a geographical imagination limited by a singularly territorial conception of spatiality.[49]

Territory is particularly associated with the spatiality of the modern state with its claim to absolute control over a population within carefully defined external borders.[50] Indeed, until Robert Sack extended the understanding of human territoriality as a strategy to individuals and organizations in general, usage of the term *territory* in English-language social science was largely confined to the spatial organization of states.[51] In the social sciences such as economics, sociology, and political science, this is still mainly the case, such that the challenge posed to territory by network forms of organization (associated with globalization) is invariably characterized in totalistic terms as "the end of geography." This signifies the extent to which territory has become the dominant geographical term (and imagination) in the social sciences.[52] It is then closely allied to state sovereignty and, sometimes, to an entirely nested, scale-based territorial conception of space (from the local and the urban through the national to the global). Thus, as sovereignty is seen to "erode" or "unbundle," so it seems goes territory. Geography having been confused with territory, the end of territory witnesses the end of geography. From this viewpoint territory takes on an epistemological monopoly that is understood as absolutely fundamental to modernity. Postmodernity, then, becomes a world without territory. In modernity, however, territory can also be given an extended meaning to refer to any socially constructed geographical space, not just that resulting from statehood, and can be used as equivalent to the term *place* in many languages including French, Spanish, and Italian.[53] Especially popular with some French-language geographers, this usage often reflects the need to adopt a term to distinguish the particular and the local from the more general global or national "space." It then signifies the "bottom-tier" spatial context for identity and cultural difference more than a simple "top-down" connection between state and territory but still within an encompassing territorialized conception of spatiality. From this perspective, territories may not aggregate together into a single state territory but can also overlap in complex ways, as with city hinterlands and cross-border regions, for example. In absolute counterpoint, some proponents of a postmodern conception of space see that space as completely "flat" without any sort of territorial division or territorial hierarchies whatsoever and thus provide a totally opposite but equally singular view of spatiality, albeit this time of localized sites in a totally networked spatial topology rather than of an absolute territorialized space.[54]

Territory in its broadest sense, then, is either the organization and exercise of power, legitimate or otherwise, over blocs of space or the organization of people and things into discrete areas through the use of boundaries. In studies of animal behavior spatial division into territories is seen as an evolutionary principle, a way of fostering competition so that those best matched to their territory will have more surviving offspring. With human territoriality, however, spatial division is more typically thought of as a strategy used by organizations and groups to manage social, economic, and political activities. From this viewpoint, space is partitioned into territorial cells or units that can be relatively autonomous (as with the division of global space into territorial nation-states) or arranged hierarchically from basic units in which work, administration, or surveillance is carried out through intermediate levels at which managerial or supervisory functions are located to the top-most level at which central control is concentrated. Alternative spatialities (modes of geographical organization) of political and economic activities, particularly hierarchical networks (as in the world-city network) or reticular networks (as with the Internet), can challenge or supplement the use of territoriality.

Territoriality as a feature within these models can be judged theoretically as having a number of different origins or sources. These would include the following: (1) as a result of explicit territorial strategizing to devolve administrative functions but maintain central control;[55] (2) as a secondary result of resolving the dilemmas facing social groups in delivering public goods (as in Michael Mann's sociology of territory);[56] (3) as an expedient facilitating coordination between capitalists who are otherwise in competition with one another (as in Marxist theories of the state); (4) as the focus of one strategy among several of governmentality (as in Michel Foucault's writings referred to earlier); and (5) as a result of defining boundaries between social groups to identify and maintain group cohesion (as in the writings of Georg Simmel and Fredrik Barth, and in more recent sociological theories of political identity in which place figures as the mediating context for a range of social influences upon the formation of political identities).[57] Whatever its precise social origins, territoriality is put into practice in a number of different if often complementary ways: (1) by popular acceptance of *classifications* of space (e.g., "ours" versus "yours"); (2) through *communication* of a sense of place and belonging (where territorial markers and borders evoke meanings for different groups); and (3) by *enforcing control* over space (by barrier construction, surveillance, policing, and judicial review).

Unfortunately, the tendency to restrict spatiality to territory and to associate territoriality only with statehood is not only profoundly mistaken but also widespread. It is worth reflecting a little here on how this has happened. I will have much more to say about this in the next chapter. The territorial state is a highly specific historical entity. It initially arose in Western Europe in the sixteenth and seventeenth centuries. Since that time, political power has come to be seen as inherently territorial because statehood is seen as inherently territorial. From this viewpoint, politics thus take place only within "the institutions and the spatial envelope of the state as the exclusive governor of a definite territory. We also identify political territory with social space, perceiving countries as 'state-societies.' "[58] The process of state formation has always had two crucial attributes. One is *exclusivity*. All of the political entities (the Roman Catholic Church, city-states, etc.) that could not achieve a reasonable semblance of sovereignty over a contiguous territory have been largely delegitimized as major political actors. The second is *mutual recognition*. The power of states has rested to a considerable extent on the recognition each state receives from the others by means of non-interference in their so-called internal affairs. Together these attributes have created a world in which there can be no territory without a state and vice versa. In this way, territory has come to underpin both nationalism and representative democracy, both of which depend critically on restricting political membership by homeland and address, respectively.

More abstractly, in modern political theory control over a relatively modest territory has long been seen as the primary solution to the "security dilemma": to offer protection to populations from the threats of anarchy (disorder), on the one hand, and hierarchy (distant rule and subordination), on the other. A major problem has been to define what is meant by "modest" size. To Montesquieu, the Enlightenment philosopher, different size territories inevitably have different political forms: "It is, therefore, the natural property of small states to be governed as a republic, of middling ones to be subject to a monarch, and of large empires to be swayed by a despotic prince."[59] Early modern Europe offered propitious circumstances for the emergence of a fragmented political system primarily because of its topographical divisions. Montesquieu further notes, however, that popular representation allows for the territorial extension of republican government.[60] The founders of the United States added to this by trying to balance between centralizing certain security functions in the federal government, on one side, and retaining local controls over many other functions in the state governments, on the other.[61] Of course, the relative balance historically has shifted to the advantage of the former. The recent history of the European Union can be thought of in similar terms as a balancing act between levels of government and functions performed, if without the formal constitutionalism (founding constitution, separation of powers, effective popular representation at all levels) of the United States.[62] In recent years lower tiers of government seem to have acquired greater autonomy and control than they had during the heyday of central state consolidation in the mid-twentieth century.[63]

SPATIAL INTERACTION

Human activities in the world, however, have never conformed entirely to spaces defined by proximity as provided by state territory. In this context, I wish to make two related points. First of all, and increasingly, as physical distance proves less of a barrier to movement because of technological change and the removal of territorially based regulative barriers to trade and investment, spatial interaction between separated nodes across networks is an increasingly important mechanism of geographical sorting and differentiation.[64] For example, the networks that connect cities (or rather enterprises within them) exhibit a "power of reach" for agents across space that facilitates the work of cities.[65] Sometimes posed today in terms of a world of flows versus a world of territories, this is perhaps better thought of in terms of territories and/or networks of flows rather than one versus the other, against the claims of both methodological territorialism and the "flat ontology" that sees human life as entirely a matter of nodes and networks. Territories and networks exist relationally rather then mutually exclusively.

Not everyone sees it this way. To some writers territories and networks represent alternative and competing rather than competing yet complementary spatialities. Thus, if on one side territories are just aggregations of networks or archipelagos of networks, on the other territories involve a distinctive spatial ontology relating to controlled and exclusive access to areas that are relatively well identified as such. Thus, according to Bernard Debarbieux, from the network viewpoint, "all territory, even with development over space, is also constituted by material networks (sentiers, routes, different infrastructures, etc.) and animated by social networks. . . . In other words, territory corresponds to an ensemble of points and contiguous areas or to an archipelago (a disjointed territory of areas connected by elements of non-territorialized networks) or a reticular/territorial space (an ensemble of areas and places linked by territorialized networks)."[66] In counterpoint, state territories can be seen as more or less homogenous socio-economic spaces, not as a fact of nature so much as a result of state activities that have reduced or eliminated internal spatial differences. Thus, in describing the diffusion of economic development under state auspices in post–Second World War Western Europe, Neil Brenner writes of administrative control as spreading "as evenly as possible across the entire surface of the national territory—much like butter on a piece of bread."[67] If the problem with the first viewpoint is that it ignores the significance of spatial continuity in defining accessibility and control (recall the continuing importance of political borders), the problem with the second one is that it misses the degree to which territories are always ensembles of places linked together dynamically and unevenly by territorialized networks as well as by areal governance. So, just as an excessive emphasis on the ontological centrality of territory is the product of an a priori methodological territorialism, the overemphasis on networks is often the result of an ideology or "cult" of movement and passage drawing on a long history, beginning at least with Saint-Simon, in which "if the tree has been the symbol of rootedness, of hierarchy and of the religious verticality that connects the earth to heaven, the network is the fetish of the contemporary cult of movement, of passing through, and of horizontality that links the present to the future."[68]

If territorial regulation, however, is in part about managing flows between places within blocs of space, the territorial governments doing the regulating have never been zero-sum entities in which the sharing of power across networks with other actors or the existence of external linkages through networks outside a given territory totally undermines their capacity to regulate territorially. If during the mid-twentieth century the governments of territorial states did severely limit the local powers of transterritorial agencies, then that this is no longer the case does not signify that the states have lost all of their powers or that everything now is solely a question of "network power": "Territory still matters. States remain the most effective governors of populations. . . . The powers to exclude, to tax, and to define political rights are those over which states acquired a monopoly in the seventeenth century. They remain the essentials of state power and explain why state sovereignty survives today and why it is indispensable to the international order."[69] Nevertheless, notwithstanding a certain ambiguity inherent in the terms, in a world in which evidence for both reinforced *territorialization* (e.g., the Israel-Palestine Separation Barrier) and *de-/re-territorialization* (e.g., the European Union Schengen passport zone) is not hard to come by, their usage suggests a dynamism to the forms of territories and territorialities and an increasing challenge from other spatialities of power, particularly the fact that most human transactions, capital flows, population movements, and so on involve point-to-point mobility or flows from place to place rather than containment within fixed territories.[70]

But some networks do not aggregate neatly into territories at all. Cities and city-networks, in particular, have long been central to many aspects of the world economy, not least finance and many producer services. Increasingly such networks have become relatively independent of the world of territories. Though still positioned across state territories, such networks rely more on relational than on immediate spatial proximity.[71] Thus, London and New York, for example, have stronger functional ties to each other in many respects than they do to more adjacent places or other cities within their state territories. In part it is the explosion of such relationships that has increased the call for increased economic regulation of market processes, particularly banks and finance, at supranational and global scales. Individual states are apparently just not up to the job, whatever their agents say about their sovereign capabilities.

PLACE-MAKING

My second point about needing to diminish the overall emphasis on state-territory as if it referred to spatiality *tout court* involves a rather different focus. This is the significance of the human experience of space reflected in English-language usage of the word *place*. Places are natural locations that have social and psychological significance insofar as they ground political outlooks and projects in the settings of everyday life. People do not live in states as such but in much smaller areas defined by the predominant and routine activities of everyday life. Places are never isolated from one another except under unusual conditions (such as in primeval forests or in Arctic vastnesses). Though they can be grouped into territories during the course of state formation, they also can be networked across larger spaces. Most importantly, they provide the physical or material basis to all human activities even as some activities become more networked over space. Political interests and identities are thus the outcome of ensembles of power relations grounded in places even as they extend beyond any particular place.[72]

In this perspective, space is bracketed, or put to one side, because its "abstractness discourages experiential explorations."[73] In his philosophical rehabilitation of place, Edward Casey notes how "place has been assimilated to space. . . . As a result, place came to be considered a mere 'modification' of space (in Locke's revealing term)—a modification that aptly can be called 'site,' that is, *leveled-down, monotonous space* for building and other human enterprises" (author's emphasis).[74] Casey's goal is to argue for the crucial importance of place in much thinking about community and the public sphere, even though the connections are often not made explicit by the thinkers in question. He wants to make place different from site and space, even though he acknowledges Michel Foucault's point that the modern world is largely one of Leibnizian sites and relations rather than Newtonian absolute spaces.[75] In rethinking space as place, his primary interest lies in phenomenologically or experientially linking places to human selves. The central issue is that of "being in place differently" conditioning the various dimensions of selfhood, from the bodily to the psychological, institutional, and architectural.[76] So, though the "shape" of place has changed historically, it is now no mere container but, rather, a taking place; its rediscovery and naming as such is long overdue. Thus: "Despite the seduction of endless space (and the allure of serial time), place is beginning to escape from its entombment in the cultural and philosophical underworld of the modern West."[77]

Symptomatic of the conceptual separation of space and place are the three dominant meanings that geographical place has acquired in writing that invokes either space or place. Each meaning tends to assimilate place to one or the other end of a continuum running from nomothetic (generalized) space at one end to idiographic (particularistic) place at the other. The first is place as location or a site in space where an activity or object is located and that relates to other sites or locations because of interaction and movement between them. A city or other settlement is often thought of this way. Somewhere in between, and second, is the view of place as locale or setting where everyday-life activities take place. Here the location is no mere address but the where of social life and environmental transformation. Examples would be such settings from everyday life as workplaces, homes, shopping malls, churches, and so forth. The third is place as sense of place or identification with a place as a unique community, landscape, and moral order. In this construction, every place is particular and, thus, singular. A strong sense of "belonging" to a place, either consciously or as shown through everyday behavior such as participating in place-related affairs, would be indicative of "sense of place."

Attempts at putting space and place together must necessarily try to bring at least two of these various meanings of geographical place together. Currently, there are four main ways in the Anglo-American and French literature in which this task has been approached: the humanist or agency-based, the neo-Marxist, the feminist, and the contextualist/performative. Each of these rejects the either/or logic in relation to space and place that has characterized most geographic and social thought from the seventeenth century to the present.[78] For the first, and the one with which I am most in sympathy, the focus lies in relating location and locale to sense of place through the experiences of human beings as agents. In one of the most sophisticated statements of this perspective, Robert Sack provides the essential thrust when he writes that his "framework draws on the geographical experiences of place, space, home, and world which people use in their lives to integrate forces, perspectives, and selves."[79] From this point of view:

> Place implies space, and each home is a place in space. Space is a property of the natural world, but it can be experienced. From the perspective of experience, place differs from space in terms of familiarity and time. A place requires human agency, is something that may take time to know, and a home especially so. As we move along the earth we pass from one place to another. But if we move quickly the places blur; we lose track of

their qualities, and they may coalesce into the sense that we are moving through space. This can happen even in my own home. If I am hardly there and do not attend to its contents, it may seem unfamiliar to me, more like a part of space than a place.[80]

In this frame of reference, cultural differences, for example, emerge because of place-based experiences and human agency but also because places are never separate but always part of larger sets of places across which differences are more or less pronounced depending on the permeability of boundaries between places as people experience them. Places are woven together through space by movement and the network ties that produce places as changing constellations of human commitments, capacities, and strategies. Places are invariably parts of spaces, and spaces provide the resources and the frames of reference in which places are made. Many states, including some of the apparently most centralized ones, exhibit a placeness in their internal political-geographical organization. Thus, and for Mao-era China, Vivienne Shue has argued that there was "a cellurality built into the peasant economic and social substructure."[81] Partly this reflects the continuing influence of the city-hinterland connections at the base of the Chinese body politic discovered by the anthropologist G. William Skinner, but it also reflects local socio-economic and cultural differences with long-established roots and a persisting "deconcentrated" pattern of authority. Even in Maoist China, therefore, place-making to pursue local interests and defend various political identities challenged the possibility of unlimited central state authority. Globalization has if anything everywhere encouraged a deepening of such cellularity, not only because most people's lives are still lived around clustered routines but also because "our visualization, our perception, of the space in-between affects our emotions, our beliefs, our attitudes, and, eventually, our behavior."[82]

In the face of globalization, partly because of distrust of distant rulers but also because of the increased salience of local conditions for economic competitiveness, local places can be expected to provide the primary settings for political organizing and economic regulation, not just in relation to local issues that may have become increasingly divergent from a "national" consensus but also because in a less singularly bounded world "old ideas of 'place,' 'land,' and 'earth' provide new sites for possible [political] metamorphosis."[83] More specifically, as Ley notes: "Maps of business and financial services in central London show a clear tendency toward geographic concentration, particularly for such activities as banking, law, and advertising where there are significant global linkages. . . . As these global players beat the bounds of their downtown parish, is their spatial behavior global or local, neither or both?"[84] Particularly important here in relation to place-making is the incentive that more direct global-local relations provide, through both connections with transnational capital and the workings of distance-spanning communications, for sub-national political units to engage in administrative and managerial activities hitherto monopolized by states.[85] Indeed, the trend across the world for municipalities and regional governments "to tax, educate, and regulate" does suggest a real rise in the importance of such sub-national units.[86]

In a recent research project on Italian electoral politics since the late 1980s, my colleague Michael Shin and I have made the case for contexts of "place and time"—changing place configurations—in accounting for what has transpired nationally in terms of the rise and fall of the various political parties.[87] We argue that these are not best thought of as invariably regional, local, or national, although they frequently have elements of one, several, or all. Rather, they are best considered as always located somewhere, with some contexts more stretched over space (such as means of mass communication and the spatial division of labor) and others more localized (school, workplace, and residential interactions). The balance of influence on political choices between and among the stretched and more local contextual processes can be expected to change over time, giving rise to subsequent shifts in political outlooks and affiliations. So, for example, as foreign companies introduce branch plants, trade unions must negotiate new work practices, which, in turn, erode long-accepted views of the roles of managers and employees. In due course, this configuration of contextual changes can give an opening to a new political party or a redefined old one that upsets established political affiliations, as the yardsticks or heuristics for judging parties change. Older geographical patterns of political behavior, particularly between North, Center, and South in Italy, have become more complex locally as a result of profound social and economic change; for example, with respect to the relative densities of public employees, the prevalence of private businesses in increasingly competitive sectors, and the incidence of criminal and illicit activities.[88] But such change as occurs must always fit in to some degree with existing cultural templates that often show amazing long-term resilience as well as slow adaptation. Doreen Massey puts the overall point best when she writes: "This is a notion of place where specificity (local uniqueness, a sense of place) derives not from some mythical internal roots nor from a history of isolation—now to be disrupted by globalization—but precisely from the absolute particularity of the mixture of influences found together there."[89]

We have used the term *place*, therefore, to capture the mediating role of such geographically located milieux. What we mean by this word are the settings in which people find themselves on a regular basis in their daily lives where many contexts come together and with which they may identify. Or, as I have made the point previously: "Places are the cultural settings where localized and geographically wide-ranging socioeconomic processes that condition actions of one sort or another are jointly mediated. Although there must be places, therefore, there need not be this particular place."[90] So, if, in this case, individual persons are in the end the agents of politics, their agency and the particular forms it takes flow from the social stimuli, political imaginations, and yardsticks of judgment they acquire in the ever-evolving social webs in which they are necessarily enmeshed and which intersect across space in particular places. Mair suggests that as political-party affiliations have weakened over the past thirty years in most European countries, voting behavior is "increasingly contingent."[91] From our perspective, this means that geographical patterns of voting turnout and party affiliation will become more unstable or volatile even as they still respond to place-based if evolving norms of participation and differing relative attraction to the offerings of different parties.

Politics, then, is never simply national-territorial. It is constituted geographically out of place-making activities in which the national is only part of the overall spatial architecture. All told, there is much more to the geography of political power—and thus sovereignty—than is captured by regarding the state territory as the singular unit of political account. All power does not emanate from a single "sovereign" site into a surrounding and well-bounded territory and outward into a spatial vacuum. Power also crosses over space and is embedded, even if always contingently, in different places.

CONCLUSION

Politics everywhere involves three different spatial modalities, only one of which is territory: territory, spatial interaction, and place-making. Yet much thinking about politics and the sovereignty that frames it has been totally related to the presumed monopoly exercised by territorial forms, especially that of the legendary "state." Today, as the focus of much writing on globalization has tended to presuppose, everything has supposedly changed. Historically, however, the workings of sovereignty have never been exclusively territorial. Nor has it ever been monopolized by states per se. A wide range of actors (persons, private organizations, international agencies, and municipalities) have long shared in the workings of sovereignty. The picture has just become more complicated rather than been transformed in a straightforward manner. The "myths" of globalization I have elucidated tend to suggest such a clean break. Problematic as these prove to be on close examination, I have argued that effective sovereignty still co-exists with the nevertheless real trends in global political economy associated with globalization. But as I will argue in chapter 3, sovereignty still takes various shapes, only one of which is intimately connected to globalization. Before getting to that, I want to explore in some detail how sovereignty and territory became so bonded together intellectually. That is the purpose of the next chapter.

NOTES

1. Thinking about politics in terms of domestic and foreign or inside versus outside has become so common as to be taken for granted in most discussions of politics. Fields such as international relations, international law, and comparative politics are meaningful only in terms of such an opposition. See, for example, R. Walker, *Inside/Outside: International Relations as Political Theory* (Cambridge: Cambridge University Press, 1993), and J. G. Ruggie, "Territoriality and beyond: problematizing modernity in international relations," *International Organization* 47 (1993): 139–74.

2. W. E. Connolly, "The complexities of sovereignty," in M. Calarco and S. DeCaroli (eds.), *Giorgio Agamben: Sovereignty and Life* (Stanford, CA: Stanford University Press, 2007), 37.

3. Connolly, "The complexities of sovereignty," 36.

4. S. Makdisi, *Palestine Inside Out: An Everyday Occupation* (New York: Norton, 2008), 1–3.

5. B. Badie, *Un monde sans souveraineté. Les États entre ruses et responsabilité* (Paris: Fayard, 1999); S. D. Krasner, *Sovereignty: Organized Hypocrisy* (Princeton, NJ: Princeton University Press, 1999); S. D. Krasner (ed.), *Problematic Sovereignty: Contested Rules and Political Possibilities* (New York: Columbia University Press, 2001); D. A. Lake, "The new sovereignty in international relations," *International Studies Review* 5 (2003): 303–23.

6. For example: J. Camilleri and J. Falk (eds.), *The End of Sovereignty? The Politics of a Shrinking and Fragmenting World* (Aldershot, UK: Elgar, 1992); T. J. Biersteker and C. Weber (eds.), *State Sovereignty as Social Construct* (Cambridge: Cambridge University Press, 1996); M. Mason, "Transnational environ-

mental obligations: locating new spaces of accountability in a post-Westphalian global order," *Transactions of the Institute of British Geographers* 26 (2001): 407–29; H. Stacy, "Relational sovereignty," *Stanford Law Review* 55 (2003): 2029–59.

7. A. B. Murphy, "The sovereign state system as a political-territorial ideal: historical and contemporary considerations," in T. J. Biersteker and C. Weber (eds.), *State Sovereignty as Social Construct* (Cambridge: Cambridge University Press, 1996).

8. K. Mills, "Sovereignty eclipsed? The legitimacy of humanitarian access and intervention," *Journal of Humanitarian Assistance* (2000), www.jha.ac/articles/ a019.htm.

9. T. Dodge, "A sovereign Iraq?" *Survival* 46 (2004): 39–58.

10. For example: M. W. Zacher, "The decaying pillars of the Westphalian temple: implications for international order and governance," in J. N. Rosenau and E-O. Czempiel (eds.), *Governance without Government: Order and Change in World Politics* (Cambridge: Cambridge University Press, 1992); J. Agnew, "Mapping political power beyond state boundaries," *Millennium* 28 (1999): 499–521; M. Hardt and A. Negri, *Empire* (Cambridge, MA: Harvard University Press, 2000); A-M. Slaughter and W. Burke-White, "Judicial globalization," *Virginia Journal of International Law* 40 (2000): 1103–15.

11. Siba Grovogui ("Regimes of sovereignty: international morality and the African condition," *European Journal of International Relations* 8 [2002]: 315–38) uses the term "regime of sovereignty" when discussing the "quasi-state" thesis and the insufficiency of the "Westphalian" account of statehood.

12. M. Foucault, *Naissance de la biopolitique. Cours au Collège de France, 1978–1979* (Paris: Seuil/Gallimard, 2004), 79.

13. B. Jessop, "From micro-powers to governmentality: Foucault's work on statehood, state formation, statecraft and state power," *Political Geography* 26 (2007): 34–40.

14. B. Stråth, "The state and its critics: is there a post-modern challenge?" in Q. Skinner and B. Stråth (eds.), *States and Citizens: History, Theory, Prospects* (Cambridge: Cambridge University Press, 2003), 178.

15. J. Agnew, *Geopolitics: Re-Visioning World Politics* (London: Routledge, Second Edition, 2003), chapter 2.

16. J. Lévy, *L'invention du monde. Une géographie de mondialisation* (Paris: Presses de Sciences Po, 2008), 70.

17. Lévy, *L'invention du monde*; S. D. Sharma, "The many faces of globalization: a survey of recent literature," *New Global Studies* 2 (2008), bepress.com/ngs/vol2/ iss2/art4.

18. *Foreign Policy*, "A.T. Kearney Globalization Index" (January/February 2003): 60–72.

19. Friedman, *The World Is Flat: A Brief History of the Twenty-First Century* (New York: Farrar, Straus and Giroux, 2005).

20. E. R. Wolf, *Europe and the People without History* (Berkeley: University of California Press, 1982); Agnew, *Geopolitics*, chapter 4.

21. S. Sassen, *Territory, Authority, Rights: From Medieval to Global Assemblages* (Princeton, NJ: Princeton University Press, 2006), 1–2.

22. T. Frank, *One Market under God: Extreme Capitalism, Market Populism and the End of Economic Democracy* (New York: Random House, 2000), 3–4.

23. J. Agnew, *Hegemony: The New Shape of Global Power* (Philadelphia: Temple University Press, 2005), chapters 4 and 6.

24. J. Gottmann, *The Significance of Territory* (Charlottesville: University Press of Virginia, 1973).

25. Gottmann, *The Significance of Territory*, 18.

26. Gottmann, *The Significance of Territory*, 22.

27. Gottmann, *The Significance of Territory*, 126.

28. Gottmann, *The Significance of Territory*, 158.

29. D. W. Drezner, "The realist tradition in American public opinion," *Perspectives on Politics* 6 (2008): 51–70.

30. For a clear example, see J. A. Caporaso, "Changes in the Westphalian order: territory, public authority, and sovereignty," *International Studies Review* 2 (2000): 1–28.

31. J. Agnew "The territorial trap: the geographical assumptions of international relations theory," *Review of International Political Economy* 1 (1994): 53–80.

32. P. Kennedy, *The Rise and Fall of the Great Powers: Economic Change and Military Conflict from 1500 to 2000* (New York: Random House, 1987), 148–49.

33. A. Pagden, *Peoples and Empires: Europeans and the Rest of the World from Antiquity to the Present* (London: Weidenfeld and Nicolson, 2001), 163.

34. Pagden, *Peoples and Empires*, 164.

35. R. V. Mongia, "Historicizing state sovereignty: inequality and the form of equivalence," *Comparative Studies in Society and History* 49 (2007): 384–411.

36. K. E. Waltz, *Theory of International Politics* (New York: Random House, 1979); R. O. Keohane, *After Hegemony: Cooperation and Discord in the World Political Economy* (Princeton, NJ: Princeton University Press, 1984).

37. M. I. Glassner and H. de Blij, *Systematic Political Geography* (New York: Wiley, Fourth Edition, 1989), 38.

38. Glassner and de Blij, *Systematic Political Geography*, 66.

39. J. Bartelson, *The Critique of the State* (Cambridge: Cambridge University Press, 2001).

40. For example: G. L. Clark and M. Dear, *State Apparatus: Structures and Language of Legitimacy* (London: Allen and Unwin, 1984); G. MacLeod and M. Goodwin, "Reconstructing an urban and regional political economy: on the state, politics, scale, and explanation," *Political Geography* 18 (1999): 697–730; B. Jessop, *The Future of the Capitalist State* (London: Polity, 2002).

41. J. A. Scholte, *Globalization: A Critical Introduction* (New York: St. Martin's Press, 1999), 18.

42. M. Van Creveld, *The Rise and Decline of the State* (Cambridge: Cambridge University Press, 1999).

43. D. Held, "Democracy, the nation-state, and the global system," in D. Held (ed.), *Political Theory Today* (Cambridge: Polity Press, 1991), 22.

44. S. Cassese, *Oltre lo stato* (Bari/Rome: Laterza, 2006), 29.

45. J. Rosenberg, *The Follies of Globalization Theory* (London: Verso, 2000).

46. Various territorialized economic ideologies undergirded these developments. Perhaps the extreme form of such an ideology would be that eighteenth-century "cameralism," which thought that territories, however deficient climatically or in other ways, could avoid both trade and imperialism by "teaching" crops and animals to grow in seemingly unpropitious circumstances (e.g., L. Koerner, *Linnaeus: Nature and Nation* [Cambridge, MA: Harvard University Press, 1999]). Such ideas have died hard notwithstanding their obvious limitations in terms of later knowledge (such as the concept of natural selection).

47. For examples of such governance beyond government, so to speak, see, for example, A. C. Cutler et al. (eds.), *Private Authority and International Affairs* (Albany, NY: SUNY Press, 1999); and R. B. Hall and T. J. Biersteker (eds.), *The Emergence of Private Authority in Global Governance* (Cambridge: Cambridge University Press, 2002). Some Foucauldians use the term *governmentality* to extend the idea of authority beyond the bounds of sovereignty as usually construed as being monopolized by a central state apparatus to include non-state actors that are intricately bound into existing webs of political power but which reflect self-management and are perceived as autonomous of central direction; see, for example, G. Burchell, "Liberal government and techniques of the self," in A. Barry et al. (eds.), *Foucault and Political Reason* (London: UCL Press, 1996). In this understanding, the role of non-state actors in governance is not a transfer of power from states but rather evidences a changing constellation of control and authority around states in which other actors have taken on crucial governmental roles (e.g., O. J. Sending and I. B. Neumann, "Governance to governmentality: analyzing NGOs, states, and power," *International Studies Quarterly* 50 [2006]: 651–72).

48. J. Agnew, "Space:Place," in P. Cloke and R. Johnston (eds.), *Spaces of Geographical Thought* (London: Sage, 2005).

49. Territories are made out of places and networks but neither simply "nests" inside them like Russian dolls. Places can sprawl across the borders of territories and networks extend across and between places in different territories. For an interesting attempt at showing how these various concepts can be made to relate to one another, see B. Jessop et al., "Theorizing sociospatial relations," *Society and Space* 26 (2008): 389–401. In human geographic terms, I would see place-making as being the most basic spatiality and the others as building on it. This is not the argument of Jessop et al. but it is of E. S. Casey ("Comments on 'Theorizing socios-

patial relations,'" *Society and Space* 26 [2008]: 402–4) in his comments on their article.

50. Agnew, "Space:Place."

51. R. D. Sack, *Human Territoriality: Its Theory and History* (Cambridge: Cambridge University press, 1986).

52. B. Badie, *La Fin des territoires* (Paris: Fayard, 1995).

53. For example, A. Scivoletto (ed.), *Sociologia del territorio: tra scienza e utopia* (Milan: Franco Angeli, 1983); T. Forsberg, "Beyond sovereignty, within territoriality: mapping the space of late-modern (geo) politics," *Cooperation and Conflict* 31 (1996): 355–86; M. Storper, "Regional economies as relational assets," in R. Lee and J. Wills (eds.), *Geographies of Economies* (London: Arnold, 1997).

54. S. Marston, J. P. Jones, and K. Woodward, "Human geography without scale," *Transactions of the Institute of British Geographers* 30 (2005): 416–32.

55. Sack, *Human Territoriality*.

56. M. Mann, "The autonomous power of the state: its origins, mechanisms and results," *European Journal of Sociology* 25 (1984): 185–213.

57. F. Lechner, "Simmel on social space," *Theory, Culture & Society* 8 (1999): 195–201; F. Barth, "Introduction," in F. Barth (ed.), *Ethnic Groups and Boundaries* (London: Allen and Unwin, 1969); J. A. Agnew, "Territoriality and political identity in Europe," in M. Berezin and M. Schain (eds.), *Europe without borders: remapping territory, citizenship, and identity in a transnational age* (Baltimore, MD: Johns Hopkins University Press, 2003).

58. P. Hirst, *Space and Power: Politics, War and Architecture* (Cambridge: Polity Press, 2005), 27.

59. C. L. Montesquieu, *The Spirit of the Laws* (New York: Hafner, 1949 [1748]), 122.

60. Montesquieu, *The Spirit of the Laws*, 151–62.

61. D. Deudney, "Publius before Kant: federal-republican security and democratic peace," *European Journal of International Relations* 10 (2004): 315–56.

62. A. Milward, "Review article: the European Union as a superstate," *International History Review* 27 (2005): 90–105.

63. See, for example, K. R. Cox (ed.), *Spaces of Globalization* (New York: Guilford Press, 1998); N. Brenner, *New State Spaces* (New York: Oxford University Press, 2004).

64. M-F. Durand, J. Lévy, and D. Retaillé, *Le monde: espaces et systèmes* (Paris: Presses de la Fondation Nationale des Sciences Politiques and Dalloz, 1992).

65. J. Allen, "Powerful city networks: more than connections, less than domination and control," *GaWC Bulletin* 270 (May 2008), www.lboro.ac.uk/gawc.

66. B. Debarbieux, "Territoire," in J. Lévy and M. Lussault (eds.), *Dictionnaire de la Géographie et de l'Espace des Sociétés* (Paris: Belin, 2003), 911.

67. Brenner, *New State Spaces*, 130.

68. P. Musso, *L'ideologia delle reti* (Milan: Apogeo, 2007), 233.

69. Hirst, *Space and Power*, 45.

70. R. Hausbert, "Déterritorialisation," in J. Lévy and M. Lussault (eds.), *Dictionnaire de la Géographie et de L'Espace des Sociétés* (Paris: Belin, 2003), 244–45.

71. P. J. Taylor, *World City Network* (London: Routledge, 2004).

72. J. A. Agnew, *Place and Politics: The Geographical Mediation of State and Society* (London: Allen and Unwin, 1987).

73. E. S. Casey, "Between geography and philosophy: what does it mean to be in the place-world?" *Annals of the Association of American Geographers* 91 (2001): 683.

74. E. S. Casey, *The Fate of Place: A Philosophical History* (Berkeley: University of California Press, 1997), x.

75. Casey, *The Fate of Place*, 298–300.

76. Casey, *The Fate of Place*, 337.

77. Casey, *The Fate of Place*, 339.

78. Agnew, "Space:Place."

79. R. D. Sack, *Homo Geographicus* (Baltimore, MD: Johns Hopkins University Press, 1997), 58.

80. Sack, *Homo Geographicus*, 16.

81. V. Shue, *The Reach of the State: Sketches of the Chinese Body Politic* (Stanford, CA: Stanford University Press, 1988), 3–4.

82. M. Berezin and J. Diez-Medrano, "Distance matters: place, political legitimacy and popular support for European integration," *Comparative European Politics* 6 (2008): 23.

83. Connolly, "The complexities of sovereignty," 41–42.

84. D. Ley, "Transnational spaces and everyday lives," *Transactions of the Institute of British Geographers* 29 (2004): 157.

85. For a specific example, see S. C. McKay, "Zones of regulation: restructuring local control in privatized export zones," *Politics and Society* 32 (2004): 171–202; and, more generally, P. Knox et al., *The Geography of the World Economy* (London: Hodder, Fifth Edition, 2008), chapter 3.

86. D. E. Paul, *Rescaling International Political Economy: Subnational States and the Regulation of the Global Political Economy* (London: Routledge, 2005).

87. M. E. Shin and J. A. Agnew, *Berlusconi's Italy: Mapping Contemporary Italian Politics* (Philadelphia: Temple University Press, 2008)

88. L. Ricolfi, *Le tre società. E ancora possible salvare l'unità dell'Italia?* (Milan: Guerini, 2007).

89. D. Massey, *Power-Geometries and the Politics of Space-Time* (Heidelberg: University of Heidelberg, Department of Geography, Hettner Lectures 2, 1999), 22.

90. J. Agnew, *Place and Politics in Modern Italy* (Chicago: University of Chicago Press, 2002), 22.

91. P. Mair, "Ruling the void: the hollowing of Western democracy," *New Left Review* 42 (2006): 44.

CHAPTER 2

SOVEREIGNTY MYTHS AND TERRITORIAL STATES

The ideal of sovereignty, in the sense of sovereign or centralized power lodged in a central place and exercised over a definite territory, has been a significant element in the view of the world as necessarily divided up into discrete territorial states. Indeed, the entire modern discourse about statehood is intimately bound up with claims to sovereignty over territory. It was not always so. Much of the cultural logic of sovereignty in the way it is often now used derives not just from the longevity of its invocation as such but from an earlier association with religious and political ideals in which the body of the sovereign/monarch served to symbolize the larger body politic irrespective of its geographic shape. Transmuted from the person of the monarch into "the people" in eighteenth- and nineteenth-century Western Europe and the United States, the body to which the state provided the head was now strictly popular and territorial rather than transubstantiated by a claim for divine appointment. Extended worldwide in the twentieth century by such claims as the right to national self-determination and the legal equality between sovereign states (ones that recognize one another), the logical association between sovereignty and territory has become virtually unassailable.

Critical to the conversion of sovereignty from a religious-monarchical principle to a popular-territorial conception of the exercise of power was the summoning of the people as a unity whose distinctiveness was the basis for the state's acting in its name. This has provided much of the mythic basis on which the claim to state sovereignty now largely rests. Myths are not simply falsehoods or mere deceptions. They are presumptions that are influential precisely because they have a long history of repetition and rehearsal. They have also entered into practice. As such, the myth of sovereignty as a product of peoplehood is invulnerable to much criticism because many of the successes of state-based activities of the recent past—democratization of everyday life, the rule of law, the self-determination of hitherto subjugated social groups, the expansion of social and economic rights, the regulation of economic activities to protect consumers and workers, etc.—have relied on popular sovereignty as both stimulus and justification. If one criticizes territorialized sovereignty as it is usually invoked, one is thereby criticizing rule by "the people." Consequently, the appeal of the idea of sovereignty as resting on popular-territorialized rule should not be underestimated. A book such as *Politics without Sovereignty* claims that recent thinking in social science (particularly the field of international relations) has too easily abandoned territorialized sovereignty for the siren song of a globalizing world (the desire for fraternity, the appeal of a world without borders, etc.) because it is sovereignty that underwrites popular self-rule.[1] Absent this version of sovereignty, therefore, democratic politics is seen as impossible. Even when the state is "captured" by this or that interest group, those left out can always look to the day when they can capture the state for their purposes, presumably, once again, those of "the people."

In this chapter I endeavor to show that discourse about territorial sovereignty often reduces to three interlocking myths. Their very longevity suggests that they are much more woven into the fabric of thought and, hence, are all the more pernicious in their effects, than are the globalization myths discussed in chapter 1. Of the three myths relayed here, if the first two relate largely to "internal" sovereignty or rule over a given territory, the third projects the presumption of absolute territorial sovereignty into the "external" realm of world politics. Much of this sovereignty discourse is often taken for granted as self-evident by both commentators and practitioners. From our earliest school days we are presented with world maps that imagine the world primarily as a mosaic of colors representing the territories of "states" into which the world is divided. This presumably "natural" fact about the world is remembered long after the details have been forgotten. The economic and political relationships (from trade and profit repatriation to military bases and colonial dominance) that transgress and subvert the map are lost from view. The easy visualization of the world political map hides the real political-economic complexity of the world. Its "obviousness," however, proves to be anything but. In the first place, I survey the history of the idea of sovereignty by reference to the idea of the "body politic," and show how this mythic idea is still far from a dead letter even in the face of the globalization trends raised in the previous chapter. The main reason for this persistence is that the idea of "the people," in the form today of the "nation," has come to embody the principle of sovereignty. This draws attention to the second myth of sovereignty. Thus, in the example I pursue, that of the making of modern Greece in Macedonia, an everyday popular nationalism has come to underpin the claim to territorialized statehood. The Greek case is particularly interesting because it is a European example with parallels to many other European (and Western) states (more broadly) and a case of a state that emerged out of the disintegration of an empire (the Ottoman Empire here) with parallels also to so many of today's states with their origins in imperial collapse.

But perhaps the true "hypocrisy" of the "game" of sovereignty has been that along with the problematic claim that it is invariably territorial (and based on the rule of "the people" in a discrete jurisdiction) have gone two other often ignored corollaries that are equally misleading: that all states have equal sovereignty over their territories (and in relation to one another) and state territories are exclusive jurisdictions with "territorial integrity" in which no other type of power than the state's sovereign power can be rooted or is capable of penetrating. These together constitute a third sovereignty myth that is at the root of that modern geopolitical thinking that admits of little or no agency beyond that of states as independent and self-contained actors. In this book as a whole I wish to show how different the actual practice of state sovereignty has been relative to the mythic ideal. The territory of the state has never anywhere been the inviolate territorialized political body that the three sovereignty myths suppose. What has happened is that focus on the ideal, largely a by-product of nationalism, has actually obscured the real practice of sovereignty.

SOVEREIGNTY AND THE "BODY POLITIC"

The image of the modern state as a bodily form has long dominated the discursive field and visual representation of political theory. Perhaps the most influential metaphor in reproducing this imaginary (in the sense of a concrete landscape of power as visualized on maps) is that of the "body politic." The shape or form of the state has been imagined as akin to that of the human body, thus naturalizing and normalizing the state in one metaphorical move. Often this is portrayed as simply an early modern European phenomenon, later resurrected by fascism, with a shift from organic to mechanistic or machine images in the seventeenth and later centuries. In fact, the notion of the body politic seems to have had a much longer life, still sustaining popular understandings of statehood today even as the king's body, the literal source of the metaphor, has been transformed into the territorial geo-body of the state. I think that this is a useful way of showing how a highly territorialized view of state sovereignty has come to prevail in much contemporary thought.

In this section, I want to trace the intellectual genealogy of the "body politic," drawing particularly on geographer Jean Gottmann's account of statehood but also with attention to more recent contributions along similar lines.[2] I also want to show how the idea of the body politic has persisted as a trope for expressing the necessary authority (legitimate power) of a state over a given territory. Living bodies must form a corporeal whole; as a result, sovereignty becomes an entirely territorial affair. Finally, I suggest that because the metaphor defies a deterritorialized or contingent sovereignty, it has served as a powerful intellectual barrier to thinking about sovereignty beyond the territorial confines of the state.

As Gottmann points out at some length, the metaphor of the body politic dominated medieval European political thought.[3] In particular, he cites John of Salisbury (1159) as defining a republic (by which he meant any type of polity) as a "mystical body" in his discussion of *pro patria mori* (accepting death for one's country) but noting that at that time, "*patria*, or the realm, or *respublica*, may still have been more closely associated with a community than with territory."[4] Community did not necessarily require propinquity or geographical adjacency. Indeed, in heavily citing the work of the German medieval historian Ernst Kantorowicz as a primary source, Gottmann endorses the idea of the transference of a corporeal language from the body of Christ to that of the body politic in which the monarch is its head and the various estates (nobility, peasants, etc.) are its members.[5] A religious image underwrote a political one. This does not mean that Christianity was inherently territorial in its conception of space. Far from it; the dominant Christian view had always been of a "universalist transcendence of place."[6] In the European medieval understanding of the *principium unitatis* binding the body of Christ to his earthly followers, in Cassirer's words: "The totality of mankind appeared as a single state founded and monarchically governed by God himself and every partial unity, ecclesiastic or secular, derived its right from this primeval unity."[7] Thomas Aquinas was the principal advocate of this view. But rather than a divinely inspired institution to remedy human sin as previous authorities would have it, Aquinas read government from Aristotle's viewpoint as originating "in the social instinct of man. It is this instinct that first leads to family-life and from there, in a continuous development, to all the other and higher forms of commonwealth."[8] This led away from "any theory of world authority, preferring instead a vision of a world of independent and equal political communities."[9] More particularly, God was not now a *primum mobile* but a *causa remota* in the organization of political authority. As a result there was a drift in medieval thought and practice from acceptance of a hierarchy of communities with specified purposes (including, of course, the Pope in Rome) to a "concentration of right and power in the highest and widest group on the one hand and the individual man on the other, at the cost of all intermediate groups."[10]

Slowly and unevenly, first France, then England, and then other proto-states began to invest in the concept of "man-centered kingship."[11] Interestingly, Gottmann sees this as a reaction to the rise of self-governing communities (such as the German and Italian city-states) in the fifteenth century and the increasing divorce of political debate from the metaphysical tradition invoking divine will.[12] Machiavelli is a key figure in this regard. He abandoned the medieval tradition of the pretended divine origin of the rights of kings to argue for a stand-alone state whose ruler's right to rule rested on the "voluntary contractual submission of the governed."[13] Despite this, even at a slightly later time, Martin Luther still adhered to the medieval doctrine of a *corpus Christianum*, in which the kingdom of God and that of the world remained largely separate if conjoined by the necessity for government to use its power "to protect the church by curbing evil."[14] By the late sixteenth century, however, what Gottmann terms the "inner divisions of Europe and the vast potential of a new and diversified overseas world" as a result of European colonialism, reinforced the direct link between monarchical sovereignty and territory.[15] In Gierke's words, "the concept of the state became the exclusive property of a community which recognizes no external superior."[16] In the philosophers Jean Bodin and Thomas Hobbes the new order of territorial states as the emerging manifestation of the historic body politic found its first modern prophets. Gottmann writes: "As the concept of a corporate national sovereignty gradually replaced the personal prerogatives of the individual sovereign, territorial delimitation acquired much more significance: it fixed limits to the spatial extent of sovereignty and outlined the size and location of it. The territory became the physical and legal embodiment of national identity, and the jurists and philosophers of the seventeenth century began to discuss how sovereign governments ought to use these prerogatives."[17]

This is very much the same story as that told in the more recent accounts of the concept of the body politic and its growing connection to territory in sixteenth- and seventeenth-century Europe. For political theorist Mark Neocleous, for example, a writer who emphasizes the role of the language used to describe the modern political imaginary as crucial to understanding the state-centric character of modern political theory and practice, "to understand the idea of the state we must grapple with the idea of the body politic" because "the image of the body has been a central way of imagining order and, as a consequence, has played an important role in legitimizing the exercise of state power."[18] He then embarks on a detailed account of the "body of the state" that follows much the same intellectual trajectory as that of Gottmann, including recourse to the argument of Kantorowicz about the king's two bodies: the mortal one subject to decay and death and the political one subject to inheritance as in the immortal phrase "the King is dead, long live the King." With Thomas Hobbes, the modern concept of the state is invented by transforming the body of the king into "an omnipotent political body-machine, an inhuman person with a force and will of his own."[19] From this viewpoint, and crucially, the sense that the "king never dies" expressed a continuity in the absolute right of a monarch to rule even if this particular one has died. Beyond the immediate symbolic role of the monarch, however, and quoting in this connection Jean Bodin, "sovereignty is that absolute and perpetual power vested in a commonwealth."[20] Thus as monarchy was subsequently undermined, the impersonal state that replaced it inherited absolute and permanent power in the form of a body politic if now without its monarchical dressing.

Moreover, if Gottmann saw the original invocation of the body-politic metaphor in the late medieval period as an assertion of aristocratic and monarchical privilege against the burgeoning power of self-governing communities, Neocleous sees the metaphor as serving a continuing function along these lines. Indeed, he claims that it became more important in underwriting sovereignty once early capitalism required the protection of private property "released from the body of the monarch" in the face of a growing and dangerous class of laborers liberated by the demise of feudalism.[21] Thus, "the sovereign 'body' of the state emerges as an attempt to resolve or defer what turns out to be *the fundamental crisis of modernity*. Concomitantly, the image of the body of the state emerges as a way of *imagining order* amidst this crisis."[22] According to Neocleous, even proponents of a radical politics who should be wary of inherited metaphors, such as John O'Neill and Donna Haraway, have been seduced by the idea of the body politic as one that can enhance democracy once turned into a vehicle for dissent and critique.[23] As Neocleous warns, in fact, it has always been a metaphor that favors order at any cost. It has always been about disciplining real, individual bodies in the interests of a fabulated one. It is thus not readily expropriated for other purposes.

The sociologist Chris Smaje also emphasizes the appropriation of Christ's mystical mediating role to "underwrite political legitimacy" and, if "this theocratic warrant for political rule did not survive the secularization of political philosophy between the sixteenth and eighteenth centuries, . . . the essentials of its structure were maintained."[24] Smaje underlines Locke's political theory as symptomatic of the main way in which the body politic was territorialized more than the arguments of Bodin, Hobbes, Petty, and Montaigne, which figure so prominently in Gottmann's and Neocleous's accounts: "Locke drew boundaries around communities not on the basis of mere subjection to government, but according to the qualities of social and political life through which the subjection was conveyed."[25] Thus was "sovereignty suffused through the social body" because Locke's theory (and the practice endorsed by the Peace of Westphalia in 1648) "was predisposed to the closure of political communities around a territorial space congruent with the cultural attributes supposedly necessary to the citizen's proper exercise of that sovereignty—in other words, to the ethnogenesis of territorial nation-states within the broader field of a European political meta-community."[26]

Gottmann for one does not return explicitly to the metaphor of the body politic once he has noted its transformation from a monarchical to a popular basis in the early modern period. But the logic of his argument certainly implies that it has remained in force ever since in bonding sovereignty to territory. For example, the obsession with "security" that Gottmann associates with twentieth-century law and politics is traced to what he calls "the consistency of thought that leads from Plato's *Laws* to Hobbes and the classic interpretation of sovereignty by many twentieth century lawyers. They see it [security] as a large sign reading 'keep off these grounds,' posted on territorial limits."[27] That the body-politic metaphor has had persisting significance is in fact a major claim of Neocleous. Even with the rise of liberalism and democracy, the metaphor of the body politic has persisted as a powerful trope underwriting territorialized state sovereignty, and not just for the "special case" of fascism (in Italy, Germany, and elsewhere) when the use of the body-politic metaphor was rampant.

The influence of Carl Schmitt's political theology, first developed in 1920s Germany but recently revived in a variety of intellectual quarters, is an example of this continuity, albeit one subject to continuous challenge from more liberal directions. Drawing directly from claims of biblical authority, Schmitt sees state sovereignty as necessarily rooted in the enmity that humanity has inherited from the Fall. From this viewpoint, what is key is to restore in a secular age the essence (if not the monarchical trappings) of the older theology-based sovereignty recognizing the need for security in the face of inevitable conflicts. In particular, the state's organic unity was under threat from the proliferation of forms of "indirect power," which Schmitt associated with a rampant liberalism and other practices that reflect the belief that "everything in the world is a human affair," and must be restored as the highest and most decisive instrument of the political.[28] An organic version of the metaphor, over and against the mechanical one envisaged by Hobbes, is thus reinstated. The biblical story of Cain and Abel, in which one brother *had* to kill the other, animates Schmitt's view that in a world of political Friends and Enemies "sovereignty (and thus the state itself) resides . . . in determining definitively what constitutes public order and security, in determining when they are disturbed, and so on."[29] This sort of thinking currently animates the Christian (Protestant) nationalist right in the United States, notwithstanding its apparent cultural distance from the Catholic Schmitt. Schmitt's explicit hostility to liberalism, in the sense of a political philosophy grounded in human-governed existence, can also appeal to those, such as Giorgio Agamben and his many recent acolytes, who see little or no difference between fascist and liberal-democratic statehood.[30] If Schmitt is the great defender of the sovereign exception, Agamben, though sharing the view that "the rule of law in a state is enabled by a practice of sovereignty that rises above the law," imagines the possibility of a politics beyond the political as defined by state sovereignty.[31] Agamben sees the ancient Roman distinction between Roman citizens, on the one hand, and the barbarians, on the other, as the founding moment of the Friends/Enemies distinction.[32] But the essentially theological roots (and territorialized conception of sovereignty) of his argument provide a weak philosophical base for a critical or progressive politics. Simply flipping around who is Friend and who is Enemy in an oppositional couplet, and seeing one side as potentially instrumental in overcoming the entire paradox of sovereignty, still leaves you trapped by the body-politic metaphor and the origins of its metaphysical genealogy in political theology. From this viewpoint, as I suggest later, even Hobbes would provide you a better start.

Citing its recent usage well beyond fascist sources, Neocleous, for his part, consequently disputes all of the usual stories for the alleged demise of the body-politic metaphor and its derivatives: from Locke's rejection of the state as a natural entity (even as he achieved much the same outcome by territorializing it); the rationalization of society presumably depersonalizing authority once the English king's head had rolled in 1649; and the replacement of the organic by mechanistic metaphors with the rise of the Cartesian mechanics so important to Hobbes and some later thinkers. In the latter two cases, Neocleous plausibly claims that the charisma of a leader was not so easily divorced from sovereignty (witness the rapid rise of Napoleon Bonaparte in the aftermath of the French Revolution) and that the body of the people or social body became the new form in which the metaphor of the body politic was perpetuated. Indeed, he argues that rather than fading, the metaphor has if anything been strengthened by its use in assimilating the state to a specific national-territorial society. It has become the means whereby states can defend themselves (as all bodies must do) from disease, contamination, and dismemberment; the very core of the physicality with which statehood is rendered manifest in everyday life. Protecting the state (and its elites) from the threat of disorder emanating from internal unruly classes and external enemies intent on challenging domestic stability by asserting some alternative political-economic model have become the contemporary justifications for the current location of sovereignty. As a result, "Playing on the doctrine of the king's two bodies, one might say that what took place in the late eighteenth century was not the death of the metaphor of the body politic, but its demise. The metaphor lives on, in another form: the sovereign body is dead, long live the sovereign body."[33]

One vital feature of Hobbes's watershed transformation of the body-politic metaphor was to point away from the political theology that had hitherto still informed its use.[34] Whether or not Hobbes saw this as a permanent resolution, short of the Millennium or Christ's Second Coming, is an open question.[35] He was in many respects a transitional rather than a completely modern secular figure. For example, unlike many other political thinkers of his era he avoided the marriage analogy in describing the relationship between subjects and sovereigns even as he could not completely accept the idea of women as autonomous political subjects.[36] But in *Leviathan* and other works Hobbes undoubtedly did try to untangle a reasoned conception of sovereignty from the religious and fabulist roots of the body-politic metaphor.[37] He set the terms of debate in which much recent academic discussion of sovereignty has been conducted even as practice has evolved in the face of dramatic socio-political change (following such events as, inter alia, the Thirty Years War, the Holocaust, the Cold War, and globalization). Hobbes clearly adumbrated the idea of sovereignty, in Daniel Philpott's words, as "supreme authority within a territory."[38] This signifies the autonomous rule over a given territory free from external interference that is the timeless definition of sovereignty in contemporary political science.

Crucial for later understanding and practice, Hobbes saw sovereignty as the consequence of a "multitude" of subjects coming together to constitute a state but that "cannot by its own volition simply dissolve sovereign power it has itself created."[39] This did not mandate absolute subjugation of subjects to the state. In other words, disobedience is one thing, dissolution of the state something different entirely. The central paradox of modern state sovereignty as commonly understood, therefore, is owed to Hobbes: that the people is not the state itself, since only individual persons can act or consent, not the people understood as a collectivity, so the state they have endowed with power cannot be limited or overthrown by them once they have called it into existence; it exists as "some ultimate authority which is sovereign and absolute."[40] Yet, even if only metaphorically, in using a family/state analogy to articulate his theory of political obligation (the subjugation of children and servants to the parents is held as akin to that of subjects to state), Hobbes reinforced the tendency to see the state, if no longer in the singular person of the monarch, as a separate social entity that could be endowed with its own power and intentionality.

As Gottmann noted, the term *territory* as connected to statehood came into its own in Europe only in the fifteenth century and it is not until somewhat later that it actually becomes intertwined with the concepts of sovereignty and the body politic.[41] But intrinsic to the modern impersonal state as it has developed since the seventeenth century has been the necessity of asserting a fixed territorial space. Sovereignty, therefore, is now regarded as necessarily territorial. Consequently, "the statist political imaginary is necessarily a territorial imaginary."[42] As well as a people occupying a given space, and supposedly giving consent to a state's rule over them, the modern territorial body politic is also closely linked to the use of force because "territory is land occupied and maintained through terror."[43] Though at first sight perhaps rather surprising, this association has an etymological basis. The term *territory* derives both from the Latin *terra* (terrain or land) and *territorium* (an area from which people are warned off). Because *terrere*, the common source, is to frighten away, *territory* and *terror* thus appear to share something of a common etymology. As Stuart Elden puts it, this seems to be more than mere coincidence: "We can see this in practice too, in that creating a bounded space is, already, a violent act of exclusion; maintaining it as such requires constant vigilance and the mobilization of threat; and challenging it necessarily entails a transgression."[44] Max Weber's famous definition of state legitimacy as being based in the state's monopoly over the means of violence within its territory follows from this elemental juxtaposition. In this perspective, sovereignty rests firstly and ultimately on an original and continuing application of force over a territorial jurisdiction rather than on just either metaphysical fiat or individual consent. Nevertheless, state violence is often endowed with a sacral quality, ascribed to the protection it presumably provides to the "body" of a national population. In distinguishing "us" from "them" we have to be purged of home-grown threats (including those exemplary traitors from opposite sides of the Atlantic, Guy Fawkes and Benedict Arnold) at the same time that the boundary between us and them is itself established through warfare. From an anthropological perspective, state-mandated violence is necessary both to cleanse the national space of potential indigenous enemies and, through the blood sacrifice celebrated as "Our Glorious Dead" on war memorials, to make it almost impossible to think about the "territory" of one's state in terms other than those of absolute loyalty. Think how much the "sacrifice" of the New York City firefighters on September 11, 2001, has been used to frame the terrorist attacks of that day as attacks on an American "homeland" and not just as assaults on discrete sites that could be given quite different interpretations (the World Trade Center Towers as the control center for global capitalism and the Pentagon as the seat of U.S. military occupation of Arab lands, etc.). Blood sacrifice and a territorialized body politic go hand in glove. "United We Stand" and "We Will Never Forget."

In much of the world, states have been introduced or imposed from outside. Until the past two centuries, non-state societies predominated just about everywhere. What has provided the incentive for states to organize? There is little or no evidence that groups of people have ever freely organized themselves into territorial states in the absence of threats of violence from others. Social contract theories of statehood, such as that of Jean-Jacques Rousseau, seem completely wrong-headed. New states seem to have arisen either because of pressure from existing states or because some societies gained an edge over others in controlling resources when they began to develop state-like institutions (such as an army). But the remote origins of the doctrine of sanctified state violence as an underpinning of state sovereignty seem to lie specifically in modern Europe. They can be found in the principle of *cuius regio eius religio* (to whom is the region, his is the religion) associated with the violent fall-out from the Protestant Reformation, first accepted at the Diet of Speyer in 1526 but only really finally settled legally by the Peace of Westphalia in 1648. Of course, today we usually associate the word *terror* and derivatives such as *terrorism* and *terrorists* with non-state (and non-legitimate) actors. In apparently challenging the state monopoly on violence, however, as Neocleous claims, terrorism ironically can serve to underwrite it.[45] From this viewpoint, terrorism serves to bring alive the threat to the body politic from shadowy and unpredictable enemies. The everyday significance of territorialized sovereignty is thereby highlighted rather than destabilized. In this way, terror directed against particular states can be an ally of state territorial sovereignty *tout court*. But, as I argue later, this is to forget that the shadowy nature of terrorism makes distinguishing between those who are protected and those who are being protected against increasingly illegible. Surveillance (telephone tapping, video taping of public spaces, systematic collection of personal and financial data) to combat external threats increasingly impinges on the freedoms of those "insiders" (the people) against whom the threats are presumably directed. Territorial sovereignty is not always readily reinforced by the invocation of and action against presumably "external" threats. They can, indeed, undermine it in a substantive sense.

Of course, once established, states are not simply "coercion-wielding organizations."[46] They can do all sorts of things for and to their populations besides threaten them. Indeed, the legitimacy of states is not just a mask behind which states hide their proclivity for violence. The word *legit-*

imacy implies at least a modicum of consent. As early modern theorists of state sovereignty from Machiavelli to Rousseau emphasized, the use of force in governing was a sign of the breakdown of a state's sovereignty rather than a symbol of its success. To Hobbes, for example, the state or "commonwealth," as he termed it, was not just something to be feared but existed precisely because it mediated between citizens in restraining their "natural passions."[47] Max Weber, typically invoked as the source of the argument that state sovereignty rests initially and finally on the threat of force against a state's own population, argued that states have many other roles also underpinning their claims to sovereignty: from public health to welfare and culture.[48] Overstating state sovereignty's reliance on a monopoly of *internal* violence contributes to overemphasizing its overall reliance on territoriality. The external threats that states use in the name of "national security" to justify military expenditures and the revenues needed to pay for them, however, clearly have continued to help define sovereignty as inherently territorial long after the "founding moment" of statehood.[49] But the idea that "the management of obedience has always been the primary task of sovereignty"[50] misses the very complexities of state sovereignty and its effects "that have inhabited it all along."[51] The real danger in confusing sovereignty with obedience and the state with violence is to assume a necessary association between liberation and statelessness. This seems to be the central assumption of much of the writing about sovereignty deriving from contemporary cultural theory.[52]

As Gottmann also points out, however, the "Platonic doctrine" of a neat correspondence between security and territory also both defies the need to "coordinate security with opportunity," as the need to trade, move, and invest may not be very territorial at all, *and* it neglects the actual historical record, which suggests strongly that the central significance of territory for political organization (at least in the form of the modern territorial state) has in fact been limited for long periods of time.[53] Individual and social allegiances beyond state borders, not to mention the needs of trade, investment, and alliance, have frequently trumped the needs of territorialized security. Not all seats of effective power over people's lives, and decreasingly so, are located within the borders of a given state. Until sovereignty and territory are symbolically disentangled, however, there is little prospect of seeing the possibility of and realizing a politics more appropriate for such an interdependent and "fluid" world. As long as the territorialized body politic of the myth of sovereignty is held inviolate as either an Act of God or a Fact of Nature, such a goal will be hard to achieve.

NATION-STATES AND SOVEREIGNTY

The nation-state as we know it today is the product of the European model that slowly emerged from the seventeenth century onward and was then progressively imposed or exported elsewhere.[54] In this historical-geographical context, the case of Greece provides some illuminating points for understanding the course of nation-statehood everywhere else. It was one of the first places where a new nation-state was made from part of an old but non-European empire. The Greek case reveals that there is nothing natural (or ancient) about the collective enmities to which hard borders are supposedly the invariable solution. Rather than emerging in response to absolute antagonism between primordial or essentialized groups, antagonism, like the groups to which it refers, has had to be made. Beyond the Platonic ideal of the body politic, therefore, sovereignty as it is usually understood also relies for its apparent veracity on the commonsense notion that in the modern world there is a clear "inside" and "outside" to society as such defined by the territorial nation to which every state has become conjoined (not the least in aspiration). This is the myth of the nation-hyphen-state.

Borders (and territory) have been crucial to embodying this myth. The original European model of the nation-state was a direct response to the religious bloodletting between Catholics and Protestants following the Protestant Reformation in the sixteenth and the early seventeenth centuries. Its projection into the margins of Europe and beyond was marketed as a solution to the problem of providing a cultural justification for statehood: the nation. Making the nation has required reaching deep into the past to provide a genealogy with which the national group can identify. In many places finding much in the way of any sort of ethnic homogeneity in situ has been difficult. Territory or *topos* has been crucial in this regard. Territory provides the ground on which to stake the claim for nation. It does so by using the authority of a common cultural heritage to establish a unified past for that bloc of space, assembling folklore traditions, associating critical historic incidents with specific sites, and using evidence from archaeological and historical studies to justify current or expansive borders, create a capital city, and sanctify national monuments. Territory, and the borders that define it, thus gives material shape to the national dream of collective emancipation. Even if a nation is without any recent history of political unity or independence, ancient sources can be discovered to give credence to contemporary claims of territorial continuity with historical precursors who either died out or became part of some other political enterprise. "Historical rights" of occupancy are invoked to justify current occupation of a given territory or an expanded one.[55] In Greece, the Western tradition of a classical Hellenic past proved especially compelling in providing the national genealogy, but this offered no ready solution to where to place the borders of the modern nation-state. This is where Macedonia acquired its significance. It provided the critical regional confluence between the national memory of a heroic Hellenic past and the existence of an uncertain present focused on the border in question. In this construction, it is borders and the threats to them from beyond (and before) that they conjure up that make the nations and not vice versa. Once the borders are tentatively geographically positioned and not before, the nation-state in its turn begins to make its place. After examining how nationalism has provided a powerful underpinning for state sovereignty through its focus on the dangers emanating from beyond the nation-state's borders, I turn to the example of Modern Greek statehood and its crucial relationship to the so-called Macedonian Question.

NATIONALISM AND TERRITORIAL SOVEREIGNTY

In contemporary social science territorial social formations are usually seen as the root of all identities. The boundaries (including nation-state borders) between territorial social groups are then viewed as defined by opposing and exclusionary identities that *pre-exist* the coming of the borders. Thus, nation-states are assimilated to a notion of social boundaries of which their borders are simply just another, if frequently more fundamental or definitional, exemplar. Yet exactly the opposite process has often been closer to the norm with respect to the relationship between identity and borders: national identities have been crafted *after* borders are more or less in place by ethnic cleansing or expulsions, forced assimilation, and other planned and spontaneous efforts at cultural homogenization by central authorities and their local agents.[56]

Reinforcing the presumption that nations always come before borders, most academic accounts of nationalism, in focusing exclusively on, say, vernacular literacy, ethnic symbolism, or national self versus other, also assume that once an exclusive national identity is achieved, it is readily perpetuated within the national population. A border is then defined *around* the national groups in question. This is to miss what is precisely one of the main sources of the political strength of nationalism: that being perpetually in question, national identity has to be constantly re-invented through the mobilization of national populations (or significant segments thereof). Borders, because they are at the edge of the national-state territory, provide the essential focus for this collective uncertainty. Even as defined strictly, therefore, but by also remaining in perpetual question, state borders provide the center of attention for more generalized elite, and sometimes popular, anxiety about what still remains to be achieved by the state for the nation.

The distinction between social boundary and state border is analytically significant. But in practice the two become fused as the simple "mental map" is conjured up by the latter and its material enforcement of "checkpoints" on the ground come to dominate the complexities of the former. State borders are not, therefore, simply just another example of, albeit more clearly marked, boundaries. They are qualitatively different in their capacity to both redefine other boundaries and to override more locally based distinctions. They also have a specific historical and geographical origin. If social boundaries are universal and transcendental, if varying in their incidence and precise significance, state borders, in the sense of definitive borderlines, certainly are not. They have not been around from time immemorial. Attempts to claim that bordering is historic in the sense of unequivocal and definite delimitation, or to take bordering as a given of state formation are, therefore, empirically problematic.

Take, for example, the borders of the United States. They seem well defined, at least in map sense. But historically the entire development of the United States has been about where the American project began and ended.[57] From its origins in colonial revolt, the United States was created through a contested process of extraordinary territorial expansion. Its borders were constantly in motion as new territories were settled and then later incorporated as new "states" into the United States. The U.S. government exerted sovereignty for long periods of time over people who did not have representation within that government. "The Constitution followed the flag."[58] But with the Spanish-American War this came to an end. In a series of Supreme Court cases from 1901 until 1922, the application of a novel legal doctrine produced fuzzy borders for the United States that have since licensed a sort of "leasehold empire" of territories and "special zones" that were "part of the United States, but not entirely so."[59] With the creation of a new class of "unincorporated territories"—Puerto Rico, Cuba, Philippines, etc.—the United States was able to both create a zone of uncertainty around its territory, and thus put the precise limits of the country legally and politically perpetually in question, and lay the groundwork for an expansive view of "its" identity that could rely on the ambiguity of its territorial limits. In the words of Bart Sparrow: "The United States did not have to have an empire based on territory; it could exert informal control instead."[60] Yet the map betrays no such ambiguity.

The model of statehood that the boundary/border distinction relies on is in fact one that was only slowly established beginning in parts of Western Europe in the seventeenth and eighteenth centuries and that has since spread worldwide. The details of how this has occurred have differed from case to case but each case is neither totally unique nor simply the result of a contagious diffusion from Europe. Rather, the "connective tissues" of capitalist expansion and European colonialism (and its breakdown) progressively incorporated different parts of the world into the logic of nation-statehood that has now become the taken-for-granted "common sense" of modernity.[61] The very idea of a "model" of anything (such as statehood) was very much a product of the European seventeenth century. Between 1610 and 1650 many leading European intellectuals, such as Descartes, Leibniz, and Newton, saw rationalism—the divorce of human reason from the details of place and time—as a necessary and revolutionary response to the religious wars and crises of governance of the times. A universal language of reason would provide general justifications for what had previously been seen as particular and local phenomena. In particular, one of the most important requirements in constructing the new "Cosmopolis" was to abandon the overlapping jurisdictions and mixed modes of political authority that had previously characterized Europe. This was undoubtedly underwritten by the pressure to improve revenue collection in pursuit of improved military capacity in an age of religious wars and the need to legitimize the territorial centralization of a wide range of administrative practices; but the novelty of the nature of the cultural logic deserves underlining. Ipso facto, borders between states would henceforth be defined in the boldest and most rigorous form rather than left deliberately fuzzy.

As a universalistic logic of clear definition replaced a particularistic conception of accumulated local practice, definitive maps of the new European states began to appear. One consequence, as Michael Biggs has noted, was that "the land was now literally cut into pieces by state boundaries: Each piece could be held in isolation from its geographical context."[62] Also, in this way, "Putting the state on the map meant knowing and imagining it as real—and, so, making it a reality."[63] Eventually, and well beyond Europe, as Neocleous notes, "sovereignty does not simply imply space, it *creates* it; left to itself, the earth has no political form. We need to therefore appreciate the political function of maps in *constructing* rather than merely reproducing the world and in *creating* rather than merely tracing borders. Borders are constructed through a socio-political process; to the extent that the map helps create the borders, so it helps create the thing which is being bordered: the geo-body created literally on paper."[64] This visualization was encouraged by developments in political philosophy that saw no political space in the "state of nature" but authorized it solely under the rigorous bounding of absolute authority (as in Hobbes), private property (as in Locke), or the general will (as in Rousseau) as sanctioned by the social contract. This emergent political territory not only separated the modern polity from the feudal, but did so by "creating a territorial grounding within which constitutional discourse and political exchange could take place."[65] The technology of the map, therefore, invented for the mind's eye the "geo-body" of the state as the prime representation of an otherwise abstract body politic.[66]

Formalized with the Peace of Westphalia in 1648 and then boosted by the American and French Revolutions at the end of the eighteenth century with their stress on territorial/national unity, in imitation of classical referents drawn from democratic Athens and republican Rome bestowed uniquely on Europe, the model state was a rigidly territorial enterprise. As a result, for the ideal-type modern state there can be neither overlaps in authority nor ambiguity in territorial sovereignty. Borders are brought into existence to hinder overlap and ambiguity. Consequently, cultures are thought of as naturally integral and territorial. Territory, the putative solution to the early-modern European crisis in political authority, thus became the leitmotif of modern "nation"-statehood everywhere. Politically ambitious elites with claims on national genealogies were drawn to the territorial model of statehood as the means for realizing their ambitions. Such "political transfer" subsequently became a long-run feature of even the most modest of institutional innovations throughout Europe. Under a later Romanticism, redolent in writers as different as Rousseau, Fichte, and Hegel, the state was defined as a political inevitability. In this way, the continuing effect of time, in the sense of the historical contingency that had produced this or that state and that could lead beyond its confines, was fatefully obscured by an emphasis on the now permanent territoriality of nation-statehood as the culmination of history. "Historical rights" to occupy a territory, and usually to expand it, were based on claims of first occupancy or on the central importance to national identity of a particular territory or of specific historic sites (battlefields, birthplaces of national heroes, etc.) within it.

Crucial to this process of hyphenating nation with state was the impact of the early nineteenth-century turn from the absolute universalism of the Enlightenment to the universalizing of the particular under Romanticism. In this manifestation, the state, now invariably hyphenated with the nation, "became the necessary form of civilized social organization. The consequently more obvious political fragmentation of Europe became the oxymoronic source of its fundamental unity, just as 'individualism' became the equally paradoxical criterion of social conformity; and in the most radical undermining of the universalist agenda, many a culture appointed itself the touchstone of European identity."[67] The exceptional character of Europe, therefore, as inherited from the ancient Greeks and Romans (and also, when laudable, each nation's own primordial ancestors), sanctioned the construction of absolute borders to distinguish each offspring's claims to superiority from the others. Yet the new borders were not simply a recapitulation of the "limits" of the ancients but ones that are always potentially labile in an increasingly dynamic (and capitalist) world. In the words of Aldo Schiavone, quoting in the last two sentences from Karl Marx's *Grundrisse*:

> The revolution of modernity meant, above all, abolishing limits—sweeping away not only the obstacles that had blocked ancient civilizations, but also the very nature of limit as an insuperable barrier and the belief that cyclicality was destiny. Boundaries were transformed into movable frontiers, continually shifted forward. The new forms of labor and science set potentialities in motion, ensuring that the history of the Western world would never again attempt 'to remain something it has become' (as in Aristides' idea of an eternal empire). Instead it would begin to be identified with 'the absolute movement of becoming' (as in our common sense notion that there is nothing that does not change).[68]

However, the model of absolute territorial nation-statehood has worked effectively, if at all, only if large parts of national populations participate in the everyday nationalism that is centered to a significant degree on the journey toward and the anxiety engendered by the fixing of borders. As Michel Foucault has emphasized, modern subjectivity or sense of self is intimately related to the development of modern statehood and its claimed fusion with nation.[69] But the achievement of personal subjectivity is not simply the result of direct coercion, as Foucault seems to intimate, or an unconscious acceptance of elite resentments and complexes by the masses, as so many popular accounts of nationalism seem to have it.[70] Rather, at the same time as "persons" become "individuals" under the gaze of the state (as a result of the constitution of modern subjects qua citizens and the establishment of a national genealogy through rooting these individuals in territory), they also have the now socially recognized capacity as individuals to invest in their own accommodations to the nation-state. Even as individual persons come to see local folklore within a national context, for example, "their *uses* of that ideology allow them to carve out personal maneuvering space within the collective."[71] Official views become subject to "semantic lability" and "disemia" as individuals and groups challenge and violate establishment terminology and rules.[72] All sorts of localized segmentary social relations, resting on familial, ethnic, and residential ties, can conflict with state-endorsed repertoires of political and social behavior. It is in borderlands, places most symbolic of the achievements of nationhood because that is where the nation is most subject to "cartographic anxiety," that the persistence and/or efflorescence of cultural variety are subject to the most systematic assault from centralized power. Such regions also acquire a mythic dimension insofar as they evoke hybridity and the possibilities of the chaos that could engulf the nation as a whole if such complex identities spread elsewhere.[73]

Nevertheless, everyday or "banal" nationalism ultimately has a corrosive impact on non-national political proclivities as the anxieties of individuals are conflated with those of the nation. As Ernest Renan famously alleged in his classic essay of 1882, "the essence of the nation is that all individuals have many things in common, and also that they have forgotten many things."[74] This emphasis on forgetting or on what cannot now be said is crucial. It draws attention to the selective retention of past social affiliations as people rhetorically fit them into the dominant narratives of the nation. As the fate of individuals, therefore, is inexorably tied to that of the nation-state, the segmentary logic of nation-statehood itself is revealed. The very claim to distinctiveness that underpins everyday nationalism needs to be constantly revisited and reinforced. The national stereotypes upon which claims to cultural distinctiveness rely are notoriously unrelated empirically to the actual personality traits of the "national" individuals to whom they allegedly apply.[75] Yet they persist because they are constantly repeated in national media, school textbooks and lessons, and everyday conversations.

Today, "almost every square inch of soil from Slovakia to Palau and back again—with the exception of Antarctica—has been shoe-horned into the sometimes pinching form of the nation-state."[76] Between 1901 and 2000, 177 new states claiming the nation-state designation were created and only twelve of these disappeared without subsequent revival.[77] Such international organizations as the League of Nations in the inter-war period and the United Nations in the years since 1944 have legitimized the whole process of state creation through hyphenation (of state with nation) by making the terms *nation* and *state* interchangeable. Thus, every flag flying outside UN headquarters in New York City is assumed to represent not only a government apparatus but also a group of people sharing a common national identity, irrespective of whether this is in fact the case. Most of the new states have appeared since the great wave of decolonization in the years after the Second World War. But the 1990s also saw a new set of nation-states as the former Yugoslavia and Soviet Union disintegrated. So the nation-state as an institutional form is far from exhausted. The doctrine of popular sovereignty is crucial to this continuing success in promising popular rule as the sequel to national independence. The borders of the nation-state are critical to the job of motivating everyday nationalism, even if only symbolically by designating where "We" begin and "They" end, as they also incessantly threaten to give way before overwhelming flows of outsiders and foreign influences. Borders are fungible, in the sense of performative phenomena that while giving the popular impression of total barriers must balance the contradictory tasks of allowing movement across them and enforcing territorial order. Consequently, border crises or threats to their integrity are fundamental to national self-definition. Borders have to be brought to mind often at great distances from where they are performed in order to imagine who is inside and who is outside their scope. This is how nations are imagined as tangible, physical entities that have an existence beyond the mere aggregation of the people who make them up. By extension, therefore, from this viewpoint there can be no nation without borders; the former follows from the latter.

With globalization, however, borders are not simply destabilized by the transnational movement of capital, people, and goods, which we might indeed expect, given my previous argument, to encourage border panics and, by reinforcing the fear of foreign contamination, to engender popular calls for the need to harden the border. The borders themselves must now be open to business if the nation is itself to prosper under new worldwide material conditions of large-scale foreign direct investment, the widely diffused appeal of globalized images of the "good life" and the consumer commodities to fulfill them, and increased flows of cross-border migrants in response to increased demand for certain categories of labor. In this regard, because of the economic necessity to allow open borders, the social distinction between those from outside and those from inside as inevitable cultural-political combatants (recall Carl Schmitt's "Friends and Enemies") loses much of its self-evident resonance. Thus, and today, previously border-specific policing activities are applied to entire populations (witness the massive use of closed-circuit television to monitor public spaces in British cities and the use of "action profiles" by police forces and private security organizations everywhere without reference to citizenship) and border procedures such as peremptory searches and on-the-spot investigations are applied to everyone with little or no discrimination between who might be citizens and who might be foreigners.[78] In this world, everyone is potentially hostile. We are all potential foreigners now, wherever and whoever we are. Identification papers are increasingly de rigueur for everyone, including well away from border zones, partly because there are so many undocumented immigrants but also because contemporary military threats come more from shadowy terrorist networks than from other territorial states.

At the same time, the benefits that accrue from the economies of scale inherent in being part of larger groupings of states or trading blocs have encouraged the emergence of a number of supranational organizations. The most wide-ranging and developed of these is the European Union, which provides a sort of prototype supranational organization akin, at least in its economic effects, to the union provided among its component units by the United States. Though it has hardly yet created any sort of political identity such as that characteristic of American nationalism, it does have a seemingly magnetic attraction beyond its borders for a large number of states, both large and small, which aspire to join. Indeed, one irony in the recent proliferation of new nation-states in Southeastern and Eastern Europe is that immediately upon independence they have all invariably set about applying to join the European Union. From this viewpoint, there is a fast emerging "crisis" everywhere lodged in the hyphen between nation and state. Though far from a dead letter, then, we should beware of confusing the continuing emotional and practical appeal of the nation-state in any particular case with either meaningful citizenship rights (all persons have ready access to real political and social rights) or the idea of effective sovereignty (that the state in question actually has control over its borders).

MAKING MODERN GREECE IN MACEDONIA

The imitation of statehood began at Europe's margins partly through local initiative but mainly through the stimulation and recognition of the European Great Powers. In one respect Europe's eastern and southern margins constituted a resource "periphery" for the capitalist "core" of Western Europe. But a philosophical geography already posited such regions as lacking in the attributes needed for self-confident, locally generated statehood. These had little if anything to do with economic development per se but reflected the taint of despotism, imported from the Ottoman and Russian empires, and, in the case of southern Europe, the need for a renewed *reconquista* for an idealized "Europe" of places that were clearly identified as the seats of that very European civilization. The Ottoman and Austrian empires that long ruled in southeastern Europe never insisted on cultural and linguistic unification. Their rule also varied in its directness and effectiveness from place to place. If in Western Europe the quintessential states such as France and England pre-existed their respective nations, in southeastern Europe the idea of the national sovereign state was imported from the west by the growing middle classes born in the empires. The coming of the modern territorial state in this region (as in most of the world beyond Western Europe), therefore, has always involved drawing borders across complex ethnic settlement patterns and sometimes using anachronistic arguments about the present-day national affiliations of long-gone polities (such as the ancient Macedonian Empire, an ancient Hindustan, or the ancient Israelites) to justify who should control a given territory and the naming rights to it. A chronological narrative of the role of Macedonia in the making of a Modern Greek nation-state provides a vivid example of the way in which borders crucially enter into the very definition of nationhood.[79]

In the Greek case, the desire to construct a state came initially from the Greek commercial diaspora scattered around the Mediterranean and Black Seas and in the cities of Central and Western Europe allied to the romantic aspiration, shared with "philo-hellenic" western intellectuals (most famously England's Lord Byron), to liberate Balkan Christians from the Ottoman Turks and, hopefully, to re-establish the glory of ancient Greece. If there was a concentration of identifiably Greek people living in the southern part of the Balkan Peninsula, many if not most Greeks (of either linguistic or religious qualification) lived scattered well beyond this territory. Of course, quite what constituted a "Greek" as opposed to a Balkan Christian or even a Turkish Christian remained very much in doubt. As Greece was made, so were the Greeks.

The numerous popular revolts against the Ottomans over the years had never taken a national cast until the early nineteenth century, but even then the first Modern Greek state was a largely foreign enterprise financed by Britain and France and in the hands of a Bavarian prince and administrators. Only in 1843, following a coup d'état by the Greek army caste that had been recruited from the *klephtes*, irregular fighters or bandits against the Ottomans, did a more truly Greek state begin to emerge; one now armed with a powerful mythic origin in peasant revolt. At that time, however, the Greek state only covered the southern part of the state as constituted today (figure 2.1A). The then-northern border was decided by French and British diplomats to arbitrarily include the places that figured in (their) historic reminders of the region as it had been in classical times and to further their policy of slowly dismembering the Ottoman Empire. A Renaissance-era imagination of Greece as a compact zone on the southwestern edge of the Sultan's Empire created an expanded perception of Greek territory that covered almost the entire Balkan peninsula, part of Asia Minor, sometimes Cyprus, and even Sicily and southern Italy. In this way, historic association and present right of occupancy became fatefully fused (and confused) in a cartographic representation justifying the "liberation" of the territories concerned and their annexation to Greece. At the same time, various apparently distinguishable groups in and around the borders of the state (particularly "Albanians" and "Vlachs" [largely Hellenized speakers of a language akin to Romanian]) were accused of "brigandage" stimulated by Turkish misrule. They could be Balkan Christians but only as Hellenized Greeks could they be rescued from their outsider status. Until this happened, they were the aliens against whom Greek nationhood could be most readily defined.

To push beyond their dependent status and to live up to the nationalist imagination of a Greece that included most Greeks within its compass and that was "true" to its Hellenic genealogy, Greek nationalists used their fusion of ethnic and historical arguments to justify territorial expansion. By the late nineteenth century this was part of what has been called a "territorial hysteria" as Greeks, Serbs, Bulgarians, and Macedonian Slavs (and others) all strove to carve out nation-states for themselves from the European rump of the Ottoman Empire. Guerrilla warfare in Ottoman Macedonia between 1904 and 1908 and the subsequent two Balkan Wars of 1912–1913 saw major efforts at expanding the northern borders of Greece. At

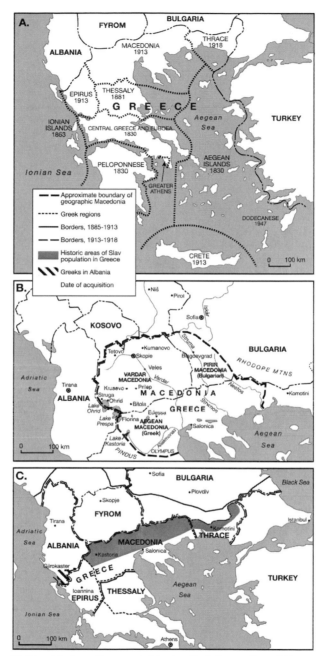

Figure 2.1.   Making Modern Greece: A. The territorial accretion of Greece, 1830–1947; B. The partition of Macedonia; C. Ethnic traces in Greek Macedonia and Albania after partition.

Source: Author.

the time, the local peasants were still immersed in religious and regional identities. In order to reply to the game of terror initiated by the Bulgarian bands, the Greek struggle aimed at forcing Exarchist peasants [followers of the Bulgarian Orthodox Church] to revert to the Patriarchate [the Greek Orthodox Church], and to protect those who still adhered to it. In doing so, the element of violence was essential.[80]

The role of nationalist violence in *creating* modern ethnic identities in Macedonia is evident in anecdotes such as the following gathered by an international inquiry into the brutalities of the Balkan Wars:

> The fugitives from Strumnitsa are simple people. One man spoke rather naively of his first horror at the idea of leaving his native place. Later, he said, he had acquiesced; he supposed the authorities knew best. Another fugitive, a village priest, regretted his home, which had, he said, the best water in all Macedonia. But he was sure flight was wise. He had reason to fear the Bulgarians. A *comitadji* early in the first war, pointed a rifle at his breast, and said: "Become a Bulgarian, or I'll kill you." He forthwith became a Bulgarian for several months and conformed to the exarchist [Bulgarian affiliated] church.[81]

It was precisely the *fluidity* of ethnicity and its complex relationship to kinship, class, trading, religion, and attachment to place in a region where many people were multilingual (if just as frequently illiterate in any language) and national preference had hitherto not been of primary significance that made the conflicts so bloody. The heterogeneity of the region, not just with respect to the distribution of discrete ethnicities but, more importantly, with respect to shared social practices and linguistic hybridity, as represented by the fruit salad that has become a well-known trope of Macedonia in a number of languages, worked against the drawing of clear borderlines. In this context, local people had to be forced by politically dominant nationalist activists into choosing sides. Violence-enforcing organizations are absolutely vital to bring people who as neighbors or indifferent strangers have no reason to kill one another into violent confrontation. On the Greek side, a Hellenic ideal of past cultural greatness in need of discovery and revival was the overwhelming thrust of the cultural redefinition involved in the process of popular recruitment to the national cause. From this viewpoint, Byzantine and Ottoman influences had corrupted the ancient mores. Local folklore studies (dances, music, clothing, etc.) were used to both reveal and teach how the masses belonged to the nation or *ethnos*. In the Greek language *nation* and *ethnos* mean the same thing. Capturing Macedonia was particularly important in re-creating the Greek nation. Not only would this bring together ancient and Byzantine conceptions of the Greek nation, thus reconciling the Church and the modern nation, it also justified a popular imperialism in which modern Greece was tied historically to Alexander the Great through the potential occupation of his homeland. Out of this confluence developed a romantic Hellenism in which Macedonia was defined as the "lung of Greece" and its possible "loss" as a mutilation. In this construction, Macedonia was potentially a repository of ancient Greek ideals as well as a pocket of cultural pollution. Paradoxically, therefore, it was at one and the same time both vital to the nation and a threat to its integrity.

Macedonia is the historic name for a large area that was shared following the border delimitations after the First World War among Bulgaria, Greece, and Yugoslavia. It comprises the watershed of the Vardar River with the two main cities of Salonica in northeastern Greece and Skopje in Yugoslavia providing the communication and transportation axis through the region. The region was populated predominantly with Slavo-Macedonians and Bulgarians at the time of the Balkan Wars (1912–1913), although the cosmopolitan city of Salonica, with its large Jewish, Muslim, and Greek populations was exceptional. Macedonia's division, into Pirin (Bulgarian), Vardar (Serbian), and Aegean (Greek) segments, left a significant Slav-Macedonian population in Greek Macedonia, particularly in rural areas and in and around Florina in the west. The fervently held nationalist goal of incorporating the whole of Macedonia into Greece came up against a complex local reality that long seemed to challenge the ideal. The border now ran through a potential zone of expansion rather than simply delimited the limit of a territorial claim (figure 2.1B). For a time Greek territorial claims in Macedonia became increasingly inseparable from a vision of a Greek state that would incorporate Crete, Macedonia, the Aegean islands, Cyprus, the west coast of Asia Minor, Constantinople (Istanbul), and areas around the Black Sea. Rather like the analogous claim to a Greater Serbia, devoted to uniting all Serbs under one government, the image of Greater Greece (known as the Great Idea) was to lead to disastrous wars against the Turks first in 1897 and then, most devastatingly, in 1922. Such an expansive irredentism was at the root of Greek "cartographic anxiety" from the founding of the state down to the 1920s. With so many potential Greeks scattered beyond the territorial limits of the state, the possibility of incorporating all of them in a territorial form was always problematic. The initial success in Macedonia compared to failure in many other places was to be reinforced, therefore, when in the aftermath of the failed attempt at expanding into Asia Minor in 1922, the Orthodox Christian population of Anatolia was exchanged for much of the Muslim population of mainland Greece, with the majority of the transplants to Greece settling in Greek Macedonia. In this way a Macedonia still ambiguously Greek at the time was ethnicized or made increasingly Greek by the transfusion of refugees.

Uncertainty about the Greek status of Macedonia, however, did not disappear (figure 2.1C). Indeed, if anything, with the incorporation of only one part of the historic region into Greece, Macedonia became even more central to the self-definition of the nation. In the 1930s authoritarian Greek governments attempted to impose a cultural uniformity in Greek Macedonia by forbidding the use of languages other than Greek and denying the contemporary existence of any degree of regional ethnic heterogeneity. In the aftermath of the Second World War, when Greece had been invaded and devastated by the Axis powers of Italy and Germany, a Communist insurgency broke out against the Royalist Greek government as it returned home from exile. The Greek Civil War came to be as much about the "Macedonian Question" as it was about a change of government in Greece as a whole. Particularly in its later phase, as the insurgent forces were forced into pockets near the Albanian and Yugoslav borders, the issue of the political future of Macedonia divided the Communist leadership as one group attempted to mobilize Slav-Macedonian support by backing an autonomous Macedonia that would then join Yugoslavia. Of course, by this time the great majority of people in Greek Macedonia saw themselves as ethnically Greek, so this meant largely abandoning whatever support they may have offered.

The U.S. military and economic assistance to the Greek government from 1947 to 1949 was the first fruit of the Truman Doctrine of U.S. commitment to back governments struggling with Communist insurgencies. Even after the defeat of the Greek Communists, collective memory of the critical position of Macedonia in the Civil War combined with the continuing dynamic of the Cold War to create a popular ideology, particularly powerful on the political right, in which leftist politics (whether truly Communist or not) was labeled as "Slavic" and its proponents as "Slavs" or "Bulgarians." This ethnicization of political ideology fits into a pattern of Greek nationalist thought that long predates the Civil War. Classical and, by extension, Modern Greek culture are associated by Greek nationalists with individualism, whereas the Slavs are associated with conformism and collectivism. Harking back to the challenge to Hellenism from the "execrable" Jakob Fallmerayer, the Austrian writer who in the 1840s had denied modern Greeks any racial affinity with the ancient ones and thus viewed them as definitely not "classically" European but as a mix of late-coming Slavs and Albanians, the recycling of the individualist/collectivist opposition serves to rescue the Greeks from such a fate. In 1950, it not only made leftist politics un-Greek, it effectively situated Greece in the modern First or "free" World of the U.S. and Western Europe in counterpoint to the Communist or "captive" Second World of Eastern Europe and the Soviet Union. The Modern Greek historical experience in Macedonia, therefore, continued to have a negatively charged valence in postwar Greece, even as the symbolism of ancient Macedonia as integral to Greece retained its hold on Greek nationalism. If anything, this latter acquired ever greater importance because of continuing difficulty on other irredentist fronts, particularly in bringing Cyprus into the national fold, and because of the disaster of 1955 when a pogrom in Istanbul was directed largely against that city's Greek minority, most of whom were forced to flee the city.

In Cyprus and Istanbul it was Turks, not Slavs, who were the barrier to Greek destiny. Turkish irredentism, however, was seen as a threat elsewhere too, including in Macedonia. Indeed, the existence of Muslim minority populations in Greek Thrace, Bulgaria, and Albania was taken as prima facie evidence for a potential encirclement of Greece by the descendants and affiliates of its historic (Ottoman) rulers. Macedonia again figured as the prime zone of contestation in which Greece itself was defined. This involved three factors during the years of the Cold War: (1) the subordination of local difference to presumed national homogeneity such that any evidence for distinctive cultural identities in Greek Macedonia was officially denied; (2) the confusion of religious and ethnic modes of identity, particularly with respect to the label "Turks," which could be applied to people of various linguistic and ethnic affinities but that thereby produced a fusion between any kind of ethnic difference and geopolitical threat from a historic enemy; and (3) the belief, encouraged by Greek national governments but with self-evident empirical plausibility, that Greece was vulnerable to attack both from an allegedly expansionist Turkey to the east and an expansionist Communist empire to the north.

This became crystal clear at the end of the Cold War. Rather than the euphoria that greeted the collapse of the Soviet Union and its sphere of influence in the U.S. and Western Europe, in Greece there was a sense of foreboding. The worry was that as its northern neighbors lost their geopolitical anchorage, Greece would be drawn into the ensuing instability. Above all, the 1980s had seen the emergence in Yugoslav Macedonia and in the Macedonian Diaspora (particularly in Australia and Canada) of a "Macedonism" or Macedonian nationalism that drew exactly opposite conclusions about the "ethnicity" of ancient Macedonia and Alexander the Great than did Greek nationalism. The Greek Diaspora around the world as well as Greeks at home felt compelled to respond both in public and in their newspapers. This controversy would not have achieved much of a critical juncture but for the breakup of Yugoslavia in 1991–1992. The declaration of an independent Republic of Macedonia, replete with symbols redolent of ancient Macedonia—such as the "Vergina Sun" and the head of Alexander the Great in profile—was widely seen in Greece as a provocation and threat to the established geopolitical order as well as to Greek nationalist aspirations.

The following four years saw a rising tide of rhetoric on both sides of the border. The slogan *"I Makedonia einai elliniki"* (Macedonia is Greek) was adopted by many Greeks. Given the fact that the former Yugoslav Republic of Macedonia (FYROM) had freely used the word *Macedonia* and that Greek Macedonia did not seem to face any sort of immediate military threat, the slogan points more to the degree to which Greek nationalism was at best ambiguous about the border rather than to the malign foreign interpretations of Greek motives. Be this as it may, what became clear was that to the majority of Greek public opinion, and across the political spectrum, no other people, apart from the Greeks, were entitled to use the Macedonian name either as a cultural-ethnic or a geographic-regional appellation. Many Greek intellectuals were particularly active in providing archaeological, textual, and historical arguments for why this should be the case.

Of course, the violent path taken elsewhere in the former Yugoslavia as the country unraveled in the 1990s understandably suggested that naming practices could become more than just that. Controlling place names has long had material consequences when, as in the Balkans, those doing the naming have mutually incompatible nationalist goals. Though the Macedonian naming and symbol dispute has now been "resolved" diplomatically, largely under external pressure and because of the dilemmas of Macedonian Slav identity in relation to the sizeable Albanian minority inside the FYROM, the Macedonian Question has long remained alive in Greece. The Macedonian naming controversy has had a continuing resonance in Greece well away from the border concerned. The seemingly ever-challenged Macedonian border is thus a critical link in the chain that connects local social practice throughout Greece to the everyday nationalism that has defined what it is to be "Greek."

Though hardly yet passing into history, the Macedonian border of Greece is one of many whose cultural logic of exclusion may seem less obvious today than at any time since the eighteenth century. For one thing, Greece is now part of the supranational European Union, which increasingly has come to superintend many of the regulatory activities once monopolized by the government in Athens. For another, the Greek economy is ever more tied into the global economy through its reliance on tourism, shipping, and financial services. These are undoubtedly powerful trends that portend diminished material pressures for the imposition of rigid national borders. In particular, with globalization the scope for the flowering of local complex identities has expanded considerably.

National identities are never given; they are produced historically under particular geographical conditions. So as those conditions change, so, even after some lag, should the continuing pressures toward reproducing national identities at borders. In Europe it has become common to ask if the nation-state is not facing a political crisis with the end of the Cold War, economic globalization, and the increased ambiguity of political identities, defined across geographical scales (European, national, local, etc.) and social groups (class, religious, ethnic, etc.). This seems particularly acute in the periphery of Europe, not least because it is here that the state has been most hollowed out by globalization since states such as Greece never did have much of the welfare orientation or history of bureaucratic development found to the north. In other words, there has been less to hollow out. With the end of the Cold War states such as Greece have also lost the political leverage they once had over their geopolitical sponsors such as Britain and the United States. Yet the European Union does not seem to have provided even the beginning of an alternative to the nation-state in the construction of a Europe-wide "nationalism."

European integration has hardly deprived EU member states of their sovereignty, as a fashionable argument would have it. Rather, the member states still successfully claim a sovereign status vis-à-vis other states and international organizations and still enjoy the rights and powers related to that status. The sovereignty debate has shifted, however, in two respects: to the issue of the borders of the EU and thus away from the continuing importance of national borders in themselves and to the position of the respective states within the institutional apparatus of the EU and other international organizations. It is the former that concerns us here. As the liberalization of trade and finance has made borders more permeable, anxieties about crime, terrorism, illegal immigration, and trafficking in women and children have increased commensurately. These concerns have taken a new shape in Europe because since the Treaty of Amsterdam (1997), movement of people within most of the EU has been freed by transferring checking to the external borders. Greece's Macedonian border is one of these.

The so-called Schengen zone has revalued the external border as defining a "security field" to keep out those foreign undesirables associated with the various anxieties that globalization has engendered. In this way the external border of the EU substitutes a new alien threat for the old (ethnic-national) one of Greece's national border. This substitution is primarily biopolitical in the sense of being about regulating populations through the filter function of border controls. Of course, borders have carried out such functions for some time, particularly since the early twentieth century. What is new is the extent to which border controls now extend throughout the national territories of the EU (enforced by national police forces and private security personnel) rather than just at the external land borders and the classification of "types" of populations who can pass through easily and others who cannot (ethnic profiling). If the Greek borderland in Greek Macedonia is today less threatening because its population has become largely Greek (of one sort or another), the border still matters but now because of new external threats, such as terrorists, smuggled humans, and so on, that can come across it. That these are threats to "Europe" rather than just to Greece would make generations of Greek nationalists smile with self-satisfaction. Greece finally belongs.

THE SOVEREIGNTY "GAME"

In the peculiar intellectual division of labor that separates the study of domestic politics from international relations, the direct result of thinking about the world in totally territorialized terms, the concern for "external" sovereignty has been largely monopolized by those focused on relations between states. From this viewpoint, the naturalness of its territoriality to state sovereignty—a state's domestic sovereignty—is underpinned by several norms or practices that have turned the European territorial state into a global standard. Here the two crucial facets of sovereignty concern recognition by other states as co-equals and territorial integrity (control over borders and autonomy in decision-making). With its roots in seventeenth-century European debates and struggles, contemporary world politics is still widely consumed by issues such as the rule of "non-interference" by one or more states in another's "domestic" affairs, the capacity of states to exercise control over cross-border flows, and the legitimacy of specific borders for a particular state. All states are engaged in a "game" of sovereignty to negotiate a position relative to other states using sovereignty claims to back it up.[82] "Sovereignty" is a tool in debate and conflict more than an actual condition.[83] It is often used to defend a scurrilous regime or as a weapon in a war of words with a more powerful neighboring state. Indeed, claims to sovereignty are invoked more often than not when the "reality" of the claim is in question. In this understanding, sovereignty is precisely the result of a system of interdependence between states in which it is the recognition (with a nod and a wink) by other states of each state's sovereignty that keeps the entire system afloat. As Stephen Krasner has argued, sovereignty in its various facets has never been "possessed" simultaneously by any state. Yet much discussion and practice presumes that this is either an actuality or a real possibility; hence Krasner's assertion that sovereignty is nothing more than "organized hypocrisy."[84]

The basic argument takes the following form. Recognition of sovereignty depends on a state having a clear territorial basis. In the modern world there cannot be a sovereign state without some sort of territory. But nominally this also implies that the state in question is an equivalent unit to all others. This follows because the presumption of territorial integrity requires that the state is autonomous politically and thoroughly controls its own borders. Sovereignty as a principle guiding relations between states thus reflects the monopoly held by states over their territories. There is no space between or around the states once the entire world is in sovereignty's orbit, as it has increasingly been over the past half century. Ipso facto, we live in a totally territorialized world in which the whole system of states is held together by the mutual recognition of state sovereignty.

This is the logical core of the Westphalian system (named for the Peace of Westphalia in 1648) that has presumably expanded from its European roots to encompass the whole world. So-called political realists (and state-centric constructivists) have made much of the self-sustaining and balancing character of this system, at least when they see it working "right." But rather like the confusion between a model of perfect competition and actual capitalism in economics, the danger here is of turning a theoretical model into an empirical description. Indeed, it is a rather poor guide to *actual* practice in relations between states. It reifies a mythology. Moreover, other configurations of authority and institutional power-structure than those of states claiming sovereignty have been and are possible.

PLAYING THE SOVEREIGNTY GAME

In the first place, and with respect to the sovereignty game in practice, the circle-of-sovereignty argument may represent the ideal but it is certainly not the practice. Krasner has pointed out that the various facets of sovereignty are rarely practiced simultaneously. They are ploys in a game played among states to gain advantage over others.[85] The various meanings of sovereignty are not logically related. In particular, certain of the claims to authority do not necessarily indicate that a state has real control. This distinction between control and authority claim is an important insight, even if Krasner is only trying to rescue sovereignty for a state-centered purpose rather than suggest the limits of thinking of sovereignty in completely territorialized terms. He is a political realist who takes as given that the political world is largely monopolized by territorial states.

Krasner distinguishes four different sovereignty claims: domestic sovereignty (public authority/control within a state); interdependence sovereignty (control over trans-border movements); international legal sovereignty (mutual recognition among states); and Westphalian sovereignty (exclusion of external actors from domestic authority).[86] Only the first involves authority and control; the second is entirely about control, and the final two involve only authority. The first of these conforms to the sovereignty claim discussed in the previous two sections, the second and fourth constitute the territorial integrity norm, and the third represents the norm of equality between states. As Krasner says, "These four meanings of sovereignty are not logically coupled, nor have they covaried in practice."[87] In practice they are unbundled. Thus, states can be ineffective domestically yet retain their international recognition (as in so-called failed states), but at the same time their Westphalian sovereignty may or may not be compromised if powerful external actors have replaced the state as an effective purveyor of public goods and services. Krasner concludes:

> Analysts and practitioners have used the term sovereignty in four different and distinct ways. The absence or loss of any one kind of sovereignty does not logically imply an erosion of others, even though they may be empirically associated with each other. A state can be recognized, that is have international legal sovereignty, but not have Westphalian sovereignty, be-

cause its authority structures are subject to external authority or control; it can lose control of transborder movements but still be autonomous; it can have domestic sovereignty, a well-established effective set of authoritative decision-making institutions, and not be recognized.[88]

Cases of such empirical complexity come readily to mind. Taiwan, for example, has domestic but not international legal sovereignty because of the widely recognized claim of China that Taiwan is a "renegade province." Iraq and Afghanistan may have international legal sovereignty but little in the way of any of the other types. Many African states have questionable domestic and Westphalian sovereignty yet are also recognized internationally as sovereign states. Increasingly, the United States and many European states have lost control of many cross-border movements, often by explicitly giving up control to international or supranational organizations ("sharing sovereignty") but sometimes simply because of being overwhelmed by numbers (as in floods of immigrants) or outflanked technologically (as in the development of global financial markets), yet still have considerable domestic and Westphalian sovereignty. Many proto- or de facto states (from Palestine to Somaliland and Abkhazia, the Turkish Republic of North Cyprus and Bougainville) are lacking in both international recognition and Westphalian sovereignty but have at least some of the trappings of domestic sovereignty. In the final analysis, perhaps the majority of the world's two hundred or so states have only international legal sovereignty. Even that does not always guarantee equal respect. How threadbare an "absolute" sovereignty is that?

Useful as it undoubtedly is, the typology misses three vitally important features of the actual sovereignty game. The first is that the territorial integrity norm (Krasner's interdependence and Westphalian sovereignty) has long been systematically violated to the degree that its status as a "norm" itself is problematic. It is difficult to see this aspect of sovereignty as having much of a substantive basis beyond a world of totally mercantilist economies. Growing up within a capitalist world economy since the eighteenth century has meant that state sovereignty has had to co-exist with the tendency of pressures to trade and invest that always push beyond state borders. If for many years attempts at restraining this behind tariff walls and constraining its expansion through empire directed world capitalism towards inter-imperial rivalry, under U.S. hegemony since the 1940s it has become much more free flowing and volatile. The most institutionalized attempts at resisting this tendency, most notably the former Soviet Union and China, finally failed to achieve a successful alternative. They have now joined in, if fitfully and with much higher elements of state direction than elsewhere. The main point is that most states have never been immune to massive external influences and are ever less so. Sovereignty has always been "shared" with other actors, foreign and domestic.

In particular, the modern territorial state system has been associated from its origins in Europe in the seventeenth and eighteenth centuries with the framework for definitions of private property rights (legal rights of ownership and use), without which global capitalism would not have been possible. States never seem so sovereign, in the conventional sense of singular entities endowed with power monopolies within their territories (domestic sovereignty), as when they are seen as definers and enforcers of property rights. The role that states have played in the growth of certain basic social practices of capitalism—defining and protecting private property rights—have inexorably led beyond state boundaries in pursuit of wealth from the deployment of "mobile property" (capital). The term *property* implies a fixity or permanence in place that modern territorial states have given a high priority to protecting. Consequently, much of the law in most Western states is devoted to establishing rights of ownership and access. It is no coincidence that property and contracts are basic courses in all law schools. But a home-territory for firms also provides a base from which to launch attempts at acquiring property elsewhere. This requires that assets be reasonably liquid and transferable over space and across state boundaries. At a certain point, however, states endure a tension, what John Ruggie calls the problem of "absolute individuation," which can give rise to an "unbundling" of territoriality when states effectively exchange control over economic flows emanating from their territories for increased access to flows coming from elsewhere.[89] As a result, when increasing proportions of property are mobile beyond any one state's boundaries, individual states provide only a partial and tenuous protection for absolute property rights. Other geographical levels of governance and regulation become attractive, as was the case with the Bretton Woods system regulating international finance from 1944 to 1972 and is now (if signally less effectively) with the annual G-8 Summits between the leaders of the Big Seven industrial countries (plus Russia). But uncertainty as to future political actions and macroeconomic changes (tariffs, interest rates, etc.) also gives an incentive to property-holders to further spread assets around rather than leave them pooled up in one state.

This process is not at all new. Its origins go back to the merchant capitalism of Europe in the sixteenth century. What is new is the increased quantitative scale and the enlarged geographical scope of the mobile property now moving to and fro across the boundaries of the world's trading and investing states. In this context, states and firms have changed their orientation from free trade to what has been called "market access" capitalism.[90] The underpinnings of the world-trade regime that prevailed in the aftermath of the Second World War are being replaced by those of a regime in which a premium is placed on the openness of borders. "Leakiness" in cross-border flows of goods and investment and in firm multinationality has become a torrent of capital, trade, and corporate alliances. Cowhey and Aronson contrast the nature of the old regime with that of the new one by identifying the six pillars that they claim have underpinned each and the policy instruments associated with the new regime.[91] The policy instruments reflect an abandonment of territorial integrity as a norm in return for guaranteed rights of access to other states' territories. The world has thus moved away from the strict association of property rights and capital accumulation with state territoriality. A range of non-territorial factors now determine the competitiveness of firms in many industries: access to technology, marketing strategies, responsiveness to consumers, flexible management techniques. All of these are now the assets of firms, not territories. Firms grow through deploying their internal assets as successfully as possible. States now compete with one another to attract these mobile assets (property) to their territories.

Three aspects of the market-access regime are particularly notable with respect to the changing spatiality of power. One is the internationalization of a range of domestic policies to conform to global norms of performance. Thus, not only trade policy but also industrial, product liability, and social welfare policies are subject to definition and oversight in terms of their impacts on market access between countries. Another is the increased trade in services, once produced and consumed largely within state boundaries. Partly this reflects the fact that many manufactured goods now contain a large share of service inputs—from R&D to marketing and advertising. But it is also because the revolution in telecommunications means that many services, from banking to design to packaging, can now be provided to global markets. This represents a significant material challenge to the domestic vs. international distinction upon which the "realism" of strictly territorial accounts of the spatiality of power relies. Finally, the spreading reach of transnational firms and the emergence of international corporate alliances have had profound influences on the nature of trade and investment flows, undermining the identity between territory and economy. Symptomatic of the integration of trade and investment are such frequently heard concerns as rules on international investment and unitary taxation, rules governing local-content and place-of-origin to assess where value was added in the commodity chains of globalized production, and rules involving unfair competition and anti-trust or monopoly trading practices.

The accelerating unbundling of state territorial sovereignty (in the sense of what is typically meant by territorial integrity) provides the most direct evidence for the reshaping of hegemony away from the more state-centered practices of a previous epoch. This does not mean to say that territorial states are (finally) withering away, only that they must now operate in a global context in which their interactions with one another must now take into account a changed military and economic environment. Indeed, in the absence of higher-level units for the enforcement of property rights and the delivery of public goods, states have a continuing and vital role to perform within the evolving world of networks and flows.[92] For example, the deregulation of financial markets requires the deliberate action of governmental authorities. It does not simply "happen." But during the Cold War between 1947 and 1990, the United States, in competing militarily and ideologically with the Soviet Union, sponsored an unprecedented opening of the world economy, partly to spread its political-economic "message" and partly to take advantage of opportunities for its businesses. The net effect has been that markets have acquired powers heretofore vested in leading states. As this process has intensified and expanded, some localities and regions within states have been privileged within global networks of finance, manufacturing, and cultural production to the disadvantage of others. The "market-access regime" ties local areas directly into global markets. Successful ones are those that can enhance their position by increasing their attractiveness to multinational and global firms. A patchwork of places within a global node and network system, from world cities such as London and New York all the way to peripheries and backwaters scattered all over the world, therefore co-exists with the territorial spatiality with which we are all so familiar. Subsequent chapters will examine the trajectory of these different spatialities of power in more detail.

The second feature of the sovereignty game neglected in Krasner's account of it is that most of the world's states are the product of decolonization. The Greeks started a trend. The issue here is that of equal sovereignty as implied by mutual recognition, the norm against interference, and international legal sovereignty. Some writers suggest that only a few states, the Great Powers and some others, actually have what is sometimes called "positive" sovereignty, in the sense of true freedom to act in international affairs.[93] The rest have only "negative" sovereignty, the freedom to demand non-interference in their domestic affairs. Jackson refers to the states with the latter as "quasi-states"; they claim to be sovereign states but they are not really. Missing from the discussion is why this description, partial as it may be, makes any empirical sense at all. The implication is that the quasi-states are to blame for their own woeful condition. They just haven't managed to follow in the footsteps of those states that have now achieved positive sovereignty, at least not yet. Of course, the states in question have simply not been able, because of the circumstances of their origin, to achieve either a nationalization of their masses in terms of common national identity or the monopoly over the means of violence that would conjointly improve their political stability and community of purpose. They may have international legal sovereignty, in Krasner's terms, but that is often about all.

In the mid-1960s, just as many of the former European colonies in Africa had come to independence, a "breakthrough" or escalation in sovereignty was widely heralded. Thirty-five states acquired the trappings of state sovereignty between 1951 and 1966. But this turned out to be illusory for two reasons. First, whatever the doubts of individual nationalists, and many such as Kwame Nkrumah and others were well aware of the poisoned chalice of ethnic-tribal politics they would inherit, they were all obliged by the imperialist policies that had first brought them into the capitalist world economy with the practical necessity of seeking independence within existing colonial territories that had neither the cultural building materials for nation formation nor political boundaries that made either economic or geopolitical sense.[94] The end result has been a pervasive politics of patronage and rent seeking as state managers—facing deteriorating terms of trade for their primary commodities against the manufactured goods they import, massive rural to urban migration, and the failure of initiatives to develop home-grown industries and a middle class—have milked state coffers (and the proceeds of exporter groups) to legitimize their rule, at least in the eyes of their beneficiaries. The import of Cold War ideologies in grotesque forms in the years following independence attracted foreign aid and advisors but proved of little long-term benefit. The ability of states to police or to develop their territories, or, in other words, to consistently exercise domestic sovereignty over them, has remained beyond their grasp. The net effect has been to make the state a barrier to more than an agent of progressive social change in large parts of Africa— and elsewhere. Civil wars, brutal dictatorships, and client regimes for foreign powers have been the frequent result. Into the political vacuum, former colonial states such as France, the U.S., and Britain have not been afraid to step, at least on occasion, and when it suits their governments of the day. Consequently, a new sort of noblesse oblige, labeled as humanitarian intervention, has openly challenged the conventions of international legal sovereignty.

Second, since independence in the 1960s and 1970s, African states have not been regarded by the world's Great Powers as the equivalents of European or other "real" states with respect to sovereignty. So it is not simply the absence of internal efficacy but also the external lack of respect or serious recognition that undermines more effective African statehood. The apparent social "chaos" of Africa is seen as calling for external intervention or management once more by Europeans. It is as if there are distinct "regimes" of sovereignty that prevail in different parts of the world.[95] From this perspective, Africa's fate was set during the Cold War. Not only did the continent become the site of much Cold War gamesmanship with episodic interventions (for example, in the Congo in 1960 and in Ethiopia and Somalia in the 1970s and 1980s) and surrogate power struggles (just about everywhere) but its recent history of settler colonialism and ineffective central administration—with continuing conflicts between natives and settlers in Zimbabwe, South Africa, and elsewhere down into the 1990s and invasions by neighbors and ethnic civil wars wracking most countries down until the present day—also marked it off as a zone in which statehood was seen as a sort of Potemkin village: a cardboard imitation of the real thing. This view—of Africa as a "wild zone" beyond the "normal" politics of Westphalian statehood—is now widely shared by both many Africans and outsiders. This lack of respect from external sources feeds back into the difficulty of building domestic sovereignty worth its salt.

A third feature of the sovereignty game given short shrift in Krasner's account is the significant role of hegemonic states and actors relative to all others. Much scholarly and popular discussion of the U.S. role in the contemporary world, for example, insists on seeing the United States as either simply just "another state" (albeit a bigger, more powerful one) or as an empire, by stretching the manifestly territorial meaning of that term to include non-territorial influence and control. Neither approach is satisfactory for understanding what has been afoot in recent years in stretching sovereignty beyond territorial limits. For one thing, the present-day world is significantly different, above all in its geography of power, from previous epochs. Often labeled as the era of "globalization," to signal the rise of actors (multinational firms, global NGOs, international institutions, etc.) and processes of development (globalized financial markets, global commodity chains, etc.) that cannot be linked to a single territorial address, this is a world that the United States has both by design and through unintended consequences helped to bring about. If this is an "empire," then it is the only de-centered one in history, which seems to suggest that it is something else. For another thing, this world has not been brought about predominantly through direct coercion or by territorial rule (hence simply by "imperialism" in its early twentieth-century sense) but through socioeconomic incorporation into practices and routines derivative of or compatible with those first developed in the United States. The best word to describe these processes is *hegemony*.[96]

The two terms *hegemony* and *empire* offer profoundly different understandings of American power and its relationship to sovereignty. Interestingly, in some usage of this language the two terms are not readily distinguished from one another; either way an Almighty America is seen as recasting the world in its image. From this viewpoint, hegemony is simply the relatively unconstrained coercive power exercised by a territorial hegemon or seat of empire. I want to suggest that this usage is problematic both historically and analytically. More specifically, the terms have distinctive etymologies and contemporary meanings in English and other languages. Some recent attempts at trying to use the term *empire* but without giving it a territorial referent fail to adequately identify the precise ways in which the U.S. has created a global imperial sovereignty. The word *empire* traps their analysis in a world of territorialized sovereign power when they hope to extend it into realms of disciplinary and biopolitical power that are both more diffuse (involving more and scattered agents practicing hegemonic ideas, respectively, about social order and regulation of bodily and mental functions) and less territorialized.

To go by way of example, it is possible to have empire without hegemony. Neither sixteenth-century Spain nor Portugal, for instance, had much control over world politics after 1600 but both did have territorial "possessions" left over from their early roles in European world conquest. But it is also possible to have hegemony without empire, as when U.S. governments after the Second World War exerted tremendous influence over world politics but with little or no contemporaneous territorial extension. U.S. governments, in line with their own republican and anti-colonial origins as well as a newfound material interest in free trade, identified themselves largely with anti-colonial movements around the world. The distinction between hegemony and empire can also help today in addressing whether securing U.S. hegemony after the end of the Cold War will require increased reliance on seeking empire. In other words, will continued U.S. hegemony depend upon creating an empire somewhat like that ruled by Britain at the end of the nineteenth century as opposed to continuing to work multilaterally through international institutions and alliances, particularly when U.S. economic troubles raise the possibility of a globalized world order in which the United States is no longer paramount?

In the present context, however, what matters most is that we continue to live in a world in which some states are more sovereign than others. But this does not mean that this greater sovereignty is always exercised territorially and coercively, as use of the term *empire* would suggest. Rather, it can be exercised through both command and assent over spatial networks that are either more or less territorialized. So, under U.S. hegemony the world as a whole has become increasingly open to material transactions, population flows, commodity chains, and financial dealings that cannot be accounted for using the conventional language of sovereignty understood in totally territorial terms.[97]

ALTERNATIVE CONFIGURATIONS OF AUTHORITY AND CONTROL

All social practices involve the application of power, the ability to engage in actions toward the completion of socially sanctioned goals. From this point of view, power is not some thing or potential vested solely in states (or associated political institutions) but the application of agency inherent in all social action to achieve chosen ends. Territorial states are one type of concentration of social power that emerged in specific historical conditions in which state territoriality was practically useful in fulfilling the objectives of both dominant and subordinated social groups.[98] Today, we see the emergence of local and regional governments and supraregional communities (such as the European Union) in the application of power for such ends as economic development and political identity, usually without the direct coercive power traditionally associated with territorial states. Of course, such alternative spatial configurations of power to that of the modern territorial state are not entirely new. The Hanseatic League, the Swiss Confederation, the Holy Roman Empire, the Iroquois

Confederation, the Concert of Europe, and the early United States (what Dan Deudney calls the Philadelphian System)[99] are familiar examples of alternative systems of power and authority to that of the Westphalian system of territorial states. Even formal (such as the British) and informal empires (such as the Soviet Union in Eastern Europe and Russia in the Caucasus) always required a balance between coercion and assent, if only to minimize administrative problems. They collapse when they fail to retain the modicum of legitimacy that they require (at least among local elites). The actual existence of these other kinds of institutional arrangements points to the range of possible ways in which control and authority can be organized spatially. They suggest that forms of power are generated, sustained, and reproduced by historically and geographically specific social practices, rather than given for all time in one mode of spatial organization: that of state territoriality. Indeed, there was nothing inevitable about the emergence of the modern system of territorial states. Until the nineteenth century even their monopoly over coercive power was easily challenged, for example by pirates, and alternative arrangements for the geographical organization of centralized power were widespread, for example in overlapping jurisdictions such as the Holy Roman Empire.

More radically, however, the power of states over their populations and in relation to one another can be understood as resting largely on power "from below." In other words, the territorial state draws its power in capillary fashion from social groups and institutions rather than simply imposing itself upon them.[100] From this point of view, power is present in all relationships among people, animals, and things and the power of any particular state relies on the wide range of sources it can tap into. Any society is necessarily a set of power arrangements based around kinship, legal, and property relations. This can be termed a non-sovereign or diffuse conception of power, in contradistinction to that view that sees power as invariably flowing from a single (sovereign) source or structure, such as the state. In this construction, power is best thought of as equivalent to the energy moving a circulatory system rather than a mechanical opposition between a source of power, on the one hand, and an obedient (or truculent) subject, on the other. At the same time, potential energy is not always translated into the kinetic version. Nevertheless, as the French language can put it in a way not available to English, "One has the *puissance* to do something, and one exercises the *pouvoir* to do it."[101] As a result, there are multiple points at which consent and resistance come into play in expanding and restricting the interplay between states and subjects and, hence, in defining the state's effective territoriality: how well it dominates and rules its claimed block of space. Authority is necessarily given rather than taken. Consent and assent are required; in other words power is vested or given up by subjects, in order for authority to be acquired. Coercion and control, in the sense of a police presence and the effective delivery of collective goods, are never enough for domestic sovereignty to prevail. Even grudging acquiescence is inadequate. The spatial monopoly of power exercised by a state, therefore, is not and cannot be total when its power derives from that given up by and potentially retaken by others.

The point here is not to suggest that all territorial states are somehow redundant or not sovereign because their power (and thus their sovereignty) rests on that vested in them by others. Technologies of power seem to have transcended their roots in popular acceptance, cession, and acquiescence, as is the case with all bureaucratic and regulatory regimes. The "pooling up" of power in state agencies is of historic proportions. But I am clearly denying that state-based power is ever everything in itself. It can be disaggregated. Eichmann, among others, both German and non-German, made the Final Solution possible. My main claim is that most discussion of sovereignty has involved seeing "it" as an entity or claim associated with a state in a given territory rather than as a set of effects involving differential impacts of combinations of authority and control, some of which can emanate from actors beyond the territory itself as well as from multiple actors (including, most importantly, the state in its various agencies) within. Even seemingly radical theories of power, such as those of Michel Foucault, are often interpreted as if they demand an equation between dominion (that of the territorial state) and power. But the state is not simply the Man directing life in a territorial Panopticon (or a global one, for that matter). As Michel Foucault has in fact said very clearly, power is "never localized here or there, never in anybody's hands, never appropriated as a commodity or piece of wealth. Power is employed and exercised through a net-like organization. And not only do individuals circulate between its threads; they are always in the position of undergoing and exercising this power."[102]

From this viewpoint, state territorial sovereignty has always co-existed, if often uneasily, with the border-busting powers of other states, all manner of private agents, and of non-state public entities, such as churches and other religious organizations, and has itself never been simply territorialized in the way the three myths suggest. Consequently, talk about the "erosion" and "relinquishing" of sovereignty in the face of globalization, when sovereignty is actually only being redefined in terms of the balance between different agents and their geographical scope, strangely accepts the prior efficacy of the sovereignty myths as much as does that of those who see only a changeless state sovereignty constantly re-creating itself.

CONCLUSION

The actual practices of sovereignty, the ways in which control and authority have been applied historically around the world, have been obscured by three sovereignty myths that have become so widely accepted that while they also still inform practice, they have become increasingly problematic in a globalizing world. It is a mistake, however, to see these myths as simply having become redundant. They have always been problematic empirically. But they also still retain a considerable hold on the political imagination. As long as nationalism has the political force that it has had for the past two hundred years, we can expect to see continued appeals to "sovereignty" as a source of liberation for this or that territorialized group from the strictures of the world economy and neighboring groups. Indeed, much of the debate about the effects of globalization is still conducted in terms of its welfare impacts on this or that territorialized national group, irrespective of the local-level distribution of costs and benefits. The language of sovereignty is invoked both to defend against the latest McDonald's franchise and to maintain the hold of national elites over national monopolies. The presumed naturalness of propinquity and territory to political and economic life continues to underpin much discussion of justice and democracy. Yet, as we all know, the world's pattern of injustices and insecurities is not so readily territorialized. The very grammar of sovereignty as rooted in its territorializing myths is a powerful barrier to seeing the world in all of its complexity. A way of mapping that complexity is the focus of chapter 3.

NOTES

1. C. J. Bickerton et al. (eds.), *Politics without Sovereignty: A Critique of Contemporary International Relations* (London: UCL Press, 2007).

2. J. Gottmann, *The Significance of Territory* (Charlottesville: University Press of Virginia, 1973).

3. Gottmann, *The Significance of Territory*, 33–52.

4. Gottmann, *The Significance of Territory*, 35.

5. E. H. Kantorowicz, *The King's Two Bodies: A Study in Medieval Political Theology* (Princeton, NJ: Princeton University Press, 1957).

6. O. O'Donovan, "Christianity and territorial right," in A. Buchanan and M. Moore (eds.), *States, Nations, and Borders: The Ethics of Making Boundaries* (Cambridge: Cambridge University Press, 2003), 131.

7. E. Cassirer, *The Myth of the State* (New Haven, CT: Yale University Press, 1946), 107.

8. Cassirer, *The Myth of the State*, 114.

9. R. Tuck, "The making and unmaking of boundaries from the natural law perspective," in A. Buchanan and M. Moore (eds.), *States, Nations, and Borders: The Ethics of Making Boundaries* (Cambridge: Cambridge University Press, 2003), 152.

10. O. Gierke, *Political Theories of the Middle Ages* (Cambridge: Cambridge University Press, 1900), 87.

11. Gottmann, *The Significance of Territory*, 38.

12. Gottmann, *The Significance of Territory*, 36–37.

13. Cassirer, *The Myth of the State*, 73.

14. H. J. Grimm, "Luther's conception of territorial and national loyalty," *Church History* 17 (1948): 82.

15. Gottmann, *The Significance of Territory*, 40.

16. Gierke, *Political Theories of the Middle Ages*, 97.

17. Gottmann, *The Significance of Territory*, 49.

18. M. Neocleous, *Imagining the State* (Maidenhead, UK: Open University Press, 2003), 9.

19. Neocleous, *Imagining the State*, 21.

20. J. Bodin, *Six Books of the Commonwealth (1576)*, (Oxford: Blackwell, n.d.), 25.

21. Neocleous, *Imagining the State*, 14.

22. Neocleous, *Imagining the State*, 15, his emphasis.

23. Neocleous, *Imagining the State*, 139.

24. C. Smaje, "Institutional history: comparative approaches to race and caste," in G. Delanty and E. Isen (eds.), *Handbook of Historical Sociology* (London: Sage, 2003), 142.

25. Smaje, "Institutional history," 142.

26. Smaje, "Institutional history," 142.

27. Gottmann, *The Significance of Territory*, 50.

28. C. Schmitt, quoted in H. Meier, *The Lesson of Carl Schmitt: Four Chapters on the Distinction between Political Theology and Political Philosophy* (Chicago: University of Chicago Press, 1998), 4.

29. C. Schmitt, *Political Theology: Four Chapters on the Concept of Sovereignty* (Chicago: University of Chicago Press, 1985 [1922]), 9.

30. G. Agamben, *Homo Sacer: Sovereign Power and the Bare Life* (Stanford, CA: Stanford University Press, 1998).

31. W. Connolly, "The complexities of sovereignty," in M. Calarco and S. De-Caroli (eds.), *Giorgio Agamben: Sovereignty and Life* (Stanford, CA: Stanford University Press, 2007), 24

32. Although, as Ralph Mathisen shows (in *"Peregrini, barbari, and Cives Romani:* concepts of citizenship and the legal identity of barbarians in the later Roman Empire," *American Historical Review* 111 [2006], 1016), things were more complex: "Being a foreign barbarian did not exclude one from access to some if not all elements of Roman *ius civile* and from other citizen privileges."

33. Neocleous, *Imagining the State*, 28.

34. S. Wolin, *Politics and Vision: Continuity and Innovation in Western Political Thought* (Princeton, NJ: Princeton University Press, Expanded Edition, 2004), 394.

35. J. R. Martel, "Strong Sovereign, weak Messiah: Thomas Hobbes on scriptural interpretation, rhetoric and the Holy Spirit," *Theory and Event* 7 (2004).

36. G. V. Shaffer, "The missing wives of Leviathan," *The Seventeenth Century* 19 (2004): 53–68.

37. Wolin, *Politics and Vision*, 246.

38. D. Philpott, "Ideas and the evolution of sovereignty," in S. H. Hashmi (ed.), *State Sovereignty: Change and Persistence in International Relations* (University Park: Pennsylvania State University Press, 1997), 19.

39. E. M. Wood and N. Wood, *A Trumpet of Sedition: Political Theory and the Rise of Capitalism, 1509-1688* (New York: New York University Press, 1997), 101.

40. Wood and Wood, *A Trumpet of Sedition*, 100.

41. Gottmann, *The Significance of Territory*, 16.

42. Neocleous, *Imagining the State*, 100.

43. Neocleous, *Imagining the State*, 102.

44. S. Elden, "Terror and territory," *Antipode* 39 (2007): 822.

45. Neocleous, *Imagining the State*, 106–7.

46. G. Steinmetz, "Introduction: culture and the state," in G. Steinmetz (ed.), *State/Culture: State-Formation after the Cultural Turn* (Ithaca, NY: Cornell University Press, 1999), 3.

47. T. Hobbes, *Leviathan* (Cambridge: Cambridge University Press, 1996), 117–20. To put the point somewhat differently, as does Srinivas Aravamudan ("Subjects /sovereigns/ rogues," *Eighteenth-Century Studies* 40 [2007]: 461): "Usurpation and self-surpassing is part of the story of sovereignty: Hobbes qualifies the Leviathan as a 'Mortall God,' hence acknowledging the inevitable entropy and finitude at the heart of any established sovereign power."

48. R. Maguire, "Guilt by association? The hazards of linking the concept of the state to violence," *European History Review* 13 (2006): 293–310.

49. C. Tilly, *Coercion, Capital and European States, AD 990-1992* (Oxford: Blackwell, 1990).

50. S. DeCaroli, "Boundary stones: Giorgio Agamben and the field of sover-

eignty," in M. Calarco and S. DeCaroli (eds.), *Giorgio Agamben: Sovereignty and Life* (Stanford, CA: Stanford University Press, 2007), 60.

51. Connolly, "The complexities of sovereignty," 23.

52. T. Brennan, *Wars of Position: Cultural Politics of Left and Right* (New York: Columbia University Press, 2006).

53. Gottmann, *The Significance of Territory*, 43.

54. J. W. Meyer et al., "World society and the nation-state," *American Journal of Sociology* 103 (1997): 144–81.

55. C. Gans, "Historical rights: the evaluation of nationalist claims to sovereignty," *Political Theory* 29 (2001): 58–79; G. Nootens, "Liberal nationalism and the sovereign territorial ideal," *Nations and Nationalism* 12 (2006): 35–50.

56. P. G. Roeder, *Where Nation-States Come From: Institutional Change in the Age of Nationalism* (Princeton, NJ: Princeton University Press, 2007), 24.

57. J. Agnew, *Hegemony: The New Shape of Global Power* (Philadelphia: Temple University Press, 2005), chapter 4.

58. B. H. Sparrow, *The Insular Cases and the Emergence of American Empire* (Lawrence: University Press of Kansas, 2006), 2.

59. Sparrow, *The Insular Cases*, 5.

60. Sparrow, *The Insular Cases*, 8–9.

61. A. Gramsci, *Selections from Political Writings, 1910-1920* (London: Lawrence and Wishart, 1977), 60.

62. M. Biggs, "Putting the state on the map: cartography, territory, and European state formation," *Comparative Studies in Society and History* 41 (1999): 394.

63. Biggs, "Putting the state on the map," 399.

64. Neocleous, *Imagining the State*, 418.

65. Neocleous, *Imagining the State*, 410.

66. T. Winichakul, *Siam Mapped: A History of the Geo-Body of a Nation* (Honolulu: University of Hawaii Press, 1994), 17.

67. M. Herzfeld, *Anthropology though the Looking Glass: Critical Ethnography in the Margins of Europe* (Cambridge: Cambridge University Press, 1987), 81.

68. A. Schiavone, *The End of the Past: Ancient Rome and the Modern West* (Cambridge, MA: Harvard University Press, 2000), 205–6.

69. M. Foucault, "Two lectures," in *Michel Foucault: Power/Knowledge: Selected Interviews and Other Writing, 1972-1977* (Brighton, UK: Harvester Press, 1980), 98.

70. For example, B. Anderson, *Imagined Communities: Reflections on the Origin and Spread of Nationalism* (London: Verso, 1983); E. Hobsbawm and T. Ranger (eds.), *The Invention of Tradition* (Cambridge: Cambridge University Press, 1983); L. Greenfeld, *Nationalism: Five Roads to Modernity* (Cambridge, MA: Harvard University Press, 1992).

71. M. Herzfeld, "The European self: rethinking an attitude," in A. Pagden (ed.), *The Idea of Europe: From Antiquity to the European Union* (Cambridge: Cambridge University Press, 2002), 143.

72. Herzfeld, *Anthropology through the Looking Glass*, 154.

73. S. Krishna, "Cartographic anxiety mapping the body politic in India," *Alternatives* 19 (1994): 507–21; M. Stokes, "Imagining 'the south:' hybridity, heterotopias and Arabesk on the Turkish-Syria border," in T. M. Wilson and H. Donnan (eds.), *Border Identities: Nation and State at International Frontiers* (Cambridge: Cambridge University Press, 1998).

74. E. Renan, "What is a nation?" in H. K. Bhaba (ed.), *Nation and Narration* (New York: Routledge, 1990 [1882]), 11.

75. A. Terracciano et al., "National character does not reflect mean personality trait levels in 49 cultures," *Science* 310 (7 October 2005): 96–100.

76. Roeder, *Where Nation-States Come From*, 347–48.

77. K. S. Gleditsch and M. D. Ward, "Interstate system membership: a revised list of the independent states since 1816," *International Interactions* 25 (1999): 393–413.

78. D. Bigo, "Detention of foreigners, states of exception, and the social practices of control of the Banopticon," in P. K. Rajaram and C. Grundy-Warr (eds.), *Borderscapes: Hidden Geographies and Politics at Territory's Edge* (Minneapolis: University of Minnesota Press, 2007).

79. Part of the narrative in the following paragraphs is drawn from the following sources: A. Leontis, *Topographies of Hellenism: Mapping the Homeland* (Ithaca, NY: Cornell University Press, 1995); D. Livianos, "'Conquering the souls': nationalism and Greek guerrilla warfare in Ottoman Macedonia, 1904–1908," *Byzantine and Modern Greek Studies* 23 (1999): 195–221; E. Kofos, "National heritage and national identity in nineteenth and twentieth-century Macedonia," in M. Blinkhorn and Th. Veremis (eds.), *Modern Greece: Nationalism and Nationality* (London: Sage, 1990); H. Jones, *"A New Kind of War": America's Global Strategy and the Truman Doctrine in Greece* (New York: Oxford University Press, 1989); A. N. Karaksidou, *Fields of Wheat, Hills of Blood: Passages to Nationhood in Greek Macedonia 1870-1990* (Chicago: University of Chicago Press, 1999); L. M. Danforth, *The Macedonian Conflict: Ethnic Nationalism in a Transnational World* (Princeton, NJ: Princeton University Press, 1995); M. Herzfeld, *Ours Once More: Folklore, Ideology and the Making of Modern Greece* (Austin: University of Texas Press, 1982); and B. C. Gounaris, "Bonds made power: clientelism, nationalism, and party strategies in Greek Macedonia (1900–1950)," in M. Mazower (ed.), *Networks of Power in Modern Greece: Essays in Honor of John Campbell* (London: Hurst, 2008).

80. For example, S. N. Kalyvas, *The Logic of Violence in Civil War* (Cambridge: Cambridge University Press, 2006); R. Collins, *Violence: A Micro-Sociological Theory* (Princeton, NJ: Princeton University Press, 2008).

81. Carnegie Endowment, *The Other Balkan Wars: A 1913 Carnegie Endowment Inquiry in Retrospect* (Washington, DC: Carnegie Endowment, 1993): 107–8.

82. W. G. Werner and J. de Wilde, "The endurance of sovereignty," *European Journal of International Relations* 7 (2001): 283–313.

83. J. J. Sheehan, "The problem of sovereignty in European history," *American Historical Review* 111 (2006): 1–15.

84. S. D. Krasner, *Sovereignty: Organized Hypocrisy* (Princeton, NJ: Princeton University Press, 1999).

85. Krasner, *Sovereignty.*

86. S. D. Krasner, "Problematic sovereignty," in S. D. Krasner (ed.), *Problematic Sovereignty: Contested Rules and Political Possibilities* (New York: Columbia University Press, 2001), 6–7.

87. Krasner, "Problematic sovereignty," 7.

88. Krasner, "Problematic sovereignty," 12.

89. J. G. Ruggie, "Territoriality and beyond: problematizing modernity in international relations," *International Organization* 47 (1993): 164.

90. P. F. Cowhey and J. D. Aronson, *Managing the World Economy: The Consequences of Corporate Alliances* (New York: Council on Foreign Relations Press, 1993).

91. Cowhey and Aronson, *Managing the World Economy*, 237.

92. J. D. Levy (ed.), *The State after Statism: New State Activities in the Age of Liberalization* (Cambridge, MA: Harvard University Press, 2006).

93. R. H. Jackson, *Quasi-States: Sovereignty, International Relations and the Third World* (Cambridge: Cambridge University Press, 1990).

94. B. Davidson, *The Black Man's Burden: Africa and the Curse of the Nation-State* (New York: Times Books, 1992).

95. S. N. Grovogui, "Regimes of sovereignty: international morality and the African condition," *European Journal of International Relations* 8 (2002): 315–38.

96. Agnew, *Hegemony*; also see J. Donnelly, "Sovereign inequalities and hierarchy in anarchy: American power and international society," *European Journal of International Relations* 12 (2006): 139–70.

97. Agnew, *Hegemony*, chapter 2.

98. M. Mann, "The autonomous power of the state: its origins, mechanisms and results," *European Journal of Sociology* 25 (1984): 185–213.

99. D. Deudney, "Binding sovereigns: authorities, structures, and geopolitics in the Philadelphian system," in T. J. Biersteker and C. Weber (eds.), *State Sovereignty as Social Construct* (Cambridge: Cambridge University Press, 1996).

100. J. Agnew, *Place and Politics: The Geographical Mediation of State and Society* (London: Allen and Unwin, 1987).

101. R. Aron, "Macht, power, *puissance*: prose démocratique ou poésie démoniaque?" *European Journal of Sociology* 5 (1964): 31.

102. M. Foucault, *The History of Sexuality. Volume 3: The Care of the Self* (London: Penguin, 1986), 234.

CHAPTER 3

SOVEREIGNTY REGIMES

The questioning of the "territorial" in state sovereignty matters not simply because of the challenge to state political-economic primacy from globalization it may presuppose but also because the equation of state with territorial sovereignty is intrinsic to the ways in which politics in general and democracy in particular have been considered in modern times. For one thing, democracy has been *historically* dependent upon the nation-state, the state as underwritten by a singular national identity. Territorial democracy and popular sovereignty grew together after the American and French Revolutions. The rise of nationalism further reinforced the link. I and others have recited some of the ways in which the deliberative nature of democracy as it developed seems to require territorial adjacency among citizens and in which its symbolic content rests on common territorial histories of struggle and social organization.[1] But is there a necessary *conceptual* dependence of each on the other? Statements such as "The ideals of citizenship clash with the sovereign nation-state in which they were first developed" imply that they no longer do.[2] Indeed, much of the so-called cosmopolitan literature on democracy holds to this viewpoint, as it rhetorically advocates a move beyond it to world citizenship. But the only way that it can do so without opening up to question the founding condition of democratic theory—the presumption of a territorialized political community—is by "scaling up" to the world as whole. In this account, therefore, normative categories of consent and legitimacy based on territorialization of those doing the consenting and legitimizing remain unaffected by globalization. This is because established democratic theory and practice have required a necessary fiction to make them possible at all: that there is absolute popular sovereignty vested in a national/territorial political community rigidly marked off from all others.[3] Absolute sovereignty thereby continues to underwrite democracy as it is typically thought of by cosmopolitan democrats, even as the contemporary world calls for attention to divisible sovereignty and deterritorialized legitimacy. Democracy's advocates will have to respond to this challenge if democracy is to survive and prosper in a globalizing world. They will need analytic concepts that offer somewhat more purchase on global complexity than nation-state versus global state or global versus local or imperialism versus self-rule. So much recent writing about globalization and sovereignty seems stuck in the terms of debate of the late nineteenth and early twentieth centuries.

My purpose is to offer a different way of thinking about sovereignty that has only become possible perhaps because thinking in terms of globalization has exposed the myths upon which dominant conceptions of sovereignty have relied. But globalization is not in itself the only cause of the incongruence between sovereignty and territory. It may have exacerbated this mismatch but it certainly did not initiate it. For example, imperial relations of subordination and other manifestations of hierarchy in world politics have long conditioned the effectiveness of sovereignty of many putatively sovereign states. The argument of chapter 2 should have made clear the idealized character of much discussion of sovereignty. Of course, globalization is also subject to its own mythology, as I have shown in chapter 1. In this chapter, I lay out a framework for understanding sovereignty in terms of a set of "regimes" in which sovereignty is viewed as organized geographically in different ways depending on the "mix" of central state authority and the degree of territoriality associated with it. Before that, however, I want to briefly review the story about how sovereignty and statehood became bonded together and the main elements of a critique of it that have emerged in recent years.

My point here is to underline the extent to which states have become not just the main but the singular subjects of world politics for most students of it. But in defining them as entirely territorial actors, the tendency has been then, at least for those not continuing to be enamored of a totally state-centric vision, to see the dynamic introduced by globalization as totally wiping out the earlier territorial order and replacing it with a completely new networked world of nodes and flows. This image of total geographical transformation is completely misleading. As I showed in chapter 1, territories, networks, and place-making have long co-existed as modalities in the workings of power. The actual story of sovereignty has never been that of an absolute territorial control, however much the conventional wisdom surveyed in chapter 2 has made it seem that way. Hence, the idea that state territorial sovereignty is now faced with total annihilation is also off the mark. "Clean break" thinking has become very popular in recent years with writers of various theoretical and political persuasions. It is attractive performatively, as an author you can declare to have discovered a new world in the making, and it also helps to simplify things for mass audiences. Whether it offers the best theoretical purchase on the world we inhabit is another thing entirely.

The core of the chapter is a proposed geo-sociological account of control and authority that puts states in a wider frame of reference for understanding sovereignty. But I also pay attention to some case studies in the "migration of authority" that does appear to have been occurring at increasing speed in recent years. A final section lays out a historical geography of sovereignty regimes as they have prevailed over the past two hundred years. Sovereignty has long taken a greater variety of forms and inspired a wider range of political-economic "games" than the conventional wisdom would frequently allow. This pluralizing of the vision of sovereignty leads us well away from the either/or logic of globalization and sovereignty (or that of imperialism and sovereignty) that has been so typical of most recent academic and popular thinking. Both past and present are more complex with respect to the workings of sovereignty than the conventional wisdom supposes.

SOVEREIGNTY AND STATEHOOD

In conventional political discourse, sovereignty is about central state control and authority. This is a relationship in which an agent of a state can make commands that are voluntarily complied with by those over whom the state claims authority. In the typical story, such internal or "domestic" sovereignty requires a source of authority (kingship, the nation, the-people-in-government, etc.) that operates effectively within the territory of the state. Explicitly, therefore, sovereignty is seen as state-based and territorial. Currently dominant understandings of state sovereignty are based on older ones in which sovereignty is associated with the physical person of a monarch. Thus, as the first part of chapter 2 argued, the manifestly incorporeal realm of the state is often described in Western thought as a "body." In early modern European absolutism, the "body politic is always an adult male body that has no history of birth and is not subject to natural deterioration. This body, whose head is a king and whose limbs and organs are subjects of various rank, can die only by violent attack or the infection of some of its parts."[4] The physicality of the sovereign has been symbolically transferred from the monarch to the state territory. This metaphor resists the idea that sovereignty can be deterritorialized. At the same time, and in the same story, sovereignty has an external dimension. Any given state must be recognized as sovereign by other states in order to qualify as such. This implies a formal equality between states in which none can exercise command over others. This "juridical" or legal sovereignty, therefore, provides the necessary geographical condition for the operation of domestic sovereignty: a rigid distinction between the hierarchy exercised by the state within its territory and the anarchy that prevails beyond it.

From this viewpoint, state sovereignty may be understood as *the absolute territorial organization of political authority.* Most accounts of sovereignty accept its either/or quality: a state either does or does not have sovereignty. They differ as to whether they see this as a foundational principle (originating in, for example, the seventeenth century with the Peace of Westphalia of 1648 or earlier) or as an emergent social practice. They also vary in accepting that there are actors in international politics (such as militarily weaker states) that are not fully sovereign. At least from Hobbes (1651) and Locke (1690) to Schmitt (1985) and Agamben (1998), to name just a few, however, modern territorial states and sovereignty have been seen as practically bonded together. Even Michel Foucault, a theorist with a less state-centered view of the world, for example, often seems to see central state authority as achieving sovereign power in the modern world with "a triangle, sovereignty-discipline-government, which has as its primary target the population and as its essential mechanism the apparatuses of security" as the exclusive political centerpiece.[5] Of course, Foucault is also the theorist who pointed to the conflict between this sovereign power of rules backed by sanctions and the actual daily experience of power exercised by a multitude of non-state sources as a fundamental element of political discourse and social practice.[6] Unfortunately, this dualist vision has rarely prevailed in critical analysis of the practices of state sovereignty. Rather, for example, when states show evidence of increasing economic and political interdependence, this is construed as either a "choice" that they have made in pursuit of self-evident interests rather than an exogenous challenge to them or sovereignty is seen as totally under threat or "at bay" from "new technologies" of power. But what if the absolute and indivisible political authority implicit in this story about state sovereignty and its presumed territorial basis is problematic to begin with?

The assumption has long been that states monopolize power that they then distribute or use to fulfill their desires. In fact, what if states are no more than coordinating devices to connect and integrate networks of power into discrete territories? From this perspective, a wide range of social actors are the sources of power and states are, at least initially, merely the vessels for the administration of the power of others. Of course, in the process of integrating power, states are able to gain their own foothold that they can then use to establish autonomy (and thus power) over the other actors. In this way, and to use a body metaphor, "the capillaries and synapses of power within the social body are gradually plugged into and connected with the central circulatory and nervous systems of the state."[7] This is an important implication of the arguments of several important recent writers on the sociology of statehood, such as Jürgen Habermas, Norbert Elias, Pierre Bourdieu, and Michel Foucault, if in each case in different ways and with different limitations.[8] If from Habermas we can borrow the centrality of praxis or practice, from Elias a focus on the social dynamics of state formation, and from Bourdieu the idea of a bureaucratic "field," Foucault offers a conception of power that is simultaneously attentive to power as both a capability *and* a medium of action *and* as both centralized and diffused. The main thrust of this chapter is to suggest that a geo-sociological approach to statehood—emphasizing how states are "produced" both materially and discursively over space, yet with powers that are always constrained and shared—provides the best basis for understanding the complexities of sovereignty.

Before proceeding to that, however, I want to explore how territorial states have acquired the much more central role they have in thinking about sovereignty and how, as a consequence, globalization has been seen as such a threat to it. This requires understanding something of how states have become the exclusive subjects of world politics by synthesizing the various elements of the argument in chapter 2 in a singular argument.

STATES AS SUBJECTS

The conventional story is based on giving the state an ontological and a moral character equivalent to that of the individual person in classical liberalism.[9] The state is thus treated as a "given." It is rooted in a grammar of fixed boundaries and identities. As a naturalized abstract individual, the state has acquired a personhood that then underwrites its special status as the locus of sovereignty. This is especially convincing because a moral claim equating the autonomy of an individual person with that of the state is masked by the natural claim that is made on behalf of the state as an individual. In this way, the historical construction of statehood as a particular type of political enterprise is given a transcendental makeover. The sovereign state is exalted as the singular solution to both the problem of human aggression, by displacing that aggression from within the territory of the state into the realm of interstate relations, and the problem of organizing economic life, by using its unique qualities to compete within a global division of labor.[10]

In fact, statehood and personhood alike are not the pre-given phenomena this story suggests. Rather, they are both subjectivities formed out of social interaction and mutual recognition. Persons and states only form as such through the interaction and recognition of households, tribes, dynasties, social movements, and such. More particularly, statehood emerges out of struggles for control; it is never a pre-existing basis for those struggles. In other words, a state is not ontologically prior to a set of interstate relations. A state emerges and is recognized as such within a set of relationships that define the rules for what is and what is not a "state." Statehood results from mutual recognition among states.[11] It is not the outcome of "isolated states" achieving statehood separately and then engaging with one another as abstract individuals. The importance of the Peace of Westphalia in 1648, for example, lay in the mutual recognition among elites of the new European territorial states as a set of equally legitimate centers of public power in the face of devastating religious wars. Yet the legitimation of state sovereignty also depended on the increased loyalty and support of populations through the cross-mapping of nation with state.[12] In the nationalist imagination the state then becomes something of a "super-person."

The view of the state as the subject of international politics, therefore, is based on the modern conception of the autonomous self as "the heroic figure of reasoning man who is himself the origin of language, the maker of history, and the source of meaning in the world."[13] It presumes that state sovereignty reflects the interests of a pre-existing subject. It sets an autonomous subject apart from the objective world, at once conceiving agency as prior to action and separating agents from their action. While rendering state action as contingent and problematic, it conceives its subjectivity as natural and given. It thereby frames the study of the state in terms of its "real" identity and interests—its subjectivity—because state action is assumed to flow from its subjectivity. It encourages questions about the effectiveness of the state as an actor, but simultaneously suppresses questions about how it is possible to conceive of the state as an autonomous actor. It thereby makes possible the dichotomies of inside/outside and self/other that are central to contemporary conceptions of politics.

Of course, this is not to say that the state is simply an illusion invented totally out of repeated invocation of the word *sovereignty*. As Werner and de Wilde say, "a claim to sovereignty attempts to establish a relation as an institutional fact (the 'fact' being the supreme or ultimate authority and the 'fact' of being an independent authority) and a set of rights and responsibilities."[14] As a result, sovereignty is more than just a word, norm, or principle; it is all of these concurrently. The recognizably institutional character of sovereignty comes about because its social construction is taken by most observers as a simple matter of fact. How has this happened?

At one time, this perspective on the state as an essential and ontologically independent subject was explicitly underwritten by an organicist conception of the state. States were seen as organisms competing for survival against one another by analogy with the struggle for survival in a state of nature. The state was connected to the nation as a mythic pre-political community, and the principle of natural selection was sometimes used to underwrite the claim that in a world of aggressive states only the strong would survive. While this approach has long since been decried in most academic circles, largely because it was seen as leading to the excesses of Nazi statism, many conventional conceptions of the state, including those of international law, also continue to see the state as the pre-given autonomous subject of world politics. It has since led to a sort of banal statism, not an explicit glorification of the state, but a more insidious commonsense view of the state as a self-evident unit. A corollary of this first-person identity is that the states are, like all organisms, engaged in competition with one another. Outside the borders of the state, the argument goes, all is anarchy. This is why territorial states must harden their borders and/or prepare actively to expand beyond them. It's a jungle out there.

In conventional geopolitical terms, therefore, the world political map is one of containers that potentially compete with one another by mobilizing their potential. This implies a cartogram of power in which each state brings its population-resources and relative location to the global game board. Figure 3.1A shows in these terms what we can expect globally around 2050. Though in nominal terms equally sovereign, therefore, each state in this representation has a differential presence within world politics. But as figure 3.1B strongly suggests, over a longer time frame, this time through 2300, the picture could well change. This map could be interpreted as relatively reassuring to the Europeans and North Americans (presuming that their descendants will be whom they think they will be) to whom figure 3.1A is anything but. Of course, both maps are premised on a state-centric view of the world that this book is actively disputing. Maps such as these stun the reader into mute acquiescence with the message their authors tell us the maps incontrovertibly convey.[15] As constructed in the ways they are, the maps explicitly exclude the possibility of ties that bind different places together.

The main point is that the presumed subjectivity of a state does not exist prior to its expression or representation as a singular entity on a map; rather, subjectivity is constituted within and through a discourse (including mapping) operating in its name. Sovereignty, then, does not express an already existing subjectivity and agency of the state. Rather, the category of the sovereign state is constructed and reconstructed through the language, practices, and the behavior of its leaders operating in its name. State actions, such as foreign policy, therefore make the very categories of national interest and identity in whose name they are conducted. The sovereign state thus emerges as the outcome of a repetitive practice of citing state sovereignty and state interests. It is through this practice of enacting the state that the alignment between territoriality and identity is brought about, so that it becomes possible to speak of a particular state as an entity or a subject with a definitive character. It follows, then, that states are necessarily always in the process of being represented and hence made as such.

My claim, though, is not the idealist one that states do not exist exter-

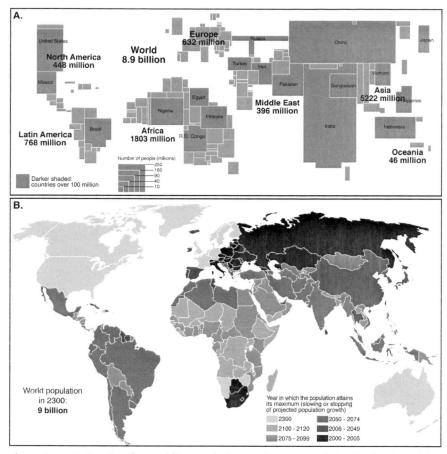

Figure 3.1.   Estimating the world's population: A. Cartogram of the distribution of the world's population by country and world region in 2050; B. Predicted period of maximum population by country between 2000 and 2300.

Source: Author from UN sources.

nally to thought or that they are not made in part, at least, through the working of material forces, although some writers who focus on the social construction of states do imply as much.[16] What I mean, rather, is that socially constructed entities such as "the state" cannot be represented and cannot do their work outside a discursive construction of some sort.[17] Thus, the materiality of state power is part and parcel of, not prior to, the discourse of sovereignty, as our understanding of its material or institutional reality is formed within the discourse. Likewise, what is under challenge from this perspective is not that states' foreign policies cannot be shaped by material interests, but that these interests necessarily exist prior to the foreign policy itself. In other words, I reject the idea that the material effects of states are derived from pre-given identities and interests that one should uncover in order to understand a later state action. The materiality of statehood emerges out of action rather than providing the pre-existing basis to it as in conventional accounts.

The process of making states as subjects has had two important underpinnings to it that bear rehearsing here, even though I have alluded to elements of them previously (particularly in chapter 2): the relationship between sovereignty and nationalism and the active role of security threats in producing the state. Nationalism is important here because sovereignty claims cannot be neatly confined to considerations of statehood alone. The view that sovereign states are the subjects of international politics relies on the assumption that the legitimacy of the state is derived from the people (see the second section of chapter 2). The doctrine of popular sovereignty proposes that states are the masters of territory and people are the masters of states.[18] It is this presumed internal homogeneity of values/norms/culture that allows the state to act in the name of "the people." There is a crucial ambiguity, however, as to how "the people" should be defined. On the one hand, the doctrine of popular sovereignty conceives "the people" as a territorial community defined by the state. On the other hand, this doctrine also evokes an image of the people as a pre-political community that establishes state institutions and has the final say in their legitimacy. "The people" is thus imagined both as existing in an already constituted state and as pre-existing the state. The state is consequently framed not only as a political but also as an organic cultural community.

Security threats constitute a second key mechanism in producing the image of the state as a separate entity. Whereas the conflation of the state and the nation inscribes the "inside" of the state as a subject, evoking national security threats designates the anarchic "outside" against which the state is defined. State legitimacy requires moral boundaries of identity and such boundaries are produced and maintained through invoking threats from the outside. Moreover, framing an entity—such as the state—as under threat also casts it as natural and unproblematic, and legitimizes emergency measures deemed necessary to deal with the alleged threat. The term *security* thereby functions as both a depoliticizing and a mobilizing tool. The whole inter-state system is based on the fusing of identity and security so that each state supposedly protects its territorially defined national identity from inroads by others. Ironically, insecurity is therefore not external to the state, but is an integral part of the process of establishing the state's identity. It is a precondition for making the state sovereign.[19]

This sense of external danger that is so vital to modern state-making has at least some of its origins in the imaginative capacity to transcend the spatial limits of everyday life and think of the world both as a whole and beyond local horizons as a picture in which you not only have a centrality as you look outward but in which dangers lurk at every turn beyond the limits of your gaze. This feat was simply not possible before the encounters of Europeans with the rest of the world beginning in the late fifteenth and early sixteenth centuries. For masses of people around the world this is even more recent with the arrival of compulsory elementary education and basic training in reading the world political map. From the outset, the world beyond the horizon was a potential source of chaos and threat. Thus, as I have argued elsewhere:

> The evil spirits and dark places decorating the borders of early modern maps, where they signified "unknown" and presumably dangerous places, moved into the world itself where they came to represent fearful religious, civilizational and political differences. The one-world picture, therefore, is not a composition of equal and pacific elements but a hierarchy of places, from known to unknown, from most friendly to most dangerous.[20]

Most importantly for present purposes, security discourse reproduces the sovereign state also in the sense that framing an issue in terms of security invariably seems to cast that issue in territorial terms. This discourse does not simply reify the idealized "inside," but also demarcates the "inside" and the "outside" as fundamentally territorial categories. This then reproduces the state as an inherently territorial subject. Although one could argue that a broadening of the security agenda decouples security from the territorial state, such a shift has not actually happened. Once an issue, such as immigration or the physical environment, is framed in terms of security, it is shifted into the realm of territorial defense and border control.[21]

The U.S. "war on terror" is a good example of how casting complex problems in terms of national security tends to give priority to the territorial conception of sovereignty over other possible spatial modalities. By way of example, the war in Iraq was arguably the direct result of confusing a terrorist enemy organized loosely over space (al Qaeda) with a territorial state (Iraq) and also an outcome of forgetting that the attacks of 11 September 2001 were as much attacks on the current world economy and all its non-territorial actors (banks, stock exchanges, investors, etc.) as symbolized by the twin towers in Lower Manhattan as they were attacks on the sovereign territory of the United States.[22]

MOVING BEYOND THE IDEALIZED STATE AS THE
ONLY SUBJECT OF WORLD POLITICS

From this broad critical overview of dominant thinking of how sovereignty is produced through the subjectivity of statehood, three aspects of the story stand in need of particular scrutiny before moving on to my geo-sociological account of sovereignty. The first two have received increasing attention from a range of writers. But the third has been largely neglected. The first is the assumption that sovereignty is acquired exogenously or in a "state of nature" rather than in an ongoing system of states. So-called social constructivists have been especially concerned with this aspect of contemporary thinking.[23] Key to their interpretation is the idea that sovereignty—both domestically and externally—is socially constructed as states interact with, imitate, and conflict with one another. "Domestic order" is thus premised on "external" disorder and danger. In this understanding, sovereignty is a social fact produced by the practices of states. So, rather than emerging from the "state-of-nature"—the war of all against all—that Thomas Hobbes used as the basis for positing the origins of the state, sovereignty comes about as a result of the "purposes" of states in interaction and can involve a wide range of actual practices and policies that change over time. The problem, of course, is that states do not occupy the world alone.[24] A society rich with all sorts of actors exists beyond the confines of a world of states. And this is definitely not new. As Michael Mann has made the point, though networks of social relations in Europe were increasingly "caged" by so-called nation-states and the state system in the nineteenth century, this is only a small part of the overall story of that time and later: "The expansion of these national and inter-national networks always proceeded alongside the expansion of certain 'transnational' power relations, especially those of industrial capitalism and its attendant ideologies (liberalism, socialism)."[25] This argument about the social construction of states (and the corollary that states have never been all there is to the world) is all well and good but even together they fail to address two further assumptions that are critical to the dominant view of sovereignty.

One of these is that of an essential equality between states claiming sovereignty, notwithstanding the obvious reality of hierarchy in power between actors in world politics. The modern world is one of major inequalities in power between states in different world regions.[26] Much of this is the result of imperialism in the past and the hegemony exercised by the United States and its allies (and other powerful states such as Russia and China) in the present. Just as sovereignty was itself emerging as a doctrine defining state subject-hood in Europe, Europeans were arrogating to themselves elsewhere "the authority to decide who or what could count as sovereign authority" underwritten by "not only complex racialized discourses of civilized versus uncivilized peoples, but superior military might and the brutal use of force."[27] Thus, although the assumption of equal sovereignty (both domestic and juridical) may have applied, at least to a degree, to the European states, their settler offspring, and later to Japan, China, and a few others, states in the rest of the world that were directly colonized have had a serious sovereignty deficit. For them, sovereignty is as yet "unrealized."[28] Many of them, such as long-subjugated groups such as Indian nations within Canada and the United States, as well as ethno-national groupings elsewhere, use allied claims to sovereignty over distinctive territories (such as Reservations) to challenge the "modular" territorial form of the modern state.[29] But even those who have acquired some type of formal statehood simply have not had the power resources to seriously challenge restrictions placed upon them by more powerful states (and other actors). Nor can they expect ready recognition of their internal political authority when they have either inherited their claim to rule from colonial powers or depend for their continuance in power on external support.[30] For example, following independence most African states were too small in population and territory to support much industrial development, yet, at the same time, many of the bigger ones in particular were prone to civil war because of their internal ethnic heterogeneity. The colonial inheritance of borders imposed from outside made the establishment of even the rudiments of territorial sovereignty next to impossible. Of course, a danger here lies in seeing state sovereignty as a largely realized phenomenon in the West and absent elsewhere when it is better thought of, as I have argued repeatedly, as "unrealized" everywhere in the form that it is usually alleged to take.

The role of imperialism/colonialism in the history of sovereignty, however, demands closer analysis. Ongoing inequality in sovereignty between colonial and (former) colonized is only part of the picture.[31] The bigger point is that modern sovereignty everywhere came out of the historical ties of colonialism. In other words, sovereignty in Europe and elsewhere was a "co-production."[32] Thus, and for example, European sovereignty was often first expressed in terms of "raising the flag" on putatively "unoccupied" or underutilized territories; of drawing borders on world maps to designate which European state owned this or that territory; of how the recognition of one another's colonial claims was intrinsic to their mutual recognition of one another as states; and of how nomads were denied the possibility of sovereignty simply because they moved around rather than occupied a given territory on a permanent basis. So the story of sovereignty in much of the world is not about the "spread" of a Western practice to incorporate "them" within its parameters as "they" became independent but about the making of sovereignty—territorialized and not—as a global phenomenon from the outset.

But the problem of lack of conformity to absolute sovereignty exercised by individual states over their territories is even more pervasive than that represented by the dominance still exerted by imperial (or hegemonic) powers over their historical subordinates simply because hierarchical dominance in world politics is much more widespread. There has always been a variety of hierarchical relationships in world politics, from empires, protectorates, and spheres of influence to dependencies, unincorporated territories and forms of indirect rule, alliances, and treaty regimes. So, even when states are nominally sovereign entities without any sort of colonial history, they are often part of other arrangements that simply vitiate the nominal claim at least in some issue areas. On a relational, as opposed to a formal-legal, conception of authority, "authority rests on a bargain between the ruler and the ruled premised on the former's provision of a social order of value sufficient to offset the latter's loss of freedom."[33] In this perspective, the existence of hierarchy comes as no surprise. It may be by no means complete. It can relate to some issues and to others. But it involves the possibility that some states will exercise more control and authority beyond (and, perhaps, within) their borders than do others. Across both economic—exchange to dependency—and security—diplomacy to protectorate—dimensions, David Lake traces how parties enter into a variety of relationships which indicate that states do not exist in an anarchic vacuum but in a world in which sovereignty is shared or pooled across a wide range of relatively institutionalized arenas and in which some states are undoubtedly more important than others.[34]

An interesting example of this hierarchy at work in the contemporary world is the "Americanization" of law enforcement beyond U.S. shores. For example, working through a variety of bilateral and multilateral channels among states, the U.S. State Department has essentially written the global agenda on drug enforcement policy. The U.S. Bureau of International Narcotics and Law Enforcement (INL) encourages foreign governments to adopt U.S. policies and sponsors training for law enforcement personnel in ninety-five countries around the world. In his book *Cops across Borders*, Ethan Nadelmann shows how:

> Foreign police have adopted U.S. investigative techniques, and foreign courts and legislatures have followed up with the requisite legal authorizations. And foreign Governments have devoted substantial police and even military resources to curtailing illicit drug production and trafficking. . . . By and large, the United States has provided the models, and other governments have done the accommodating.[35]

David Lake's point about the relational character of sovereignty is well worth reiterating more broadly. Around the world many situations completely violate the rule of formal-legal sovereignty. In the first place are situations of what can be called "shared sovereignty" (such as one China, two systems in Hong Kong; the strange mutual sovereignty claims of China and Taiwan; the emergence of supranational systems such as the European Union; and the ceding of economic power into the hands of international institutions such as the IMF in the case of heavily indebted underdeveloped countries).[36] Other seeming anomalous but all too typical situations (such as that of the Palestinian National Authority in the occupied West Bank and Hamas in Gaza, the bi-partite government of Bosnia, the apparent lack of reach of Pakistan's central government in Pakistan Tribal Regions, land conflicts at West African borders, and the British/Irish collaboration over Northern Ireland) also suggest how widespread exceptions to the rule of absolute, indivisible sovereignty exercised equally by all states can be. Sovereignty is divisible across different areas (economic, security) and seems increasingly so across the world. Authority can also be delegated or pooled to international and supranational organizations. In the overall context of subordination and delegation, international lawyers increasingly distinguish between a historic insular sovereignty, which emphasizes a right to resist, and an emerging relational sovereignty, which is the capacity to engage.[37] They use this distinction as the basis for explaining the proliferation of networks of government officials who share information and coordinate their activities around the world. This "disaggregated sovereignty" points to the willingness of states to share authority in the face of environmental, economic, and social problems that go well beyond their individual capacity to manage on their own.

This brings us to the third problematic assumption, one that has received much more limited attention from scholars and commentators. This is the assumption that sovereignty is invariably territorial or exercised over blocs of terrestrial space. Modern political theory has long regarded geography as simply territorial: the world is divided up into contiguous spatial units with the territorial state as the basic building block from which sometimes other territorial units (such as alliances, spheres of influence, empires, etc.) derive or develop. This is the opposite of the historical situation in the field of geography considered as a whole, where, outside the confines of the small subfield of political geography, as Robert Sack once noted, "conventional spatial analysis has largely ignored territoriality."[38] Fleeting, if important, exceptions such as the impressive work of Jean Gottmann referred to at length in chapter 2 only help to prove the rule. More recently, however, particularly under the influence of a certain statist reading of Foucault and the strange revival of interest in the Nazi philosopher Schmitt, it is as if power cannot be thought of except in terms of territoriality.

Much of the speculation about "the decline of the state" or "sovereignty at bay" in the face of globalization is posed as the "end of geography" because geography and territory are read as one and the same thing by most political theorists and international relations specialists. Yet, and in the first place, the historical record suggests that there is no necessity for polities to be organized territorially. As Hendrick Spruyt claims, "If politics is about rule, the modern state is verily unique, for it claims sovereignty and territoriality. It is sovereign in that it claims final authority and recognizes no higher source of jurisdiction. It is territorial in that rule is defined as exclusive authority over a fixed territorial space. The criterion for determining where claims to sovereign jurisdiction begin or end is thus a purely geographic one. Mutually recognized borders delimit spheres of jurisdiction."[39] Territoriality, the use of territory for political, social, and economic ends, is in fact a strategy that has developed more in some historical contexts than in others. Thus, the territorial state as it is known to contemporary political theory developed initially in early modern Europe with the retreat of non-territorial dynastic systems of rule and the transfer of sovereignty from the personhood of monarchs to discrete national populations.[40]

But even then: "Territorial sovereignty was . . . never a hard and fast rule. Numerous exceptions to strict territoriality existed and even thrived." For example, "prior to World War II, western powers regularly maintained 'consular courts' within non-western nations such as Turkey, Morocco, and China. These courts, typically founded on coercive treaties, adjudicated claims among western citizens abroad as well as between western citizens and locals, on the theory that local law was barbaric, unpredictable, and strange."[41]

THE GEOGRAPHY OF EFFECTIVE SOVEREIGNTY

Without historically very specific economic and political conditions, sovereignty—in the sense of the socially constructed practices of political control and authority—may be exercised non-territorially or in scattered territorial pockets connected by flows across space-spanning networks. From this viewpoint, sovereignty can be practiced in networks across space with distributed nodes in places that are either hierarchically arranged or reticular (without a central or directing node). In the former case authority is centralized whereas in the latter it is essentially shared across the network. All forms of polity—from hunter-gatherer tribes through nomadic kinship structures to city-states, territorial states, spheres of influence, alliances, trade pacts, seaborne empires—therefore, occupy some sort of space but not always contiguous territories. What is clear, however, if not widely recognized within contemporary debates about state sovereignty, is that political control and authority is also not necessarily predicated on and defined by strict and fixed territorial boundaries.

It follows from this argument that political control and authority are not necessarily restricted to states and that such control and authority are thereby not necessarily exclusively territorial. Final authority is often ascribed to the state as a type of irresistible power. But in fact the foundation of control and attribution of legitimacy to different political entities has changed historically. By way of example, the legitimacy of rule by monarchs in the medieval European order had a different meaning (primarily that of social obligations of various sorts) from that of later absolutist rulers (greater recourse to fear and divine right) and from that operating under more recent democratic justifications for state power (allowing for public deliberation and delivering public goods).[42] In no case, however, has the authority of any state ever been complete. There have always been competing sources of authority, from the Church in the medieval context to all sorts of non-territorial actors today.[43] In terms of criteria for establishing authority, rather than simply ascribing authority to central states as a natural feature they all must share as if by definition, transparency, efficiency, expertise, accountability, and popularity are all as much foundations of legitimacy as are nationality and democratic process and can be characteristic of many types of social groups and organizations.[44] Indeed, and reflecting the application of such criteria by populations, private organizations can be given as great or even greater authority than are states.

Phrases such as "divisible" and "graduated" sovereignty are often now used to give the sense of an increasingly labile sovereignty (political authority) not immediately associated with territorialized state power. Thus, for example, Aihwa Ong claims that

> globalization has induced a situation of graduated sovereignty, whereby even as the state maintains control over its territory, it . . . lets corporate entities set the terms for constituting and regulating some domains. . . . Weaker and less desirable groups are given over to the regulation of supranational entities.[45]

It is not the existence but the nature of sovereignty, therefore, that is transformed by the workings of graduated sovereignty. Authority is vested in agents who manage flows through space or through action at a distance as much as in those who manage territories. Adjacency and territorial division of space as modalities of power thus face the challenge of coercive power and authority emanating from scattered sites. The spatiality of authority, therefore, cannot be entirely reduced to the territorial template of state sovereignty. Indeed, with globalization the transactional balance is increasingly tipping in favor of a networked system of political authority that challenges territorialized state sovereignty as the singular face of effective sovereignty. Of course, as I have been at pains to point out, none of this is entirely new.

In this regard, the terms *territory* and *space* need to be very carefully distinguished from one another. This conflation is not unusual in even the most sophisticated of theoretical arguments. Simply because the former (territory) might be superseded or supplemented in the organization of political authority does not mean that the latter (space) disappears. Territory is not geography *tout court*. Indeed, "states" of one type or another can continue to serve as a locus of political authority even as their power is deployed by networked flows rather than by territorial control penetrating other nominally sovereign states. For example, relatively powerful states today can supervise security threats in distant places and financial transactions in "offshore" centers (even as they have little direct regulatory control) by rewarding and/or punishing actions that they judge in relation to the spatial efficacy of their authority. Of course, in such situations sovereignty is not absolute. But, then, as is increasingly clear, and as criticism of the first two assumptions about conventional views of state sovereignty (taken-for-granted subjectivity and "state-of-nature" equality) implies, state sovereignty rarely ever has been or is absolute, even when apparently neatly territorialized.

The main issue is that territoriality is only one of the ways in which space can be constituted socially and mobilized politically (see chapter 1). Territoriality always has two features: blocks of rigidly bordered space and domination or control as the modality of power upon which the bordering relies. This may well be legitimate power, that is, exercised with authority (either bureaucratic or charismatic), but it ultimately rests on demarcation through domination. It works through territorial division of space, boundary control, and the hierarchical dissemination of authoritative commands.[46] Yet space and power have other possible modalities (see chapter 1).[47] *Centralized* power, involving command and obedience, can operate over long distances as well as over territorial blocs, for example through the deployment of military assets, but this may have less possibility of sustained, and legitimate, impact on the people with whom it comes into contact. But this is then still a networked form of centralized power. It is based on flows through space-spanning networks, not privileged access to blocks of space. On the contrary, *diffused* power refers to power that is not centered or directly commanded but that results from patterns of social association and interaction in groups and movements (as, for example, in NGOs and global social movements) or through market exchange (e.g., credit rating agencies such as Moody's are one example).[48] Diffused power can also be territorialized and authoritative, but only insofar as the networks it defines are territorially constrained by central state authority. Otherwise, networks are limited spatially only by the purposes for which they are formed. In this way, power is generated through social and market-based association, affiliation, and reticular diffusion rather than through authoritative command or domination. This is power that comes into existence through association and assent. When not sustained through legitimate collective action, however, the power networks thus created will disintegrate. Today, both centralized and diffused powers are arguably less territorialized by state boundaries than at any time since the nineteenth century.

Sovereignty as the *legitimate* exercise of power (as authority), therefore, is necessarily about ceded, seduced, and co-opted diffused power as well as coercion by (and acceptance of) centralized power. The precise combination of power mechanisms (coercion, assent, seduction, co-optation, etc.) involved in the exercise of authority can be the same for all issue areas (trade, security, currency, etc.) or differ across them and operate solely within a state's territory or more widely either territorially or non-territorially. But without at least a modicum of active collaboration by collective actors on both sides of borders, state sovereignty can be neither sustained nor undermined. In short, as John Allen remarks, "domination is not everywhere."[49] Indeed, even demarcation through borders, the essence of state territoriality, relies to a considerable degree on the extent to which networks of association and affiliation (diffused power) parallel the boundaries of domination. Even the seemingly most Westphalian of states, then, are riddled with authoritative power networks whose extension beyond territorial boundaries can render claims to absolute sovereignty moot but whose continuing presence inside the boundaries is critical to their credibility.

EFFECTIVE SOVEREIGNTY AND SOVEREIGNTY REGIMES

The political authority at the heart of sovereignty is the legitimate practice of power. In other words, it is the myriad effects of an ascribed asymmetry between actors that permits some actors to not just command but also to enroll others in their desires and activities. *Ascribed* is the key term. As Bruce Lincoln puts it, "Persuasion and coercion alike are constitutive of authority, but once actualized and rendered explicit they signal—indeed, they are, at least temporarily—its negation."[50] Today, it requires both communicative and infrastructural resources and a high degree of popular acceptance to operate effectively. More specifically, political authority qua state sovereignty requires (1) a governmental apparatus to serve as a final seat of authority and (2) an accepted definition of functional and geographical scope (territorial and non-territorial) beyond which its commands go unheeded and unenforced.

THE GEO-SOCIOLOGY OF STATEHOOD

One thing that has been lacking in discussing the range of social practices associated with sovereignty has been a means of identifying the effects of co-variation in the effectiveness of state authority, on the one hand, and its relative reliance on state territoriality, on the other. Another has been a resistance to thinking in terms of different states having distinctive experiences with sovereignty. One size fits all has tended to prevail with the "model" to which others are held to correspond or aspire (usually France, Britain, or the United States) gaining central billing. It is not difficult to see the "international" as involving overlapping and interconnected histories rather than singular state experiences following some European precursor or a single universal trajectory. What is needed is what Philip McMichael has called "incorporated comparison" by which he means that the particulars of each state's sovereignty are established within a world-historical context.[51] This approach views "comparable social phenomena [such as sovereignty] as differentiated outcomes or moments of an historically integrated process, whereas conventional comparison treats such social phenomena as parallel cases."[52] Sovereignty has traveled in different ways in different parts of the world, so to speak.

A useful method for dealing with both of these issues—the central state authority/territory nexus and the problem of comparison—comes from some famous writing on the historical sociology of power. Specifically, the terms *despotic* and *infrastructural* power have been used by Michael Mann to identify the two different ways in which a governmental apparatus acquires and uses centralized power. In other words, these terms identify, respectively, the two different functions that states perform and that underpin their claims to sovereignty: (1) the struggle for power among elites and interest groups in one state and between those and elites and interest groups in other states and (2) the provision of public goods that are usually provided publicly (by states).[53] In Mann's own words:

> Let us clearly distinguish these two types of state power. The first sense [despotic power] denotes power by the state elite itself over civil society. The second [infrastructural power] denotes the power of the state to penetrate and centrally co-ordinate the activities of civil society through its own infrastructure.[54]

Historically, infrastructural power has risen in importance since the eighteenth century. Infrastructural power is the quintessential indicator of modern statehood. This is because elites have been forced through political struggles to become more responsive to their populations and, as a result, rising pressure groups have demanded more infrastructural goods. In turn, this gave a boost to the territorialization of sovereignty. The populations calling for more infrastructural goods were concentrated territorially. Until recently, the technologies for providing public goods have also had a built-in territorial bias, not least relating to the capture of positive externalities. This is as far as Mann goes. He is after all constructing an argument for why states have acquired power independent of the elites who founded them and who still tend to work through them. A state's command over a territory is precisely what provides the basis to its autonomy because it is within its territory and by means of the infrastructural power deployed there that the state can trump the elites and interest groups who would otherwise dominate it.

Increasingly, however, and this is to adapt Mann's argument in directions he probably would not choose to go, infrastructural power can be deployed across networks that, though located in discrete places, are not necessarily territorial in the externality fields that they produce. Thus, currencies, systems of measure, censuses, trading networks, legal arbitration, educational provision, regulatory activities, and welfare services need not necessarily be associated with exclusive membership or residence in a conventional nation-state. New deployments of infrastructural power both de-territorialize existing states and re-territorialize membership around cities and hinterlands, regions, and continental-level political entities such as the European Union.[55] International organizations, both private (NGOs) and state-run (IGOs), likewise have developed the capacity to deliver a wide range of public goods associated with infrastructural power. There is a simultaneous scaling-up and scaling-down of the relevant geographical fields of infrastructural power depending on the political economies of scale of different regulatory, productive, and redistributive public goods. The U.S. states, for example, "have surged back in recent years, reclaiming broad swaths of sovereign power and right after a long eclipse."[56] Consequently, "the more economies of scale of dominant goods and assets diverge from the structural scale of the national state—and the more those divergences feed back into each other in complex ways—then the more the authority, legitimacy, policymaking capacity, and policy-implementing effectiveness of the [territorial] state will be eroded and undermined both within and without."[57]

Good case studies of the contribution of various agencies, both private and state-based, to the non-territorial delivery of public goods would be credit rating firms such as Moody's and the hybrid of public and private organizations involved in establishing and enforcing standards for communication and information technologies. These are both cases of how the "performance of globalization," though there are also important historical precursors, involves its own active regulation beyond state borders.[58] Though credit rating agencies have recently been embarrassed by scandals over their ratings of certain firms (which were also paying them for their services) during the sub-prime mortgage crisis of 2007–2008, they can still be viewed as veritable "superpowers" of infrastructural power in the contemporary world economy. With the worldwide liberalization of financial markets since the 1980s, rating of credit risks has become an important part of private and public regulation because the private agencies involved (the Big Three: Moody's, Standard and Poor's, and Fitch) can rate both private firms and sovereign (i.e., state) bond issuers for the risk they pose to possible investors. If at one time commercial banks carried out this task (and largely within local and national contexts), as a result of financial innovation and the growth of worldwide markets, judgments about who is creditworthy have increasingly been concentrated in the hands of the credit raters.[59] Communication has also gone global, even though it has long been international in various ways. This worldwide extension of communication is one of the most familiar truisms of globalization. Less often noted, however, regulation in the form of standardization of rules of access and technological compatibilities has followed suit. It has always involved both private and state-based actors. But today it involves a much more coherent "regime" of actors who come and go but who together create an authority based on what Liora Salter calls common "expectations."[60] After all, standards are voluntary but to the extent that they inform the making of products they become relatively coercive. Many other examples of such collaborative private/public regulation and delivery of public goods from beyond state borders could be described.[61] One particularly poignant example, given its centrality to life itself, is water, which has historically been a public good provided territorially. Increasingly, however, in the face of local shortages and global imbalances in population growth and water availability, water is becoming commoditized. The inelasticity of demand for water (people will pay high prices because it is necessary for existence) suggests that as it becomes less available in some places, it will become traded across places and international borders. This does not necessarily signify just privatization but also the possibility of collaborative cross-border provision by public agencies as well.

At the same time as infrastructural power can de- and re-territorialize, despotic power (in Mann's sense) has historically come to rely much more on establishing its legitimacy than once was the case. Direct coercion is simply less effective as a mode of rule in most modern states. Authority has long rested on someone or other's ability to "deliver the goods." Formal-legal authority follows from this rather than provides the basis to sovereignty *tout court*. Legitimacy thus has social more than directly legal origins. In this construction, obligation follows from potential reward more than from the threat of force. Though force can be used against recalcitrant minorities, large segments of the population must be placated and pleased rather than coerced. Rulers need to establish at least a modicum of popular authority before they can achieve their goals. Constant coercion limits that possibility. But state legitimacy is also fragile. It cannot be taken for granted. But this need not always involve a singular focus on fixed state territories if elites and pressure groups adjust their identities and interests to other territorial levels (such as city-regions, localities, and empires) or shift loyalties to non-territorial entities such as international organizations, corporations, social movements, or religious groupings.

This shift in emphasis could involve the enhancing of territorial hierarchy in pursuit of, for example, an imperium, or the attenuation of territorial sovereignty in the form of the diffusion of authority across a multinodal financial network involving transnational corporations, banks, other states, credit-rating agencies, and NGOs. There is no necessary association, therefore, between despotic power and central state authority. Both despotic-governmental and diffuse social power can work together to challenge central state authority based on the territorial distribution of public goods. There is no single pattern to the possible operations of despotic power. Consequently, either an up-scaling or a fragmentation of the sources of sovereignty can result as elites and social groups pursue their goals in ways that potentially territorially expand or undercut the authority of the central governmental apparatus, respectively. David Smith et al. put the overall challenge for the governments of states very well when they write: "A key problem in the present era is the perceived need of national leaders to navigate between the demands of acquiring and maintaining internal legitimacy, on the one hand, and the necessity of securing and ensuring financial backing that appears—in a time of enhanced global interaction among states—to underwrite that legitimacy, on the other."[62] The current heavy reliance of U.S. governments on foreign (particularly Chinese and Japanese) purchase of their bonds to pay for a variety of public expenditures, including wars in Iraq and Afghanistan, is an important example of such a (perhaps Faustian) compact.

By way of recent example of the shifting contours of despotic power, the use of U.S. military forces to invade Iraq in 2003 without benefit of sanction from the United Nations had a number of shifting rationales: "weapons of mass destruction" that threatened the United States, Iraqi ties to al Qaeda, and so on. Most of these turned out to be based on poor or false intelligence. One outcome, however, has been to deploy U.S. despotic power toward a sort of imperium as the U.S. government destroyed the authority (what there was of it) of the government of Iraq. But this in turn had a number of devastating side effects including a bitter war of resistance inside Iraq, the prospect of internal disintegration along ethnic and religious lines, and a general worldwide diminution in respect toward the U.S. government. This is because the invasion has been bereft of legitimacy not only in the eyes of most Iraqis but also in those of much of the rest of the world and of large segments of U.S. public opinion. Coercive power as an element of effective sovereignty, therefore, has limited possibility of long-term success unless it can simultaneously enroll and gain the consent of others. It can actually undermine effective sovereignty, as it seems to have done for the United States in Iraq and more generally in terms of its reputation around the world. Through its stimulus to recruitment into anti-American terrorist networks it certainly seems to have made the territory of the United States itself an even greater target than it was before the events of 11 September 2001 that started the rush to war.

A second example indicates a different aspect of the sovereignty-territory nexus. In Britain in the 1980s, financial elites using their long-term political ascendancy within Britain pushed the government for regulations that would enhance the performance of London as an international banking center.[63] Though such regulations (for instance, relaxing capital controls and deregulating commodity markets) benefited London's financial sector, they had generally negative macroeconomic effects on the state territory as a whole. In the long term they may also have had an unintended negative effect on the ability of the government to move in contrary directions because they generated powerful interests whose loyalties now link them to other financial centers rather than to their nominal home state. British government anxiety about joining the European Monetary Union (the Euro) has been exacerbated by the despotic power now exercised most effectively within British politics by London's financial center, even though such a move might be helpful to manufacturing and agricultural interests elsewhere in Britain.[64] This is related to the "Who is 'us'?" question raised about nominally U.S.-owned businesses that pay low or no taxes in the United States, invest heavily in jobs in other countries, and yet depend on American consumers for final demand for what they produce.

CASE STUDIES IN THE CONTEMPORARY
MIGRATION OF AUTHORITY

But the recasting of the territorial basis to sovereignty and the challenge to central state authority through de-territorialization at the state level and re-territorialization at local and supranational scales of infrastructural and despotic power are uneven around the world. Neither, as I have been at pains to emphasize, are such processes entirely new. But the world has been changing, if not entirely in tune with the myths about globalization addressed in chapter 1. There is no single trend everywhere toward what some have called the "migration of authority" across levels of government and between territories and networks.[65] But some consequences are becoming clear. I use the examples of the emergence of the European Union, the shift from interstate to civil wars, and the redefinition of the novel as a literary genre away from exclusively national confines to illustrate some of these recent consequences.

The first and most frequently noted is the emergence of the supranational authority of the European Union, which has gone from six member states in 1957 to the twenty-seven states that currently belong. This represents from one point of view a major pooling of sovereignty for a wide range of issues, though some still remain largely in the hands of the member states. There is a sense in which the EU has begun to develop common norms that imply, in an institutional context at least, that there may be an emerging European political space. This has been thought about in three ways. One is with respect to how the "soft borders" that serve to direct the institutionalization of the EU and its policies on immigration, human rights, product liability, antitrust, and so on have increasingly taken "hard" forms in which Europe is mobilized as a set of stories about what can and cannot be done *where* that gain increasing circulation and currency across Europe (and into adjacent regions). In this way, at the very minimum, "Europe may be presented as a cognitive project of constructing a collective identity carried by elites."[66]

Another way of thinking about the EU is that, within given policy areas, there is convergence in norms and expectations across member states such that common "cultures" develop among practitioners and bureaucrats. Thus, Meyer, for example, finds strong evidence of increasingly common strategic norms in relation to national security and defense policies in Europe with respect to international authorization of force, preferred modes of cooperation, and goals for the use of force.[67] The actual content of the common norms, however, is not directly European, but often reflects the pre-existing norms of a dominant state. As Paul Ruttley has established for the EU overall, the two defeated European Axis powers of World War II, Germany and Italy, were initially unable to provide much leadership; and given the relative weakness of the other founding members, such as Belgium and the Netherlands, it has been the French government and its administrative models that have channeled the course of European identity.[68] As late-joiners to what later became the EU, the British, for example, have thus faced something of a fait accompli in many areas where they would like to be more influential. A common view is that, in response, they block proposals or opt out of policies rather than participate in establishing common norms, thus weakening the overall European project.

Finally, various European philosophers, from Jürgen Habermas and Jacques Derrida to Etienne Balibar and Massimo Cacciari, have proposed rethinking Europe precisely as a borderland or incongruous zone whose identity should be that of challenging "binary distinctions."[69] Alternatively, Europe might serve as a "mediator" because the region has not and cannot have an absolute identity distinct from those around it. In this construction, as the world economy is seen as operating increasingly as a set of flows through networks that resist traditional bordering, the possibility of territorializing a separate "European" identity makes less and less sense if only because of the massive violence (and, thus, self-evident barbarism) it would now take to impose it. Geo-philosophy ex cathedra and powerful economic practices thus mutually reinforce an evolving image of Europe as no longer capable of adequate representation as a singular culturally homogeneous territorial space but one decreasingly capable of understanding adequately as simply a collection of territorial states.

Another less noted trend relating to the migration of authority is the increasing incidence of conflicts and wars within states relative to wars between them.[70] Though there are still numerous potential "flash points" in territorial disputes between states, these have shrunk in comparison to the proliferation of civil wars over the past twenty years (figure 3.2). Some of the shift has to do with the changing social and technological conditions for the military viability of states and their impact on the possibility of war serving reason-of-state. The advent of nuclear weapons has meant that security now "derives from the paralysis of states rather than from the exer-

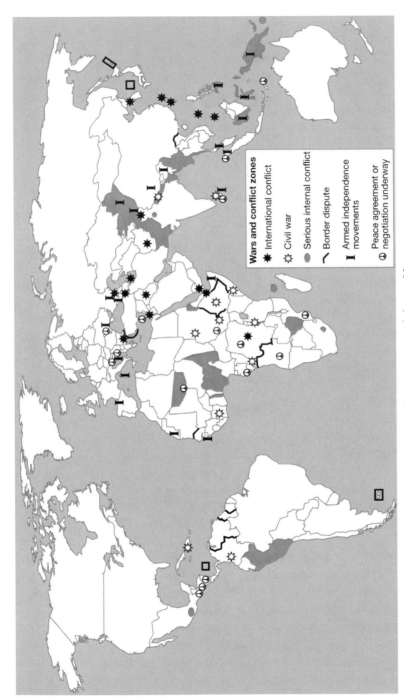

Figure 3.2. From inter-state to civil wars. Wars and conflict zones around the world, 2008.

Source: Author.

cise of state power, and from the acceptance of the impossibility of territorial violence monopolization rather than its pursuit."[71] At the same time, the spread of easy-to-use conventional weapons (Kalashnikov machine guns and Stinger surface-to-air missiles, for example) has made it much easier for local populations to resist the designs of apparently more powerful adversaries. As Dan Deudney puts it in summarizing the point about contemporary military practices, "It is nearly impossible to protect territory from annihilation; but it is easier than ever to prevent conquest."[72] The recent American experience in Iraq and Afghanistan is exemplary.

Perhaps even more of this change is owed to both the dampening effects of globalization on inter-state conflict, because the economies of the world's leading states are becoming ever more interdependent, and the liberation of suppressed nationalities, particularly in Eastern Europe and the former Soviet Union, in the aftermath of the Cold War.[73] Unfortunately, however, much of it also reflects a more widespread "instability" of existing states—from group grievances and demographic pressures to failed delivery of public services, factionalized elites, and external interventions. Some of this instability may be due to globalization but much of it reflects the historic fragility of many states. Particularly in some world regions, a significant number of states have more or less ceased to exist as sources of territorial authority. Their populations have had to get by for many years without much in the way of a central state apparatus. Often they are better off without it. Somalia is the poster case, but many other states that appear as such on the world map are in similar straits, particularly in Africa (figure 3.3 and table 3.1).

These are obviously extreme cases. The actual erosion of state sovereignty *tout court* of whatever spatiality is absolutely not a worldwide phenomenon. Many of the states in table 3.1 have been hollow either for some time or since they were actually first named as states. To understand the current realities of sovereignty around the world we need more than a map of instabilities or claims about globalization hollowing out states and/or imperialism undermining them. The entire discussion of "failed" or "quasi-states" rests on the illusion that the world of states can be neatly divided into two categories signifying "success" and "failure" with each determined by a territorial calculus of what a state is and is not capable of doing. After the U.S. intervention in Iraq with no apparent plan of occupation and the pathetic response of U.S. governments at all levels to the aftermath of Hurricane Katrina, we can no longer be sure about such casual categorizations even in the case of the apparently most successful states. Even widely ad-

Table 3.1.   **The Top Twenty States in** *Foreign Policy Magazine's Instability Ranking* **(2008)**

1. Somalia	11. Guinea
2. Sudan	12. Bangladesh
3. Zimbabwe	12. Burma
4. Chad	14. Haiti
5. Iraq	15. North Korea
6. D.R. Congo	16. Ethiopia
7. Afghanistan	16. Uganda
8. Ivory Coast	18. Lebanon
9. Pakistan	18. Nigeria
10. Central African Republic	20. Sri Lanka

Source: Foreign Policy Magazine, Failed States Index, 2008. www.foreignpolicy.com.

vertised as a "hyper-power," "empire," and "imperial formation," the United States is increasingly vulnerable not only to asymmetric attack from terrorist groups but also to the depredations, both licit and illicit, unleashed by a globalization that does not always favor those who are presumably its greatest proponents. Consider, for example, the massively increased impact within the U.S. of the activities of increasingly globalized criminal networks in the areas of drug smuggling, money laundering, prostitution, and gambling.[74] Misha Glenny shows how cybercrime, particularly that involving identity theft and phishing for bank account data, targets the U.S. (and Western Europe) primarily from computers sited in Moscow, Beijing, and Sao Paulo.[75] In this context, U.S. Homeland Security is something of an oxymoron. The dual corruption and ineffectiveness of politicians, police forces, and the criminal justice system that have followed along have seriously undermined the legitimacy of the larger states as they have, of course, everywhere else in at least equal measure.

Finally, by way of a third case study in the migration of authority, so-called canonical literature is still largely categorized by specific nation-state territories. Much of this has had to do with linguistic competence on the part of scholars studying different literary genres and the ways in which literature came to be studied in the nineteenth century in terms of exclusive national "schools." The novel has been a literary form particularly linked to the cultural authority of the nation-state. This categorization was always problematic. Was Walter Scott, for example, an English or a Scottish novelist? But the larger question of whether the presumed mapping of novels onto particular national territories was often a shotgun marriage has only recently received the attention it deserves.[76] Most modern

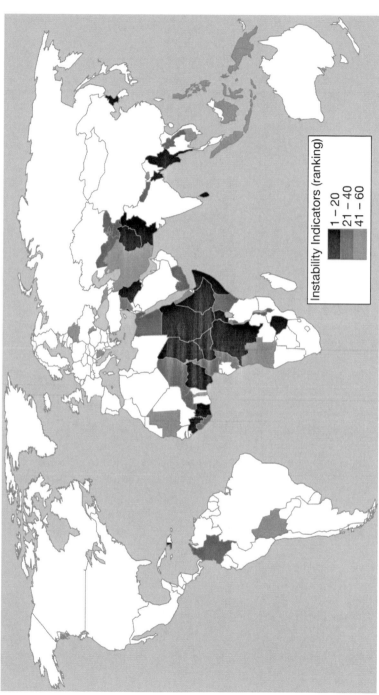

Figure 3.3. Mapping the instability index. Rankings based on twelve political, economic, and social indicators of instability (e.g., demographic pressures, factionalized elites, external intervention, weak or non-existent central government, etc.) for sixty countries, mapped in three groupings: most unstable (1–20), intermediate (21–40), and more stable (41–60). Other countries are defined as "stable."

Source: Foreign Policy Magazine, Failed States Index, 2008. www.foreignpoicy.com.

European novel writing grew up in parallel with European empire building. While expressed in a given European language, many novels were strongly influenced by the fact that they were not purely national in either inspiration or scope. India, the Middle East, and the Caribbean, for example, figure powerfully in many eighteenth- and nineteenth-century English novels. They are not, therefore, strictly English at all.

Two trends, however, signal the extent to which the historic association of the novel, as a specific literary form, with the modern territorial state is undergoing something of a renewed challenge.[77] One of these is the increased importance of works frequently translated and immediately on publication on worldwide best-seller lists. These works can be called post-national novels. Examples would include Umberto Eco's *The Name of the Rose*, Salman Rushdie's *The Satanic Verses*, Milan Kundera's *The Unbearable Lightness of Being*, and Margaret Atwood's *Lady Oracle*. Though each of these can be readily linked to specific national contexts, they all aspire to move beyond such limits. In particular, they all address themes relating to potential placelessness, local versus national identities, and rapid movement across cultural worlds (diaspora, existence losing its meaning under multiculturalism, etc.). In terms of their physical production, they also appear almost simultaneously in multiple languages and are distributed globally. Beyond the long-standing trading of global genres in cinema, therefore, some of the hitherto much more nationally inflected genre of literature also seems to be going global.

Yet, at the same time, a second contemporary trend in literary production is the revival of local and so-called ethnic literature. In orientation and substance this literature predates Literature (of the national kind) but has existed in its shadow ever since the nation-state took hold in Europe and the Americas. Its very existence was once an embarrassment to the national genre. Often expressed in dialects or local vernaculars distinct from official national ones, it called the putative monopolies exercised by the national forms into doubt. Its characters are drawn from local "types," and its perspectives are located in the place-making activities of people without aspiring to fit into national themes. Local novels and poems obviously appeal primarily to local audiences. But, as with the post-national novels, they also call into question, though this time from "below" rather than from "above," the established social identities of a national kind that dominate the national genre. In emphasizing particularities, local novels and poems, such as Chicano short stories, Italian dialect poetry, and the Glasgow novels of Alasdair Gray and James Kelman, in focusing on alternative subjectivities, expose all social and political identities as constructs rather than as natural categories. The cultural authority of the national is thus challenged by the flexing of local and ethnic identities at the same time as the wide circulation of post-national novels calls into question the fixity of the territorial spaces upon which so much literary production has hitherto been based.

SOVEREIGNTY REGIMES

What is needed, and following on from the earlier discussion, is a typology of the main ways in which sovereignty is currently exercised to take account of (1) its social construction; (2) its frequent association with hierarchical subordination; and (3) its deployment in territorial and non-territorial forms. The two basic dimensions to the typology are defined by the relative strength of central state authority (state despotic power) on one axis and its relative consolidation in state territoriality (state infrastructural power) on the other. The former involves judgment about the extent to which a state has acquired and maintains an effective and legitimate apparatus of rule. The latter refers to the degree to which provision of public goods and operation of markets is heavily state regulated and bounded territorially. Regarded as social constructions, these dimensions define both the extent of state autonomy and the degree to which it is territorial in practice. Intersecting continua rather than discrete categories, four extreme cases can be identified nevertheless as ideal types for purposes of theoretical discussion and empirical analysis. These are relational in character, referring to how sovereignty is exercised effectively over time and space, rather than discrete territorial categories into which existing states can be neatly slotted.

I refer to these four ideal types as "sovereignty regimes," recognizing that any actual real-world case might not exactly conform to a particular regime but involve mixes of them (table 3.2). By *regime* I mean a dominant calculus of rule relative to a given state or set of states. In this regard the term anchors sovereignty to state-based authority. But it does so in full acknowledgment of the role of other sources of authority operating beyond the purview of the particular state in question. This usage should be clearly distinguished from that which uses the term *regime* to refer only to explicit agreements between states in certain issue areas, though such agreements, to the degree that they involve sharing or pooling sovereignty, would also be covered by this conception of the term.

Table 3.2. Sovereignty Regimes

		STATE TERRITORIALITY	
		Consolidated	*Open*
CENTRAL	*Stronger*	Classic	Globalist
STATE	*Weaker*	Integrative	Imperialist
AUTHORITY			

Of the four exemplary cases, the *classic* example is the one closest to the story frequently told about Westphalian state sovereignty, though even here there can be complications (for example, Hong Kong and Taiwan for China). The sense is one of both despotic and infrastructural power still largely deployed within a bounded state territory (even if increasingly dependent on foreign direct investment and overseas markets for its exports) and a high degree of effective central state political authority. In broadly political-economic terms, classical sovereignty is also perhaps best thought of as akin to the doctrine of mercantilism in its totalizing of territorial borders and its emphasis on central state regulation of all transactions entering and leaving the state's home territory. Contemporary China is a good test case for how long such absolute sovereignty can survive pressures for divisibility and the need to establish the state's democratic legitimacy when increasingly open to the rest of the world.

The second case resembles most a story that emphasizes hierarchy in world politics but with networked reach over space increasingly supplementing or replacing direct territorial control. This *imperialist* regime is in all respects the exact opposite of the classic case. Not only is central state authority seriously in question because of external dependence and manipulation as well as corruption and chronic mismanagement; state territoriality is also subject to separatist threats, local insurgencies, and poor infrastructural integration. Infrastructural power is weak or non-existent and despotic power is often effectively in outside hands (including international institutions such as the IMF as well as distant but more powerful states). It is imperialist, if also reliant on the assent and cooperation of local elites, because the practice of sovereignty is tied ineluctably to the dependent political-economic status that many states endure in the regions, such as the Middle East, sub-Saharan Africa, and parts of Latin America, where it prevails. Territorial incursions by a dominant external power, such as the United States in Central America and the Caribbean, may also bring with them permanent military bases.[78]

The other two cases are less familiar in relation to both conventional and critical perspectives on state sovereignty. The third regime is the *integrative*, represented here by the European Union. In this case sovereignty has complexities relating to the co-existence between different levels or tiers of government and the distinctive functional areas that are represented differentially across the different levels, from EU-wide to the national-state and sub-national regional. But the territorial character of some of its infrastructural power is difficult to deny (consider the Common Agricultural Policy, for example), even if central state authority for both the entire EU and the member states is weaker than when each of the states was an independent entity. Quite clearly, many of the founding states of the Westphalian system have thrown in their lot with one another to create a larger and, as yet, politically unclassifiable entity that challenges existing state sovereignty in functionally complex and oftentimes non-territorial ways.[79]

Finally, the fourth regime is the *globalist*. Perhaps the best current example of this is the effective sovereignty exercised by the United States within and beyond its nominal national boundaries when it enrolls other states in its policies. Certainly, Britain in the nineteenth century also followed a version of this regime. But in both cases attempts have been made to recruit other states, by co-optation and assent as much as by coercion, into the regime. Indeed, globalization can be seen as the process (along with necessary technological and economic changes) of enrolling states and other actors in the globalist sovereignty regime.[80] From this viewpoint, the globalist state relies on hegemony, in the sense of a mix of potential coercion and active consent, to bring others into line with its objectives. The revolution in information technologies and telecommunications has allied with the end of the Bretton Woods monetary system in the early 1970s to lower transaction costs in financial centers and spur the deregulation of financial markets to the extent that the networks connecting the various global financial centers (in New York, London, and Tokyo, in particular) are increasingly the collective center of the globalist regime. As a result, this regime relies more than any of the others on non-territorial mechanisms of power. It is under its auspices that markets have tended to challenge the authority of states through the privileged role of the world-city network as a system of authority and control.

Although U.S. central state authority remains relatively strong (notwithstanding the problems of its republican constitutionalism in coping with its global role and the widely recognized inefficiencies of its various governments, both federal and local), its centrality to world politics catches it between two conflicting territorial impulses: one that presses toward a scattered imperium (as in Iraq) and one that pushes toward keeping the U.S. as an open territorial economy. The basis of its hegemony is a historical welcoming of immigrants and foreign investment and goods and encouraging of these tendencies elsewhere, but at the same time being increasingly subject to fiscal over-extension as it endeavors to intervene globally yet also serve the demands of its population for, among other things, pensions and healthcare benefits. States other than the hegemonic one that enter into the globalist regime are not as likely to experience the tension because they can restrict their military expenditures and thus can benefit from it as long as they retain a relatively high degree of central state authority. In other words, open borders can be beneficial as long as states retain the potential capacity to close them down. Otherwise the danger is always that the globalist regime becomes imperialist for states other than the dominant one.

In no specific case can exactness of fit be expected between specific states and the classification of sovereignty regimes. Thus, the contemporary U.S. exhibits classic sovereignty at home while being the base for the globalist regime elsewhere. At the same time, while the European Union is an integrative regime internally, it exhibits a mix of features of the globalist and classic regimes in relation to the rest of the world: globalist in relation to the U.S. and classic, for example, in relation to Russia. Some European states, for example France, also have an imperialist relationship to some former African colonies. The classification is a guide to understanding the variety of forms that sovereignty can take, not a simple set of categories that each state slots into neatly and completely.

THE HISTORICAL GEOGRAPHY OF SOVEREIGNTY REGIMES

None of the sovereignty regimes identified above is totally new, although the precise form that each takes has varied over time and from place to place. For example, the U.S. today is itself the product of an integrative regime that began with political independence in 1787 but only came to a close after the U.S. Civil War in 1865. The imperialist regime was once much more pervasive when the big European empires stretched across the continents. The globalist regime is only characteristic of periods when "free-trade imperialism" prevails under the auspices of a relatively open state providing public goods as well as the capacity to coerce others. The terms themselves, recall, are ideal-types or models that cannot map exactly onto real-world cases. Given this caveat, however, a strong case can be made for a historical pattern to their co-appearance.

The purpose of this section is to give a sense of the historical geography of effective sovereignty since the presumed emergence of the modern state system in the early nineteenth century. Perhaps four periods can be identified from the early nineteenth century to the present in which different combinations of the sovereignty regimes have prevailed with distinctive geographies to them. Not surprisingly, these periods coincide with general trends in world history that result from a complex mix of economic, geopolitical, and technological change. Needless to say, the periods are used for heuristic rather than definitive purpose in exploring the relative incidence of sovereignty regimes over time and space. Any periodization is inherently contestable. Philip Bobbitt, for example, provides a different periodization from the one adopted here based on the outcomes of wars since the sixteenth century rather than any other criteria such as economic downturns or the complex of political-economic and discursive factors underpinning that of Agnew and Corbridge.[81] Other authors, Saskia Sassen and Jacques Lévy, for example, operate on an altogether much longer timescale than does the present discussion, going back, respectively, to the European Middle Ages and the Ancient World.[82] The present purpose is merely to historicize and contextualize the relative appearance of sovereignty regimes over time and space, not to provide a total account of world history over the past two hundred years and where globalization fits into the big picture.

The classic regime is, of course, closely associated with the so-called Westphalian version of state sovereignty, though it really only emerged as a potentially practicable form in the nineteenth century. If the Concert of Europe is its main historical legacy as new states formed a "balance of power" in Europe in the years after the defeat of Napoleon, it co-existed from the outset outside of Europe with imperialist regimes (such as the British in India, the French in Africa, and the Dutch in the East Indies) and with a relatively weak British globalist regime that through a commitment to free trade and a gold-sterling standard deployed some types of infrastructural power well beyond Britain's boundaries. This geopolitical order was undermined in the late nineteenth century by the emergence of a set of rival imperialist projects as Germany, the United States, and Japan in different ways challenged Britain's globalist regime. Sassen refers to this period as one of developing "national economies centered on imperial geographies."[83]

The net effect over the entire period of 1875–1945 was to encourage the consolidation of classic and imperialist regimes at the expense of the globalist one. Borders hardened even as they were threatened by the expansionism of those powerful states that saw themselves as closed out of or disadvantaged by the previous imperialist and globalist regimes. The Great Depression of the 1930s reinforced protectionist pressures to seal off territorial economies from foreign economic competitors. Plausibly, this simply deepened the economic misery. But it also encouraged nationalist sentiments. This period reached a crescendo with the Second World War.

The outcome of that war ushered in a period in which an overarching Cold War led to two competing imperialist regimes of which one (the U.S.) had incipient globalist elements. The countries of Western Europe and Japan, however, retained a relatively high degree of central state authority and the rapid expansion of welfare states across states in these regions created something akin to the classic regime. The Bretton Woods monetary system based on a fixed exchange rate between the US$ (backed by gold) and the main currencies of Western Europe and Japan tended until its disintegration in the late 1960s and early 1970s to reinforce the territorial basis to sovereignty in those states whose currencies were convertible within it, notwithstanding its dependence on a foreign (U.S.) currency as the datum of monetary value. Capital controls and central bank dependence on central governments combined to turn the apparent dependence on a transnational currency into a shield or defense against external dominance. As former colonial countries achieved independence from the late 1940s down into the 1970s, they explicitly aspired to classic sovereignty. Unfortunately, the terms of trade for their main products and the weakness of their central state authority worked against this, reproducing in many cases the imperialist regime. Only where states could steer a course between their past dependence and the globalist regime incipient in U.S. sovereignty (as in East Asia) was this path avoided.

When the United States government acted in the early 1970s to protect its domestic economy from a series of external shocks initiated in the 1960s (by abrogating the Bretton Woods Agreement of a dollar-gold standard), it inadvertently furthered the opening up of the U.S. and other economies to relatively unregulated flows of capital, goods, and services. Along with the actions of a range of new policies from existing U.S.-dominated international institutions, such as the IMF and the GATT (after 1994, the WTO), this stimulated the worldwide spread of a new "market-access" model of global trade and investment (described in chapter 1). Together with the end of the Cold War, as the Soviet Union and its allies essentially abandoned their imperialist regime because of its failure to deliver economic growth and political participation, this liberated the U.S. for unrestricted pursuit of a globalist sovereignty regime. In many parts of the world, however, the perception is that this is simply a new version of an imperialist regime.

In Europe the deepening of the European Union since the late 1980s represents the major example of the construction of an integrative regime. There are, however, a number of possible candidates for such a sovereignty regime should the U.S.-sponsored globalist regime falter (e.g., Free Trade Area of the Americas, ASEAN, etc.). States such as China, India, Brazil, and possibly Russia, all large countries, remain as the best surviving examples of the operation of the "classic" sovereignty regime. Yet all have very important ties to the globalizing world economy, including in some cases export-market and financial dependencies.

Previous periods of "balance" between different regimes faded away. There is no good reason to think that the present one has unlimited staying power. So what might bring it to an end? The major conflict potential today lies between the beneficiaries of the globalist regime who extend well beyond the borders of any particular state, on the one hand, and those states and people trapped in the imperialist and globalist regimes, on the other, that are not experiencing many if any benefits. From their perspective, there isn't much difference between the two regimes. Even though still asymmetric in orthodox security terms, the globalist regime has the biggest guns; this tension lies at the heart of much contemporary global conflict in, for example, the Middle East and Latin America, where religious revivalism (as in militant Islamism) and attempts at rehabilitating state-socialist claims (such as the Venezuela of Hugo Chavez) are based upon a sense of loss of state-territorial control in a globalizing world where uneven geographical outcomes in economic development are very much still the order of the day.

The classic and globalist regimes, however, are also basically antithetical in their operations. The current U.S.-China conflict over trade and exchange-rate valuation is an example of this tension. Vladimir Putin's fears of Russia's "encirclement" by the integrative and globalist regimes (in the form, respectively, of the EU and NATO), even as their relatively open markets serve as its main trading partners, suggest that the classic regime still has much ideological mileage in it yet. If the integrative regime in Europe gives rise to a globalist regime incompatible with the current one, then this too could produce a major conflict of interests as two globalist regimes compete for global reach. A range of sovereignty regimes does not signify a stable world. It never has. The globalist regime built under the aegis of U.S. hegemony may be in the ascendancy at the moment, but there are no guarantees that this will last. Other possibilities are waiting in the wings.

CONCLUSION

Sovereignty is not just one thing. Its application takes various geographical shapes. The idea of sovereignty regimes is an attempt at providing a template or schema by which to consider the dominant shapes that sovereignty has and continues to take. The four basic types I identify—classic/territorial, globalist, integrative, and imperialist—provide a frame of reference for discussing how globalization relates to sovereignty. These are all relational forms in which sovereignty in a particular case is always established in relation to other states and actors. If one conclusion is that globalization and its "challenge" is not all there is to contemporary effective sovereignty, another is that no single or binary model fits all states at all times. It is not, then, a simple question of classic versus imperialist or classic versus globalist. Rather, in a world in which various migrations of authority and control are under way, understanding sovereignty should start from a presupposition of pluralism rather than of a single model for the whole world. Unfortunately this has not been the tendency, irrespective of the relative emphasis on the impact of globalization. One size, so to speak, has been presumed to fit all. If pluralism is indeed the case, though, how does this work in practice? That is the focus of the next chapter.

NOTES

1. For example, J. Agnew, *Making Political Geography* (London: Arnold, 2002), 166–67; W. Thaa, "Lean citizenship? The fading away of the political in transnational democracy," *European Journal of International Relations* 7 (2001): 503–23.

2. A. Linklater, *The Transformation of Political Community* (Cambridge: Polity Press, 1998), 182.

3. D. Chandler, "New rights for old? Cosmopolitan citizenship and the critique of state sovereignty," *Political Studies* 51 (2003): 332–49; D. Runciman, "The concept of the state," in Q. Skinner and B. Stråth (eds.), *States and Citizens: History, Theory, Prospects* (Cambridge: Cambridge University Press, 2003).

4. D. Shemek, "Introduction," to A. Caverero, *Stately Bodies: Literature, Philosophy and the Question of Gender* (Ann Arbor: University of Michigan Press, 2002), 5.

5. M. Foucault, "Governmentality," in G. Burchell et al. (eds.), *The Foucault Effect: Studies in Governmentality* (Chicago: University of Chicago Press, 1991), 93.

6. M. Foucault, "Two lectures," in *Michel Foucault: Power/Knowledge: Selected Interviews and Other Writings, 1972-1977* (Brighton: Harvester Press, 1980).

7. P. S. Gorski, *The Disciplinary Revolution: Calvinism and the Rise of the State in Early Modern Europe* (Chicago: University of Chicago Press, 2003), 23–24.

8. J. Habermas, *Theory and Practice* (Boston: Beacon Press, 1988); N. Elias, *State Formation and Civilization* (Oxford: Blackwell, 1982); P. Bourdieu, "The force of law: towards a sociology of the juridical field," *Hastings Journal of Law* 38 (1987): 209–48; and M. Foucault, *Sécurité, territoire, population. Cours au Collège de France, 1977-1978* (Paris: Seuil/Gallimard, 2004). More generally on the potentials and limitations of these writers see, e.g., G. Steinmetz (ed.), *State/Culture: State-Formation after the Cultural Turn* (Ithaca, NY: Cornell University Press, 1999); P. Dews, *Logics of Disintegration: Post-Structuralist Thought and the Claims of Critical Theory* (London: Verso, 1987); Gorski, *The Disciplinary Revolution.*

9. N. Jacobson, "The strange case of Hobbesian man," *Representations* 63 (1998): 1–12; Q. Skinner, "Hobbes and the purely artificial person of the state," *Journal of Political Philosophy* 7 (1999): 1–29.

10. N. Inayatullah and M. E. Rupert, "Hobbes, Smith, and the problem of mixed ontologies," in S. Rosow et al. (eds.), *The Global Economy as Political Space* (Boulder, CO: Lynne Rienner, 1994).

11. T. J. Biersteker and C. Weber (eds.), *State Sovereignty as Social Construct* (Cambridge: Cambridge University Press, 1996).

12. J. Gottmann, *The Significance of Territory* (Charlottesville: University Press of Virginia, 1973).

13. R. K. Ashley, "Living on border lines: man, poststructuralism, and war," in J. Der Derian and M. J. Shapiro (eds.), *International/Intertextual Relations* (Cambridge, MA: Lexington, 1988), 264.

14. W. G. Werner and J. de Wilde, "The endurance of sovereignty," *European Journal of International Relations* 7 (2001): 292.

15. On the politics of cartography more generally see the important collection of J. B. Harley, *The New Nature of Maps: Essays in the History of Cartography* (Chicago: University of Chicago Press, 2001).

16. A. Wendt, *Social Theory of International Relations* (Cambridge: Cambridge University Press, 1999).

17. D. Campbell, *Politics without Principle: Sovereignty, Ethics, and the Narratives of the Gulf War* (Boulder, CO: Lynne Rienner, 1993), 9.

18. B. Yack, "Popular sovereignty and nationalism," *Political Theory* 29 (2001): 517–36.

19. D. Campbell, *Writing Security: United States Foreign Policy and the Politics of Identity* (Minneapolis: University of Minnesota Press, Second Edition, 1998).

20. J. Agnew, *Geopolitics: Re-Visioning World Politics* (London: Routledge, Second Edition, 2003), 16.

21. D. Bigo, "When two become one: internal and external securitizations in Europe," in M. Kelstrup and M. Williams (eds.), *International Relations Theory and the Politics of European Integration: Power, Security, Community* (London: Routledge, 2002); S. Dalby, *Environmental Security* (Minneapolis: University of Minnesota Press, 2002).

22. *Economist*, "Winning or losing: a special report on al-Qaeda," (19 July 2008).

23. E.g., Wendt, *Social Theory of International Relations*.

24. H. Lacher, "Putting the state in its place: the critique of state-centrism and its limits," *Review of International Studies* 29 (2003): 521–41.

25. M. Mann, "Has globalization ended the rise and rise of the nation-state?" *Review of International Political Economy* 4 (1997): 476.

26. D. Slater, "Geopolitical imaginations across the North-South divide: issues of difference, development and power," *Political Geography* 16 (1997): 631–53.

27. R. V. Mongia, "Historicizing state sovereignty: inequality and the form of equivalence," *Comparative Studies in Society and History* 49 (2007): 396.

28. N. Inayatullah and D. L. Blaney, "Realizing sovereignty," *Review of International Studies* 21 (1995): 3–20.

29. For example, T. Biolsi, "Imagined geographies: sovereignty, indigenous space, and American Indian struggle," *American Ethnologist* 32 (2005): 239–59.

30. E. Keene, *Beyond the Anarchical Society: Grotius, Colonialism, and Order in World Politics* (Cambridge: Cambridge University Press, 2002).

31. D. Gregory, *The Colonial Present: Afghanistan, Palestine, Iraq* (Oxford: Blackwell, 2004); A. L. Stoler, "On degrees of imperial sovereignty," *Public Culture* 18 (2006): 125–46.

32. Mongia, "Historicizing state sovereignty," 397.

33. D. A. Lake, "Escape from the state of nature: authority and hierarchy in world politics," *International Security* 32 (2007): 54.

34. Lake, "Escape from the state of nature." But as Jack Donnelly argues (in "Sovereign inequalities and hierarchy in anarchy: American power and international society," *European Journal of International Relations* 12 [2006]: 139–70) however open to considering hierarchy theorists may be, they still often presume (as in Lake's "state of nature") an idealized world of anarchy in which there is sovereign equality when in fact anarchy may not have equality at all.

35. E. A. Nadelmann, *Cops across Borders: The Internationalization of U.S. Criminal Law Enforcement* (University Park: Pennsylvania State University Press, 1993), 470.

36. S. D. Krasner (ed.), *Problematic Sovereignty: Contested Rules and Political Possibilities* (New York: Columbia University Press, 2001).

37. A-M. Slaughter, "Disaggregated sovereignty: towards the public accountability of global government networks," *Government and Opposition* 39 (2004): 159–90.

38. R. D. Sack, "Human territoriality: a theory," *Annals of the Association of American Geographers* 73 (1983): 56.

39. H. Spruyt, *The Sovereign State and its Competitors: An Analysis of Systems Change* (Princeton, NJ: Princeton University Press, 1994), 34.

40. M. Neocleous, *Imagining the State* (Maidenhead, UK: Open University Press, 2004).

41. K. Raustiala, "The geography of justice," *Fordham Law Review* 73 (2005): 2510.

42. P. Bobbitt, *The Shield of Achilles: War, Peace, and the Course of History* (New York: Knopf, 2002).

43. J. J. Sheehan, "The problem of sovereignty in European history," *American Historical Review* 111 (2006): 1–15.

44. J. Delbruck, "Exercising public authority beyond the state: transnational democracy and/or alternative legitimation strategies?" *Indiana Journal of Global Legal Studies* 10 (2003): 29–44.

45. A. Ong, *Flexible Citizenship: The Cultural Logics of Transnationality* (Durham, NC: Duke University Press, 1999), 217. Also see, for example, D. A. Lake, "Delegating divisible sovereignty: sweeping a conceptual minefield," *Review of International Organization* 2 (2007): 219–37.

46. R. D. Sack, *Human Territoriality: Its Theory and History* (Cambridge: Cambridge University Press, 1986).

47. M. Mann, *The Sources of Social Power, Volume II: The Rise of Classes and Nation-States, 1760–1914* (Cambridge: Cambridge University Press, 1993); J. Allen, *Lost Geographies of Power* (Oxford: Blackwell, 2003).

48. T. J. Sinclair, *The New Masters of Capital: American Bond Rating Agencies and the Politics of Creditworthiness* (Ithaca, NY: Cornell University Press, 2005).

49. Allen, *Lost Geographies of Power,* 159.

50. B. Lincoln, *Authority: Construction and Corrosion* (Chicago: University of Chicago Press, 1994), 6.

51. P. McMichael, "Incorporating comparison within a world-historical perspective: an alternative comparative method," *American Sociological Review* 55 (1990): 385–97.

52. McMichael, "Incorporating comparison within a world-historical perspective," 392.

53. M. Mann, "The autonomous power of the state: its origins, mechanisms and results," *European Journal of Sociology* 25 (1984): 185–213.

54. Mann, "The autonomous power of the state," 188.

55. K. R. Cox (ed.), *Spaces of Globalization* (New York: Guilford Press, 1998); A. J. Scott, *Regions and the World Economy* (Oxford: Oxford University Press, 1998).

56. K. M. Johnson, "Sovereigns and subjects: a geopolitical history of metropolitan reform in the USA," *Environment and Planning A* 38 (2006): 164.

57. P. G. Cerny, "Globalization and the changing logic of collective action," *International Organization* 49 (1995): 621.

58. A. Amin, "Regulating economic globalization," *Transactions of the Institute of British Geographers* 29 (2004): 225.

59. Sinclair, *The New Masters of Capital*.

60. L. Salter, "The standards regime for communication and information technologies," in A. C. Cutler et al. (eds.), *Private Authority and International Affairs* (Albany, NY: SUNY Press, 1999), 122.

61. See, for example A. C. Cutler et al. (eds.), *Private Authority and International Affairs* (Albany, NY: SUNY Press, 1999); and R. B. Hall and T. J. Biersteker (eds.), *The Emergence of Private Authority in Global Governance* (Cambridge: Cambridge University Press, 2002).

62. D. A. Smith et al., "Introduction," in D. A. Smith et al. (eds.), *States and Sovereignty in the Global Economy* (London: Routledge, 1999), 2.

63. See G. Ingham, "States and markets in the production of world money: sterling and the dollar," in S. Corbridge et al. (eds.), *Money, Power and Space* (Oxford: Blackwell, 1994), on the long-running conflict between "the City" and the rest of the British economy.

64. This is not to mention the increased openness to external financial volatility this creates for the entire *British* economy, as evidenced by the import of the shocks from the U.S. credit squeeze and sub-prime mortgage fiasco in 2007–2008 because of *London's* centrality to the "global" packaging of mortgage-backed securities.

65. M. Kahler and D. A. Lake (eds.), *Governance in the Global Economy: Political Authority in Transition* (Princeton, NJ: Princeton University Press, 2003).

66. K. Eder, "Europe's borders: the narrative construction of the boundaries of Europe," *European Journal of Social Theory* 9 (2006): 257.

67. C. O. Meyer, "Convergence towards a European strategic culture? A constructivist framework for explaining changing norms," *European Journal of International Relations* 11 (2005): 523–49.

68. P. Ruttley, "The long road to unity: the contribution of law to the process of European integration since 1945," in A. Pagden (ed.), *The Idea of Europe: From Antiquity to the European Union* (Cambridge: Cambridge University Press, 2002).

69. J. Derrida, *Une Europe de l'espoir* (Paris: Flammarion, 2004), 3.

70. S. David, *Catastrophic Consequences: Civil Wars and American Interests* (Baltimore, MD: Johns Hopkins University Press, 2008).

71. D. Deudney, "Nuclear weapons and the waning of the real-state," *Daedalus* 124 (1995): 219.

72. Deudney, "Nuclear weapons and the waning of the real-state," 219.

73. M. Kahler and B. F. Walter (eds.), *Territoriality and Conflict in an Era of Globalization* (Cambridge: Cambridge University Press, 2006).

74. W. van Schendel and I. Abraham (eds.), *Illicit Flows and Criminal Things: States, Borders, and the Other Side of Globalization* (Bloomington: Indiana University Press, 2005); M. Glenny, *McMafia: Crime without Frontiers* (London: The Bodley Head, 2008).

75. Glenny, *McMafia*, 313.

76. For example, F. A. Nussbaum, *Torrid Zones: Maternity, Sexuality, and Empire in Eighteenth-Century English Literature* (Baltimore, MD: Johns Hopkins University Press, 1995); E. W. Said, *Culture and Imperialism* (New York: Knopf, 1993).

77. B. Allen, "From multiplicity to multitude: universal systems of deformation," *Symposium* 49 (1995): 93–113.

78. The imperialist regime can take a variety of forms, only some of which deserve the territorial term *empire*. For discussions of the range of hierarchical regimes, covering everything from spheres of influence to protectorates, often occluded by the language of empire and imperialism, see, for example, Donnelly, "Sovereign inequalities and hierarchy in anarchy."

79. H. W. Hofmann, "Mapping the European administrative space," *West European Politics* 31 (2008): 662–76.

80. Two authors as divergent intellectually and politically as Carl Schmitt and Antonio Gramsci first noted the emergence of what Gramsci (*Selections from the Political Writings, 1910-1920* [London: Lawrence and Wishart, 1977], 81) termed "Anglo-Saxon world hegemony" and what I am here terming the globalist sovereignty regime. Their arguments came from very different theoretical premises and reflected very different sensibilities as to the consequences of globalism. On Schmitt's logic see W. Rausch, "Human rights as geopolitics: Carl Schmitt and the legal forms of American supremacy," *Cultural Critique* 54 (2003): 118–29; and on Gramsci, see A. D. Morton, *Unravelling Gramsci: Hegemony and Passive Revolution in the Global Economy* (London: Pluto, 2007), chapter 3. I have developed a neo-Gramscian argument about the origins and historical course of the contemporary globalist regime at some length in *Hegemony: The New Shape of Global Power* (Philadelphia: Temple University Press, 2005).

81. Bobbitt, *The Shield of Achilles*; J. Agnew and S. Corbridge, *Mastering Space* (London: Routledge, 1995).

82. S. Sassen, *Territory, Authority, Rights: From Medieval to Global Assemblages* (Princeton, NJ: Princeton University Press, 2006); J. Lévy (ed.), *L'invention du monde: une géographie de la mondialisation* (Paris: Presses de Sciences Po, 2008).

83. Sassen, *Territory, Authority, Rights*, 88.

CHAPTER 4

SOVEREIGNTY REGIMES AT WORK

This largely abstract argument needs some effort at empirical demonstration. In this chapter I use two different empirical examples to illustrate some of the theoretical points made in previous chapters. I make no pretense that my examination of the two examples I use, currencies and immigration, is by any means complete. My purpose is not to provide an encyclopedic account of either but only to show how they illustrate important features of the arguments made earlier.

The first example is that of national currencies and the ways they are related to one another through exchange-rate mechanisms of various types. Currencies are not only an economic phenomenon, though that is the main emphasis in much of the scholarship about them, but they are also deeply political. They are important practical and symbolic representations in everyday life of the presence and power of the nation-state. Paper currency and coinage alike are covered with symbols of the states that issue them. More practically, a currency is a lever of authority: it fuses the desire both to further the collective image of the state as an operational concern and to manage the economy of the state as defined by the territory in which the currency circulates. When a currency suffers a huge devaluation against others, as in Weimar Germany in the 1920s and in Zimbabwe in recent years, it comes to stand for both the overall decline in power of the state in question and the fecklessness of its current government in particular. Of course, as we all know, not all currencies are equal. Over the years, and under different political-economic conditions in different places, even as most states have maintained their own currencies they have had to manage these in ways that either deposit effective sovereignty in the hands of financial markets or of states with more powerful (harder) currencies.

Much of my discussion of this example will be taken up with showing the various ways in which all currencies today exist increasingly in a global relational space rather than in the absolute territorial space with which they are symbolically associated. Some of this relates to the impact of global financial markets operating from global cities, while some of it relates to how central banks and governments have differential effects on the operations of monetary sovereignty in different countries. This is thus an excellent example of how effective sovereignty today is something else again from the sovereignty of the sovereignty game outlined in previous chapters (above all in chapter 2).

My second example is that of immigration management and control. Again, the typical image of the classic sovereign state is of a territory with a relatively culturally homogenous population that has been present from time immemorial with strict border controls filtering who can and who cannot enter and reside in the national territory. Alternatively, with, at least as typically idealized, French and settler-state conceptions of nationality as something that can be gained through political conversion rather than acquired by inheritance, citizenship is given as a reward or as a stimulus for cultural-political assimilation by immigrants who are literally populating the state. Yet few states have ever had complete cultural homogeneity and most have had, and increasingly have, flows of immigrants who disturb the national self-image and who challenge the self-evident identification between one culture and a singular territory. No states any longer have officially open borders to all comers. Nevertheless, migration is an excellent example of how the world has always involved interaction across space over long distances, rather than containment in discrete territories and, in the way immigrants adjust to new situations, how through place-making immigrants can adapt existing places to fit their needs and wishes. Immigration, then, is a useful example for illustrating all of the limits of thinking in terms of a totally territorialized world. As refugees and as economic migrants, immigrants search not just for a territorial jurisdiction in which to acquire safe haven and citizenship but for opportunity denied them where they come from. They go to specific places within destination countries, not to a state as a whole. At the same time, they do not invariably cut off all ties with where they come from; far from it. They often support their families back home with remittances and their "home" governments may cultivate them to influence politics back home and that of where they now live. Migration, therefore, is almost never simply a matter of moving from one national territory to another and abandoning those left behind or smoothly assimilating into a totally separate territorial world.

Quite how immigration is regulated and citizenship acquired differs considerably across states. As is well known, some of the flow of migrants at a global scale is from poor to much richer countries as poorer people move to take advantage of better opportunities. Classically, international migrants have also followed in reverse the paths beaten by the various empires, both formal and informal, that led their regions into the world economy in the first place. But there is also now a large migration from very poor to more recently rich countries, as with the flows of economic migrants from South Asia to the Persian Gulf region. Within states of large land area and massive population there is also considerable internal migration. Currently, for example, it is plausible that more people are migrating within China, given the size of the country, than across borders in the rest of the world. So it is important to bear this in mind in what follows. Across borders, there are very well-established migration corridors (for example, between Mexico and the U.S.). Many of these follow routes established over generations with flows from particular source places to determinate destinations inside the destination country. Once they have arrived, however, and whether they have done so under official state sanction or not, immigrants are faced with different legal situations in different countries when it comes to acquiring official membership. As with currencies, then, as with immigration: the process of effective sovereignty is expressed through a range of regulatory mechanisms operating both territorially and non-territorially.

CURRENCIES AND SOVEREIGNTY REGIMES

In the context of state sovereignty, currencies are interesting for three reasons. In the first place, they are a key material and symbolic feature of central state authority.[1] National currencies only rose to prominence in the mid-nineteenth century as state authority in Western Europe and North America was firmly established. Local and trading currencies without government sanction were once widespread. This is not to say that markets and money grew up separate from states that then co-opted them. Rather, the point is that the rationalization of money in the form of national currencies occurred remarkably recently, given how important a money economy was to political power in, for example, European antiquity and medieval Europe.[2] The new national currencies contributed to firming up national identities, reduced transaction costs within national economies, raised revenues through the minting of currency ("seigniorage"), and provided a means for states to pay for their purchases through taxes on the increasing incomes emanating from industrial capitalism.[3] As a result, currencies are also, then, one of the main examples of infrastructural power. But many currencies also seem to be losing their national character; either because they have much enlarged geographic scope or because they have been effectively replaced by foreign currencies for a wide range of transactions (not least the storage of wealth).[4] In scattered places, local currencies, often based on scrip and so on, have also come back into favor. Particularly under inflationary conditions, when the value of a national currency sinks against others, local currencies potentially can substitute for national ones. More typical in such conditions, as we shall see, is the adoption of a foreign currency, usually informally or on the black market. There are microfoundations to the use and acceptance of currencies.[5]

Second, "it is in the monetary realm," according to Helleiner, "where challenges to the practice of [sovereign state] territoriality are particularly apparent in the present age."[6] Thus, the various impacts of globalization on the territoriality of state sovereignty should be most immediately obvious in relation to the geographical dynamics of national-state currencies. Because it is primarily a medium of exchange, "money is a belief that has to be shared with other people."[7] This makes it a relatively fluid medium in which authority over its issuance and management is always vulnerable to challenge from an array of actors (central banks, investment banks, transnational corporations, speculators, etc.) and yet, because of its symbolism (not least that displayed on coins and banknotes), it is frequently one of the most visible examples of a claim to state sovereignty.

Finally, decisions by governments and other actors about whether to maintain a national currency, share a new one, substitute a global one for a national one, and how to manage a global one provide a common metric for examining the descriptive merits of the typology of sovereignty regimes. In other words, the contemporary geography of money provides a way of both illustrating the typology of sovereignty regimes and showing the territorial and non-territorial ways these regimes work.

TYPES OF MONETARY SOVEREIGNTY

To be more specific about the connections between globalization and monetary sovereignty first requires identifying the processes whereby currencies take on distinctive relationships with particular states and mapping these onto the sovereignty regimes identified previously. Since the collapse of the Bretton Woods Agreement in the early 1970s, no single worldwide exchange-rate arrangement has prevailed.[8] It is the exchange-rate mechanism that is central, when put together with associated institutional forms such as central bank independence and capital controls, to the ways in which currencies articulate with one another and thus to the extent to which any individual currency either monopolizes or extends its purview beyond a particular state territory.[9]

Since the 1980s a number of different exchange-rate models have prevailed, with some countries switching between them while others have maintained a commitment to a single one over time. Typically, exchange-rate arrangements are classified into four or so categories: soft pegged or relatively fixed exchange rates, with a foreign currency serving as the anchor but with government intervention to maintain the peg; independently floating, in which a currency is allowed to find its own exchange rate in open market trading (if with occasional intervention by single or several governments); managed floating, in which a government attempts to influence the exchange rate but without a predetermined rate path or target; and other arrangements, defined here as (1) a shared currency (with external floating), (2) a currency board, with a domestic currency fixed permanently (hard peg) against foreign exchange and fully backed by foreign assets thus eliminating government control, and (3) adoption of a foreign currency (such as the US$) as sole legal tender.

In the 1980s soft pegged arrangements were widespread with two-thirds of all exchange rates set this way (figure 4.1). This was probably a hangover from the Bretton Woods system of the post-war period in which all convertible currencies were pegged to the US$ backed by gold. By the mid-1990s, however, a significant shift was afoot, with a huge expansion in the number of independently floating currencies at the expense of pegged and other arrangements. In the 1980s the spread of monetarist ideas among governments involved among other things the belief that governments should not actively intervene to direct their exchange rates. The most avid proponents of liberal globalization have been the biggest fans of floating currencies. The presumption is that floating currencies will better reflect the willingness of investors to "bet" on the value of a given currency as a judgment about the overall condition of its national economy. Free floating also has always involved the lifting of capital controls and the establishment of central bank independence, thus facilitating the "retreat of the state" mandated by a generous faith in the relative efficiency of market mechanisms. By 2004 a new pattern had emerged with a further retreat of soft-pegged currencies but with an expansion of managed floating and other arrangements (mainly due to the arrival of the Euro as a shared currency in 1999) and a net waning of independent floats. Since 2004 the number of pegged rates and managed floats has increased further relative to independent floats. Even with a declining dollar (in free float) between 2006 and 2008, there was no rampant retreat from soft pegging.[10] Some countries diversified their soft pegs from the US$ to include the Euro but that was about all. One interpretation might emphasize the relative eclipse of pegged arrangements over the forty years since the demise of Bretton Woods, but another would stress a continuing and dynamic pluralism of arrangements. The world of currencies does not seem to be on a single path away from pegged or toward a norm of independently floating currencies. This would be the either/or of state sovereignty converted to the realm of currencies. In fact, the picture painted in figure 4.1 suggests that a variety of political-economic processes are at work, not simply a persisting territorial currency system mediated by an anchoring currency (or gold standard) versus a free floating (and globalized) market capitalism.

Some confusion is possible relative to my view of soft-pegged currencies as expressed above. From one viewpoint, pegged currencies represent a decision to subordinate the national currency to a foreign one and thus to give up monetary sovereignty.[11] It is then seen as merely a milder version of the hard peg of a currency board. The corollary is that under free floating a currency is freed from a hierarchical relationship to another currency. This thereby signifies "freedom" in monetary affairs. From my perspective, this argument is totally perverse. Pegging is in fact a way of trying to shield

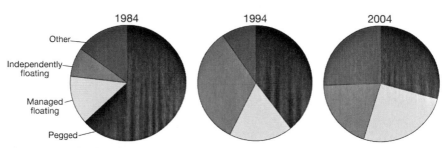

Figure 4.1. The distribution of exchange-rate arrangements in four broad categories: soft pegs, managed floats, independent floats, and other (including hard pegs such as currency boards and integrative currencies), 1984, 1994, 2004.

Source: IMF.

a currency from both markets and states other than the anchor and, when combined, as is typical, with capital controls and an absence of central bank independence, the best way of maintaining state control over a national currency. If the anchoring currency is a major trading partner or the one in which your state's exports are invoiced then so much the better. The general perception of governments seems to be that pegged (and managed) rates generate both more net policy autonomy and better exchange-rate stability. The danger of importing inflation from and having to follow the monetary policies of the anchor is seen as mitigated by all of these other advantages. The currency board and the substitution of a foreign currency are in fact the real candidates for monetary subordination to another state. Independent and managed floats represent, in various degrees, subordination to the markets. Now, whether soft-pegged exchange rates really do offer all the autonomy and stability that they are perceived to is something else again.[12]

A truism of contemporary open-economy macroeconomics, if not of that monetarism that always prefers floating exchange rates, is that there is no "magic" to any exchange-rate arrangement. No single arrangement can guarantee capital mobility, a targeted exchange rate, and independent monetary policy at the same time. This is the so-called open-economy trilemma. Indeed, with increased worldwide trade and massive international investment, the trade-off between exchange-rate volatility and domestic price stability has become tougher than ever. According to some research, even when some states are officially committed to independent floating, in fact they really have "soft pegs" of some sort or another.[13] Overall, however, the empirical evidence is that despite the difficulties of classifying exchange-rate arrangements, there is a wide range of such arrangements, official and actual, rather than dispersion around a central or median type.[14] From a political perspective it is the cross-mapping of dominant exchange-rate arrangements and sovereignty regimes that is of prime concern. This is reflected in the discussion that follows. What is the best exchange-rate arrangement from an economic perspective is not relevant to the present discussion.

There are four ways in which currencies tend to work with respect to any given national territory, paralleling the four sovereignty regimes. This in itself suggests that, at least for the geography of money, there is something useful theoretically about the fourfold schema of sovereignty regimes. The four currency processes are as follows:

1. the *territorial*, in which a national-state currency dominates a state territory and the population has restricted access to currencies of wider circulation except through a pegged exchange rate controlled by central state authority; a managed float represents an intermediate case between this and reliance on a transnational currency;

2. the *transnational*, in which the currency issued by one state (invariably a powerful one) circulates widely among world financial centers, floats freely, is a standard (or reserve) currency in relation to which other currencies are denominated, and is a preferred currency for transacting global commerce;

3. the *shared*, in which a formal monetary alliance operates either through full monetary union (as with the Euro and the EU) or through an exchange-rate union among economic equals with an internal managed float and, in both cases, an external floating exchange rate;

4. the *substitute*, in which a transnational currency substitutes either officially or unofficially in all or many transactions for the nominal territorial currency of a given state. The substitute currency is particularly important as a store of wealth in local banks, hedge against inflation in the national currency, and medium of capital flight to foreign financial centers for local elites. Given the dominant economic role of the U.S. in some world regions, this is usually a process of dollarization.

These processes map onto the four sovereignty regimes with the four cases taken from table 3.2 (see table 4.1). As noted earlier, however, there

Table 4.1. Sovereignty Regimes and Currency Processes (examples along the diagonal)

		SOVEREIGNTY REGIME			
		Classic	Globalist	Integrative	Imperialist
DOMINANT	Territorial	China			
CURRENCY	Transnational		U.S.		
PROCESS	Shared			EU	
	Substitute				Latin America

is no sense in which these various "solutions" are fixed for all time. Exchange-rate arrangements have been almost as volatile as floating exchange rates! They reflect decisions on the part of state and other influential actors based on socialized understandings of their "monetary interests."[15] These understandings reflect, to one degree or another, views of state and market performance in relation to the different structural positions vis-à-vis the world economy that states and local actors find themselves in and the institutional and political characteristics of particular states. They also reflect judgments about the state's capacity to manage or direct a currency and its associated exchange-rate system. Thus, the classic case can be seen as based on the Keynesian logic that states can mitigate market failures, the globalist represents a neo-classical approach that states should retreat and let markets work their magic, the imperialist stresses the classical monetary theory that state failure necessitates radical decoupling of domestic and monetary policies, and the integrative is a mix of Keynesian/inside and neo-classical/outside the grouping of states in question. Currency processes, therefore, are not the direct result of materialist pressures but are mediated by the perceptions and understandings of exchange-rate mechanisms and other monetary policies governments and other actors bring to their material situations.

What is the worldwide distribution of the different combinations of sovereignty regime and currency process as defined in table 4.1? In the contemporary world there are still examples of territorial currencies that reflect "classic" state sovereignty.[16] But the net trend of the past forty years has been away from this singular regime toward the other ones. As of 2004, pegged rates were a shrinking part of the overall exchange-rate arrangements pie, though they have made something of a comeback latterly (figure

4.1). Managed floats have everywhere emerged as a "balance" between the territorial and the transnational arrangements (figure 4.2). In 2005 China finally made this move. The 2004 world map of exchange-rate arrangements as classified by the IMF shows a wide variety of outcomes. In Asia managed floats prevail with China (at that time) as the main example of a soft-pegged currency. Elsewhere, pegging is closely associated with oil-exporting countries (e.g., Saudi Arabia) and countries overtly jealous of their sovereignty (e.g., Ukraine, Malaysia, Syria). Independent floats prevail, unsurprisingly, in the most globalized countries (compare figure 1.1) including the Eurozone (the Euro floats externally).

One of the best examples of the closest to a classic sovereignty regime today is perhaps China, whose currency, the renminbi (or yuan), was pegged against the US$ until July 2005 and has been in a very carefully managed float since then and whose economy is thereby insulated to a certain degree from monetary shocks emanating from the wider world economy. The only contemporary example of an intersection between a transnational currency process and a "globalist" sovereignty regime is the United States. The US$ is the main metric of transnational trade and commerce and the main currency that other states (including China) hold as a reserve. As a result, the US$ is also the currency that is the main instrument of globalization. The exchange-rate mechanism most closely associated with the globalist regime is the free or independent float.[17] The best current example of a shared currency is the Euro, associated as it is with the project of pan-European unification, though there are others, such as the CFA franc zone in West Africa and the ECCU currency board arrangement in the Caribbean. Historically, many national currencies such as the US$ emerged out of the unification of more geographically variegated currency systems.[18]

Finally, to the extent that certain territorial currencies reflect the weakness of their national economies and are heavily dependent on foreign capital flows, they are substituted for by the use of transnational currencies. Currently, the US$ is the most important of the transnational currencies, either through informal or formal dollarization, and, more infrequently, through so-called currency boards or some variant thereof, which insulate monetary decisions from domestic political pressures. In both cases any pretense at territorial monetary sovereignty is essentially sacrificed to dampen inflation, increase foreign investment, and reduce the proclivity for growth in government spending. Many Latin American countries have recently experienced this intersection between currency substitution and what I call the imperialist sovereignty regime even though relatively few countries have

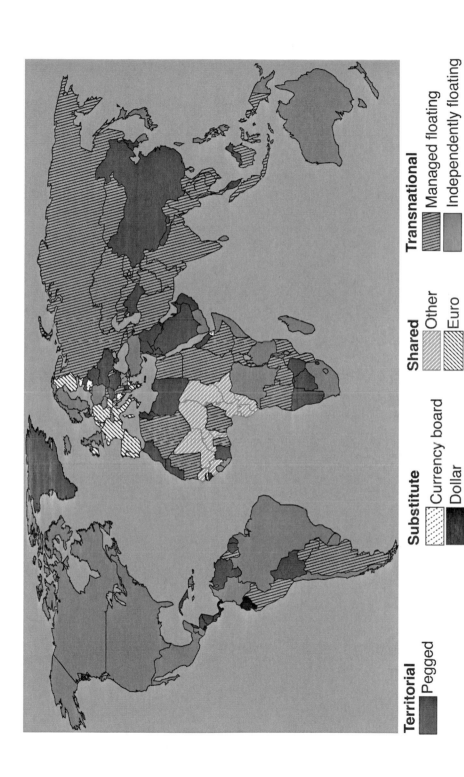

Territorial

Pegged

Substitute

Currency board

Dollar

Shared

Other

Euro

Transnational

Managed floating

Independently floating

Figure 4.2. Mapping exchange-rate arrangements by currency category (see text), 2004.

Source: IMF.

engaged in full-fledged or official dollarization. Each of the four currency processes is discussed below with reference to the specific example.

But before turning to this more detailed examination, how do the currency processes operate geographically relative to a given sovereignty regime? The territorial and shared currency processes are the most evidently territorialized. But even they are hardly totally closed monetary spaces. They must co-exist with a transnational currency that breaks down borders and challenges the hold of national currencies over a range of transactions, not the least by encouraging the development of currency markets at financial centers within their territories. This is an opening up of possibilities for the redistribution of political authority beyond capital cities whose central banks and finance ministries must now work to share power with other actors in the monetary realm. Of course, much of the monetary flow across territorial boundaries today tends to be between financial centers in the richest countries. Wall Street (in New York) and the City (in London) are the key places of authority with affiliates and collaborators scattered all over the world economy but with the densest presence in North American, European, and East Asian cities.[19] This is because most global flows are involved in "diversification finance," "intended to reduce risk through the fine-tuning of portfolios."[20] One hundred years ago a significant proportion of world capital flows moved from rich to poor countries. Of course, much of this was within colonial currency blocs that used the same or closely pegged currencies.[21] That this is no longer the case suggests that the use of substitute currencies today is more a question of subordinate state elites looking for a monetary port in an economic storm than of a hegemonic state actively looking to use currency as a mechanism of subordination. Imperialism today is not a simple facsimile of imperialism in the 1890s. Yet susceptibility to the demands of foreign capital provides a major incentive for some states and local actors to find shelter, however problematic, in the holding of a less volatile transnational currency such as the US$, as evidenced by the large domestic and foreign holdings of such currencies (in offshore and other "dollar salting" centers) by the nationals and governments of many countries.

CASE STUDIES IN EXCHANGE-RATE ARRANGEMENTS AND EFFECTIVE SOVEREIGNTY

CHINA

If the industrialization of Asia was the "most spectacular economic happening of the second half of the twentieth century," then it has been China's rapid emergence since 1978 as a major global economic actor that is perhaps its most remarkable feature.[22] Closed off to the capitalist world economy from 1949 until the late 1970s, China has quickly become a major presence in both the world's trading and financial economies. In particular, China has become an incredible exporting machine based on massive foreign as well as domestic investment. China's exports grew tenfold between 1990 and 2006. Between 2000 and 2006 this represented an increase from 3.9 to 10 percent of the world total. Allied to domestic consumption, this export explosion has generated a huge demand for raw materials as local firms and foreign investors have vastly increased production capacity in such sectors as steel and cement. As of 2006, China consumed more steel (31.3 percent of the world total) than the EU (16.8 percent) or NAFTA (16.0 percent). In 2006 China accounted for 19 percent of the growth in the world economy, second only to the United States. By 2008, its manufacturing sector was estimated to be larger in value-added terms than that of the U.S. Along with this, there is some evidence that domestic consumption has become more important than exports in driving economic growth.[23]

Since 1978, but especially since 1987, the Chinese economy has gone from a command-and-control model to a state-managed but market-driven one. Undoubtedly, however, China has entered into the world economy largely on its own terms. A considerable proportion of its growth has been driven by foreign direct investment (FDI), which accounts for over 40 percent of GDP (compared to a minuscule 1.1 percent in Japan). But the central government has retained much more control over its national economy than is characteristic of most contemporary states. One of the main mechanisms for continuing central control was a soft peg (from 1994 to 2005) and since 2005 a managed float of the Chinese renminbi (sometimes called the yuan) against the US$. This has served both to keep Chinese goods competitive in the U.S. market as those of other countries have become less so because of the appreciation of their currencies against the US$ since 2001 and to build up massive US$ reserves that the Chinese government has been investing in, inter alia, U.S. Treasury bonds and thus helping to finance both the U.S. federal budget and current account deficits. Indeed, as the U.S. trade deficit with China expanded monotonically between 1996 and 2006, the Chinese purchase of U.S. Treasury securities climbed at a much faster rate, especially after 2000.[24] This makes the U.S. economy very vulnerable to any Chinese decision, for instance, to diversify its peg or float

from the US$ to a basket of currencies. This could lead to a dramatic de-
cline in the credit the Chinese government has come to extend to the U.S.[25]

China, then, uses the monopoly of the renminbi within the country to
keep out external currency shocks and to cultivate itself as a destination
for massive foreign direct investment premised on low labor costs and a
stable exchange rate against the US$. To the Chinese government the ex-
change rate is "an issue of national sovereignty" in which foreign actors are
not viewed as having an equal interest.[26] Two major questions arise: how
does the exchange-rate arrangement work and is it sustainable in a world
where monetary sovereignty such as that claimed by China seems under
considerable pressure?

The Chinese pegged system effectively began in 1994. Prior to that date
the renminbi was severely overvalued at about 1.7 to the US$ to segregate
the planned Chinese economy from the rest of the world. The official exchange rate was pegged in 1994 at 8.4 to the US$ but only in December
1996 did the Chinese government accept the IMF Article 8 and set about
making the renminbi convertible for current account transactions.[27] From
1996 until July 2005 the rate against the US$ was fixed at Rmb 8.28. This
encouraged both exports and FDI inflows denominated in U.S. dollars.
Much of China's growth since the mid-1990s owed much to this exchange-
rate system. It allowed China to profit externally while maintaining internal currency homogeneity and stability. The renminbi was a territorial currency whose value was more or less fixed against the currency of its main
export market and the main currency of world trade.

By way of example for this critical monetary insulation, during the
Asian financial crisis of 1997–1998 the Chinese economy remained largely
unaffected because the renminbi was not convertible on capital accounts
so investors could not suddenly withdraw their funds as they could elsewhere. Though there was some pressure from international business to devalue the renminbi, not least from the ethnic Chinese business networks
that provide foreign capital for Chinese development from San Francisco
and Vancouver, Canada, as well as from Taiwan, Hong Kong, and Southeast
Asia, the Chinese government resisted this. Wang claims that this was
mainly a question of maintaining the government's self-image of control
and autonomy.[28] But she also points to the role of commitment to low inflation and the lack of influence on government policy of local and foreign-
owned enterprises in China that lobbied unsuccessfully for devaluation.
So, even in the face of increased dependence on FDI, the Chinese govern-

ment was more concerned about other largely political goals than pleasing its foreign investors.

This currency system proved unsustainable in its purest form. As a result in July 2005, the Chinese government moved to a rigorously managed float. This maintained a high degree of government control over appreciation of the renminbi to the US$ but also allowed for a greater flexibility in managing the currency. One problem with the strict pegged currency had come from overheating of the manufacturing sector. As fixed asset investment grew by 31.1 percent in China for all sectors in the first half of 2003, three times the rate for the whole of 2000, consumption grew only at 8.8 percent.[29] This disparity indicated a high degree of excess capacity. The fixed exchange rate encouraged the growth of foreign exchange reserves, which then pushed up the money supply (up from 12 percent in 2001 to 20 percent in 2003). In turn, this encouraged more fixed asset investment by speculative capital, thus exacerbating the problem of shrinking profit margins as more investment chased stagnant or shrinking demand. At this point the Chinese monetary authorities would have had to strengthen capital controls and intervene in foreign exchange markets to suppress the appreciation of the renminbi.[30] They chose instead to redesign their exchange-rate arrangement, keeping state control but allowing for steady adjustments in value.

A second threat to the pegged system had come from the efforts of foreign political leaders, such as the U.S. secretary of the treasury, to persuade the Chinese government to move to a freely floating renminbi in order to avoid the imposition of trade and financial sanctions. Disturbed by China's ability to exploit the US$ by "hiding" behind a currency pegged to the US$, those who would dramatically change the Chinese monetary system, however, should note how much U.S. businesses investing in China have lower labor costs and reap higher profits and U.S. customers/workers receive lower prices and low-paying jobs from the current system. China has also increased its imports (largely raw materials) at a higher rate than its exports over the period 1998–2006. But the pressure to move toward a free float is likely to continue. A territorial currency and a globalizing world economy are not easily harmonized, one with the other, particularly for a country such as China with an increasingly heavy presence in world trade.[31] As of summer 2003, the renminbi was approximately 40 percent undervalued against the US$. From the shift in 2005 until late 2007, however, the renminbi appreciated by 14 percent against the US$.[32] Even this "stealth" revaluation still hands businesses operating in China an enor-

mous competitive advantage over businesses in the United States, resulting
in a major loss of American jobs in relevant sectors. Many of the three
million or so manufacturing jobs lost in the U.S. between the beginning of
the George W. Bush presidency in 2001 and 2008 disappeared because of
competition from China: an amazing one out of every seven jobs in U.S.
manufacturing. No U.S. president ever presided over such a hemorrhaging
of jobs over such a short period of time. That this occurred at a time when
even many service-sector jobs were also becoming vulnerable to relocation
from the U.S. and Europe to countries such as India and China (e.g., soft-
ware programming and call centers) only makes the political tension that
much greater. Only a radical restructuring of the Chinese monetary system
through relaxing capital controls and allowing the US$ and other currenc-
ies to freely circulate between Chinese financial centers such as Shanghai
and Hong Kong and foreign ones is likely to assuage the critics. Whether
this is possible for a government seemingly still intent for political reasons
on maintaining a classic sovereignty regime—keeping the political monopoly exercised by the Communist Party and re-establishing the prestige lost
when China was subject to the depredations of colonial powers in the
nineteenth and early twentieth centuries—remains to be seen.

THE UNITED STATES

As one of the victorious powers after the Second World War, the U.S.
was the main agent of imposing a fixed exchange-rate system on the international economy of the time. This system, known by the name of the
place in New Hampshire where it was negotiated (mainly between the U.S.
government and British government representatives in 1944)—the Bretton
Woods Agreement—pegged exchange rates against a dollar-gold standard
for the period from 1945 until 1971. Although full convertibility of European currencies against the US$ did not occur until 31 December 1958,
political acceptance of the system in the U.S. and elsewhere rested more
on its stimulus to open, multilateral trade than on its particular properties
as a strategy for organizing international monetary relations.[33] Although
the system can be seen as part of the "embedded liberalism" that the U.S.
extended to its sphere of influence during the Cold War, it was a deeply
territorialized way of managing currencies.[34] It rested initially and finally
on the capacity of governments (and central banks) to regulate their currencies against an external standard provided by the US$ pegged against a
fixed price of gold.

By the 1960s the system was in deep trouble. The problem was the increasing leakage of dollars beyond American shores through the accumulation of dollar reserves by foreign central banks and the emergence of the so-called Eurodollar market. On the one hand, the economic recovery of Europe and Japan meant that they accumulated large dollar reserves, but "this was attractive only as long as there was no question about their convertibility into gold. But once foreign dollar balances loomed large relative to U.S. gold reserves, the credibility of this commitment might be cast into doubt."[35] As early as 1947 the economist Robert Triffin had predicted that this would be a problem. By 1960 U.S. foreign dollar liabilities exceeded U.S. gold reserves. If foreign countries wanted to convert their reserves there would a rush to cash in dollars before the U.S. authorities could devalue. This threat became a major refrain of international monetary debate in the 1960s.

On the other hand, the dollar increasingly became a transnational rather than a territorial currency in the sense it had to be for the Bretton Woods system to function properly. Beginning in 1958 a Eurodollar market had sprung up in London to service dollars beyond the regulatory domain of both the U.S. and Britain. As a result, dollars flowed into this market where they were then lent out without reference to capital controls. U.S. Banking Regulation Q, which capped interest rates in the U.S., encouraged investment in the Eurodollar market from the United States. Multinational businesses parked dollar funds in Eurodollar accounts to avoid U.S. taxes and to gain interest-rate differentials relative to U.S.-located banks. Attempts by U.S. governments to correct the imbalances by manipulating the U.S. capital account did slow down the development of the offshore dollar market. But the Eurodollar market "enabled private financiers to engage in exactly the type of hot-money transactions that the Bretton Woods regime had sought to eliminate. As predicted by Triffin's dilemma, the opportunity for arbitrage profits against the dollar and the other major currencies was overwhelming. Speculation consequently worsened, and ultimately the system collapsed."[36]

The action taken by President Nixon in 1971 in unilaterally abrogating Bretton Woods can plausibly be seen as an attempt at reasserting classic sovereignty. In other words, given that a fixed exchange-rate system seemed to deliver decreasing benefits to the U.S. territorial economy, it would be best to abandon it.[37] Whatever the intention, the outcome was a system in which the dollar was liberated from gold and after 1973 floated freely against other major currencies.[38] Rather than a return to the US$ as a territorial currency, therefore, the US$ has become an even more transnational currency than that inaugurated by the Eurodollar market of the 1960s.

Arranged in discussion among the finance ministers of the G-5 (the U.S., Japan, France, Germany, and Britain) in 1975, the floating exchange-rate system was formalized in 1978 by a Second Amendment to the Articles of Agreement of the IMF. This removed the role of gold, legalized floating, and obliged countries to promote stability in exchange rates by authorizing the IMF to oversee the monetary policies of members. This was all something of a "leap in the dark."[39] No one really knew how it would work. In the 1970s many established monetary policies co-existed with the new system, such as capital controls and concerted intervention. New financial devices designed to cope with increased volatility in exchange markets, such as futures and options, bred speculation and further volatility.[40] The large quantity of dollars introduced into world financial markets by the OPEC-inspired increases in the price of oil had an additional stimulative effect, given that world oil prices were denominated in US$. This led to the spate of lending by international banks that produced the debt crisis for countries that received loans but then were faced with declining terms of trade plus large interest-rate increases in the 1980s as the U.S. Federal Reserve tried to wring inflation out of the U.S. economy. But in the 1980s, partly in response to persisting stagflation and partly to the increased popularity of ideas of market superiority over state regulation, most industrialized countries moved toward greater exchange-rate flexibility by abolishing targeting and reducing interest rate interventions. Policy coordination among countries did help to some degree in reducing volatility in foreign exchange markets.

The net effect of the post–Bretton Woods turn of events, therefore, has been to make the US$ into a transnational currency. In a sense the dollar has inherited its role from Bretton Woods when it was "the central numeraire" for the system as a whole.[41] As the currency of the world's largest territorial economy with a long-established and dominant presence in world financial markets, the U.S. dollar was not "dethroned" when the official exchange rate parities collapsed in 1971. If anything, the opposite has happened. The US$ has become "the vehicle currency in the interbank spot and forward exchange markets, the currency of invoice for primary commodity trade and for many industrial goods and services, and the main currency of denomination for international capital flows—particularly at short term and interbank. Outside of Europe, governments use the dollar as their prime intervention currency—often pegging to the dollar, and U.S. Treasury bonds are widely held by foreign central banks and treasuries as official exchange reserves."[42] This is because, as McKinnon and others have argued, providing transnational money to the world economy is a natural monopoly. For one thing, in a world of 150 or more territorial currencies, tremendous savings in transaction costs occur if just one currency is chosen as a vehicle currency. All foreign-exchange bids and offers can be made against the one currency. For another, significant economies of scale accrue from pricing and invoicing goods and services in international trade in one territorial currency. The fact that many of the world's major commodity exchanges are also located in the U.S., in Chicago and New York, gives a further fillip to the dollar.

The dollar, therefore, is not just a matter for America, because the dollar is not just America's currency. Over one-half of all dollar bills are held outside U.S. borders. Almost one-half of U.S. Treasury bonds are held as reserves by foreign central banks, particularly those of Japan and the People's Republic of China.[43] Other currencies cannot, at least as yet, rival this global reach. Consequently, to some economists, the world is now on a de facto dollar standard.[44] Certainly, more nominally territorial currencies now float freely against the dollar (and other currencies) with the US$ as the common unit of comparison than before 1980. The percentage of IMF members with either soft- or hard-pegged exchange arrangements declined from about 77 percent in 1977 to 36 percent in 1997 and 34 percent in 2001, while the percentage with floating arrangements increased from 12 percent in 1975 to 25 percent in 1997 and to 32 percent in 2001.[45] But the trend from fixed exchange rates to more flexible arrangements can be exaggerated both in general and with respect to free floating against the dollar in particular. Rather than *freely* floating against the dollar, many currencies still take the form of managed floats or relatively fixed pegs. Moreover, the coming of the Euro offers a potential alternative currency of wider use to the dollar. As of 2004, forty-one countries had no independent currency (i.e., relied totally on a foreign currency such as the Euro or US$), seven had currency boards, forty-two had soft-pegged exchange rates, thirteen had fixed exchange rates adjusted by indicators (inflation or exchange-rate targets), forty-eight had managed floats, and thirty-six freely floated.[46]

What is more important about the dollar than its role as a monetary standard is the revolutionary hollowing out of other territorial currencies that it has facilitated. It is now a direct means of exchange in many countries that still have their own territorial currencies. Indeed, in many financial centers irrespective of country it is the currency of most transactions. Its authority, and that of those actors who command it, is often greater than that of the nominally sovereign state. This is one of the main features of the transnational uses of the US$. At the same time, the dollar is still also the currency of the United States. Specifically, the U.S. uses its dollar to finance its large current account and federal budget deficits. Of course, all those foreigners holding dollars have a stake in keeping up the flow of dollars into the rest of the world. They have an interest in keeping the whole system in motion. For this reason, as McKinnon argues, America's creditors have a stake in preserving the dollar's role as a transnational currency even as the U.S. current account deficit balloons. As a country with a large financial services sector, the United States also benefits indirectly from the globalist regime that the US$ serves as a transnational currency. This sector has a vested interest in seeing use of the dollar expand around the world. They also are powerful political proponents—as is the financial sector in Britain, the only other country that has both a chronic current account deficit and a major financial services sector—of liberalized global capital markets.

The Achilles' heel of the US$ as a transnational currency is that although it gives the U.S. a "uniquely soft credit line with the rest of the world," it also (as in relations with China) opens up the U.S. economy to competition in sectors where it is less competitive internationally (as in labor-intensive manufacturing) and portends a future in which the U.S. will have to rely on foreign-owned capital and foreign central banks (even if in dollars) to finance its domestic economy.[47] As a net importer of 70-plus percent of total global capital flows in 2006, the United States risks unbalancing its own economy (through the loss of certain kinds of jobs, etc.) in order to provide a transnational currency to the rest of the world. Foreigners may not need to care that much about the U.S. current account deficit, therefore, but Americans are a different matter entirely.

THE EUROPEAN UNION

Though what today is known as the European Union can trace its roots back to the European Coal and Steel Community of the early 1950s and the European Economic Community of 1957, it was not until the disintegration of Bretton Woods in 1971 that much effort was made to implement some sort of managed currency system among member states. And it was not until the late 1980s, in fact, that a fully fledged monetary union became a major objective of the organization. European monetary unification through the creation of a shared currency, therefore, has had two distinct origins. One is as an economic response to the end of Bretton Woods. The other is much more clearly political: building European integration on monetary unification.[48]

In the European Community attempts at reducing volatility among European currencies gave rise first to "the Snake" or managed float in the early 1970s. This was a collective arrangement whereby the six original members pegged their exchange rates within 2¼ percent bands. The Snake did not last long, mainly because the oil shock of 1973 had devastating effects on the weaker currencies and as governments adopted expansionary fiscal policies, such as France did in 1976, they had to leave the Snake. Eventually, by 1978, the idea of pegging currencies within unchanging bands had run its course, particularly when the European currencies were simultaneously floating against the dollar. The European Exchange Rate System (ERM) replaced the Snake in 1979. Under this arrangement, the German mark assumed the strong-currency role that the dollar had performed under Bretton Woods. Eight of nine EC countries participated in the ERM (Britain was the sole exception). Italy was allowed to have a 6 percent band for a "transitional" period because of persisting high inflation whereas the system as a whole had ones of 2¼ percent. There were no withdrawals during the 1980s but the first four years were turbulent mainly because the Mitterrand government in France embarked on an expansionary fiscal policy. Once this was abandoned, however, policy convergence across members made it easier for the system to respond to the relative strengthening of the dollar in the late 1980s. "Europe's 'minilateral Bretton Woods' appeared to be gaining resilience."[49]

It was precisely at this moment, however, that a set of non-monetary concerns emerged across the countries of the European Union. These included the ability of European firms to compete with the U.S. and Japan, reduce unemployment, maintain European welfare programs in the face of pressures exerted through the floating dollar to liberalize labor markets and pension programs, reinvigorate the "European project," and create a single European market through the removal of capital controls. A new vision of Europe based on these concerns found expression in the Delors Report of 1989 and in the Maastricht Treaty of December 1991. Eliminating currency conversion costs was one of the ways of forging an integrated market. Concurrently, one way of liberalizing trade among members without stimulating protectionism was to remove the threat of member governments engaging in exchange-rate manipulation. The only way to do these two things was to create a shared currency for the entire EU. Without moving forward to monetary union the fear also was that the political project of European unification would founder in the face of the transnational threat to Europe from U.S. and Japanese economic competition.

The Maastricht blueprint for monetary union threw continuing political commitment to the ERM into immediate doubt. Along with the global recession of 1990–1992, the decline of the dollar against the mark, and the rise in German interest rates following German reunification, this sealed the fate of Europe's experiment in managing currencies.[50] What replaced it in the 1990s was the movement toward a shared currency by declaring a set of fiscal and monetary criteria for accession to monetary union. These criteria—freeing central banks from political control; setting inflation, government debt, and government spending targets, etc.—should be understood not just as goals in the pursuit of price stability and trade benefits. Rather, "European monetary integration can be best understood as a political compromise involving divergent ideas and preferences within Europe, specifically between France and Germany."[51] If the French government desired to enhance France's and Europe's independence from the United States, Germany wanted to see its reunification accepted as unthreatening to the rest of Europe. If the Bundesbank-like role assumed by the European Central Bank (ECB) represents what the Germans wanted out of the system, an independent bank devoted to keeping inflation under control, the French have acquired a currency that can potentially challenge the US$ as a transnational currency.

The transition to a shared currency has gone through three stages as foreseen in the Delors Report and agreed to in the Maastricht Treaty.[52] The first stage from 1990 to 1994 saw the removal of capital controls among potential members, political independence for central banks, and convergence toward treaty obligations. The second stage from 1994 to 1999 saw the convergence of macroeconomic indicators and policies and planning for introduction of the new currency. Finally, the third stage has seen the introduction of the new currency, first alongside the existing territorial currencies and then instead of them. The implementation went remarkably smoothly. Since January 2002 the Euro has been the sole legal tender in all of the EU countries at that date except Britain, Denmark, and Sweden, who have chosen to remain outside for the time being.

In a sense, of course, the shared currency is simply a new territorial currency for a larger area. But it also has a couple of other features that do set it apart from being just that. One is that it is already a transnational currency, in that after the dollar it is now the most important currency for worldwide financial transactions. Its existence seems to have reduced monetary policy autonomy for countries that trade heavily with the Eurozone and that presumably could be candidates for membership in it.[53] Critically, inside Europe it has replaced the mark and the dollar as the two previously most important currencies in cross-border flows. Second, it is peculiar in that individual states have retained control over fiscal policy even as they have ceded control over monetary policy to the ECB and the foreign exchange markets. If the latter has tended to lead toward a more "Anglo-American" market capitalism in Europe's financial centers (though these are still underdeveloped compared to London and New York), the former has created serious problems as some member countries, notably France and Germany, have violated the excessive government deficits rule (no more than 3 percent of GDP) that they agreed to follow when planning the shared currency.[54] The EU's fiscal rules, therefore, appear simultaneously unenforceable and unchangeable. Until there is some parallelism in Europe between the levels at which fiscal and monetary policies are made, this is likely to be a continuing problem for the shared currency and any deepening of its role as a transnational one.

LATIN AMERICA

The U.S. has long had a strong influence over monetary policy in Latin America. In the early twentieth century this took the form of encouraging the use of the US$ as part of a "gold standard diplomacy" that would bring monetary stability to the region and make it easier for U.S. business to operate once countries possessed currency units that were identical in value to the dollar.[55] In Rosenberg's words, the idea was to "create a gold dollar bloc, centered in New York, to rival the de facto [British] sterling standard."[56] At the same time, dollar diplomacy also could involve encouraging straightforward adoption of the dollar itself. This dollarization, however, usually meant the use of the US$ alongside the territorial currency, not exclusive use of the dollar in its place.[57] By the 1920s dollar diplomacy of both species had largely peaked. Increasing Latin American nationalism, the various advantages of issuing a territorial currency (identified earlier), and serious current account crises that the economic thinking of the time suggested needed activist monetary policies conspired to limit the substitution of national currencies by the dollar.

After the Second World War, official U.S. policy was to discourage use of the dollar as a substitute for territorial currencies in the region. The new priority was national economic development, so the best monetary policy should be an independent one with each country having its own currency. Of course, this fit into the conventional economic wisdom of the times as manifested in the Bretton Woods Agreement and many other U.S.-sponsored policies in the late 1940s and 1950s. Indeed, U.S. governments even endorsed economic nationalist policies such as import-substitution industrialization, partly as a tool to undermine left-wing groups and co-opt nationalists to the American side in the Cold War, but also because large American manufacturing firms wanted to build factories behind high tariff walls to serve local markets.[58] This illustrates how much U.S. monetary policy in Latin America at the time reflected U.S. foreign policy interests and the relative influence of large-scale U.S. manufacturers compared to financial and U.S. investors in mines and agriculture.[59] But it also suggests strongly that the state territories were seen by locals and Americans alike as very much the basic building blocks for all economic policies. In this regard, U.S. policy in Latin America differed considerably from British and French policies in Africa and elsewhere that often pushed for currency blocs (such as the Franc CFA zone in former French colonies in West Africa) or currency boards to limit the monetary discretion of the local governments.[60]

Beginning in the 1970s dollar diplomacy returned to the American agenda in Latin America. Price stability replaced economic growth as the central goal of U.S. policy toward the region. This was obviously part of the ideological shift toward neo-liberalism that followed the freeing of currencies from fixed exchange rates after the collapse of Bretton Woods. But economic conditions in Latin America also made the change seem more imperative than it otherwise might have appeared. In particular, a number of factors played a role in making price stability a higher priority than formerly. Two were especially crucial: the extremely high inflation rates in the countries of the region and the growth of export-oriented FDI as the motor of economic development in place of import-substitution. As a result, the elimination of exchange-rate risk had come to be widely seen as likely to foster U.S. trade and investment throughout the region.[61] In 1999 a bill devoted to the spread of official dollarization throughout Latin America was actually introduced in the U.S. Senate. But after a flurry of interest enthusiasm seems to have faded. Cohen maintains that, from a U.S. perspective, it is likely that U.S. governments will remain passively neutral about official dollarization.[62] Although there are seigniorage, transaction cost, conversion cost, prestige, and geopolitical advantages, many of these can be gained by unofficial and surreptitious dollarization. Official dollarization has the major drawbacks of exposing the U.S. politically if economic growth stalls and imposing costs if the U.S. has to intervene in financial crises. Only if the Euro came to challenge the status of the dollar as the pre-eminent substitute currency in Latin America, the currency Latin Americans really want to have, does Cohen think that U.S. policy might become more aggressive in pushing official dollarization.

In Latin America itself, Ecuador and El Salvador have enacted legislation in recent years to fully dollarize their economies. Panama has been largely dollarized from its origins as an American dependency at the time of the construction of the Panama Canal. Elsewhere, however, full dollarizations (either official or unofficial) have not occurred. From 1991 until 2002 Argentina did employ something like a currency board to maintain a fixed exchange rate between the peso and the US$ but the charter of the board allowed considerable discretion to the monetary authorities. This cannot be seen as a true case of official dollarization. Many other Latin American countries in fact now float their currencies against the dollar and other currencies. From this point of view, Latin America is now relatively less dollarized officially than it was in the late 1980s when many of its countries had currencies that were closely pegged to the dollar or adopted so-called intermediate mechanisms such as crawling pegs and bands.[63] In other words, the continent is stuck between the globalist and the imperialist regimes even though many governments, if given a choice, would aspire to classic sovereignty.

Unofficial dollarization is a different matter entirely. Although much more difficult to document than official dollarization, this is clearly substantial in amount and effects.[64] For example, in Argentina in 1992, one study estimates that the dollars in circulation amounted to $26 billion or around 11 percent of Argentine GDP.[65] In Bolivia and Uruguay in the same year, the ratio of paper dollars to local currency was reported as an incredible three or four to one.[66] Bank deposits in different currencies are easier to track than physical flows of cash. Many Latin American countries allow dollar-denominated deposits in domestic banks. Cohen reports figures that suggest perhaps as much as 80.9 percent of all deposits in domestic banks in Bolivia in 1992 were of foreign currency (almost entirely dollars one surmises).[67] In the same year in Argentina the comparable figure was 41.5 percent. In 2000, the range went from a high of 92.5 percent of all deposits in US$ in Bolivia to a low of 4.9 in Mexico with a mean of 49.2 percent across all countries in Latin America that allowed foreign currency bank deposits.[68]

All this adds up to a major unofficial (or spontaneous) dollarization. The reasons for this are not difficult to find. They range from the fact that drug trafficking, one of the Andean countries' main economic activities, is an entirely dollar business through remittances from migrants to the United States (this is particularly important in Central America) to the salting away of dollars as a defense against inflation and to aid in the acquisition of dollar assets abroad (i.e., capital flight to offshore banking centers in the Caribbean and to Miami). The fact that many states, particularly in Central and Andean America, fail to raise enough tax revenue to pay for even the barest of modern states, including adequate monetary regulation, also leads their own elites to look to the dollar as the best guarantee of future wealth. Lying behind much of the unrealized sovereignty of Latin American states is the fact that Latin America is now oriented almost completely toward the United States both as a source of investment and as the destination for many of the region's commodity exports, migrants, and capital. It is Latin America's dependence on the U.S. economy that has produced the substitution of the dollar for territorial currencies throughout the region. Although this is mainly unofficial or the result of diffusion of the dollar into the economic fiber of the region rather than the outcome of a formal adoption of the dollar as a replacement for the territorial currencies, it is nevertheless a significant strike against the possibility of real monetary sovereignty on the part of Latin American countries. In this regard, effective sovereignty lies to *El Norte* and is exercised through privatized network flows of U.S. dollars rather than through explicit state adoption of the dollar as a territorial currency.

IMMIGRATION, CITIZENSHIP, AND SOVEREIGNTY

The period between 1970 and 2000 has sometimes been referred to as the "Age of Migration" to contrast with the previous sixty years or so when rates of international migration slowed down considerably from a previous epoch of expansive migration in the late nineteenth and early twentieth centuries.[69] Of course, people have always moved from place to place. Some human societies have been entirely nomadic. Even sedentary societies have experienced periods of disruption in which people have moved around in response to shifts in economic and social opportunity. Indeed, a case can be made that movement has been much more characteristic of human history as a whole than has fixed settlement in particular places. But certainly over long distances there has been a recent revival in migration that makes it generally more global in character than migration in previous epochs when flows either were more regionalized (as within Europe or within specific countries) or had well-defined source and destinations areas (e.g., flows from southern Europe to the U.S. and Argentina in the period 1890–1915). The era of globalization has produced a much more variegated pattern of flows with a quantitatively significant increase as a whole in migration over relatively long distances.[70]

Given that the primary objective of this chapter is to illustrate how the sovereignty regimes work, I wish to emphasize the intersection between migration, state regulation of movement, and citizenship. The purpose is to show how states have coped with the recent explosion of migration in different ways that reflect different histories of migration and approaches to citizenship or state membership. After a brief overview of contemporary trends in global migration, I turn to a classification of approaches to migration regulation and citizenship in relation to the four sovereignty regimes. A final section illustrates this classification using some empirical case studies.

THE COMPLEXITY OF CONTEMPORARY INTERNATIONAL MIGRATION

An important feature of globalization is the dramatic increase in movement of people as well as of goods and capital. The barriers to mobility of people remain much more restrictive than are those to goods and capital. But aging populations and low birth rates in more developed countries coupled with huge disparities in incomes and increased education in poorer countries provide the basis for a long-term pressure for increased human mobility around the world. The 190 million or so people who were estimated to live outside their countries of birth in 2005 (up from 82.5 million in 1970) are still only about 3 percent of the world's total population. But they have significance well beyond their numbers.[71]

Immigration is now the major contributor to demographic change in the world's most affluent countries where declining birth rates, aging populations, and increased educational levels predisposing people against manual labor make it the only antidote to population decrease, possible declines in economic growth, and fiscal disaster if the aged receiving pensions expand without a commensurate increase in the working population paying taxes. Japan, the one developed country with little immigration, is expected to lose 26 million people from its population by 2050. Who will pay for the increasingly high percentage of the Japanese population on retirement pensions as the postwar baby boom reaches retirement age? In the U.S., the population will likely grow by 129 million between 2005 and 2050 if immigration continues at the present rate but would go up by only 54 million if immigration stopped. With their higher birth rates, recent immigrants would continue to give the U.S. a growing population. Immigration, therefore, matters enormously in relation to prospects for future economic well-being (and continuance of welfare state benefits) in developed countries as well as in source countries where remittances from migrants provide an important source for both current spending and capital accumulation.

The range of relative distances traveled by migrants and the complexity of connections between source and destination areas have also all increased over the past forty years. In the past, many flows were largely between adjacent countries (e.g., Ireland to England); from Europe to settler countries such as the U.S., Australia, and Argentina; or within the confines of historic empires (e.g., Algerians to France, Pakistanis to Britain). But now the patterns are much more variegated. Major migration corridors today are often worldwide rather than geographically contiguous or culturally defined. Many previous source countries have become destinations (e.g., Italy), and some countries, often on opposite sides of the world, are both sources and destinations for immigrants (e.g., China and the U.S.). The net effect has been to produce more culturally diverse immigrant populations who, because of ease of movement and modern telecommunications, also often remain bonded to their places of origin. What is also new is that movement is not just between overpopulated areas and underpopulated ones. Neither is it just, as many would still have it, between a poor global South and a rich global North. Indeed, perhaps a third of contemporary international migrant flows per year are between countries in South Asia and the Gulf States (including Saudi Arabia). Within China around 15 million people now move on average each year from rural to urban areas. Within that vast country the global pattern of rich and poor areas is recapitulated at a national scale.

A proportion of all international immigrants also move either temporarily or without official sanction. The past image of the immigrant is of someone who intends to move permanently and selected the destination as one of choice. In fact, many immigrants have always moved without the intention of putting down roots in the place to which they have moved. For many years, for example, seasonal immigrants moved to and fro across the U.S.-Mexico border to harvest crops in the U.S. Many Italian immigrants to the U.S. also moved back to Italy on retirement. Many of the illegal or undocumented immigrants to the U.S. today remain so because they have no intention of staying permanently and because of the difficulties of acquiring legal status. They are readily exploited by employers who can avoid paying them official pay rates and social security contributions. About 8 to 10 million illegal immigrants currently reside in the U.S., living overwhelmingly in the states of California, Texas, and Arizona. Such immigrants include not only those who "slip over the border" deliberately but also those who arrive legally and overstay their visas. As of 2005 there were around 2 million international students in circulation. The World Tourism Organization estimates that there were 760 million tourist arrivals in 2004. These groups provide important recruitment pools for both legal-permanent and illegal immigration.[72]

The biggest destination country is the U.S., where more than 31 million foreigners over the age of fifteen account for 14.5 percent of the population as of 2007.[73] This is still a significantly lower percentage than that of the late nineteenth century when in 1890 the percent foreign-born in the U.S. population peaked at around 24 percent. Overall, foreigners account today for 9 percent of the population over the age of fifteen in the world's richest countries (members of the OECD). The range is from a high of 36.6 percent in Luxembourg to a low of 4.3 percent in Italy. In Germany immigrants account for 12.7 percent of the population, compared to 11.7 percent in France and 9.4 percent in Britain. Mexico is the largest source of migrants, sending more than 8 million of its citizens to live abroad, overwhelmingly to the U.S. The next largest are the UK with 3.2 million and Germany with 3.1 million citizens living in other OECD countries. China and India provide about 2 million migrants apiece to the rich countries. Many of the British and Germans living abroad are over sixty-five (in other words they are retirees), whereas most of the other immigrants are much younger, looking for work or political asylum. Interestingly, many of these immigrants have a relatively higher level of education than do the natives; 23.6 percent of immigrants have tertiary education compared to 19.1 percent of the native-born. The poorest people on earth tend not to migrate.

They cannot afford the airfare or the payment to a smuggler. It is typically the better off and better educated who move, even among the unskilled. Although immigrants from other rich countries account for many of the best educated in many countries, only the U.S. receives more skilled immigrants from other rich countries than it loses to them. The effect of the "brain drain" of the relatively skilled from poorer to richer countries seems to have the most impact on small African and Caribbean countries. But the U.S. also has a much higher percentage of the low-skilled among recent immigrants. It remains more open to unskilled immigrants, intentionally or not, than do most other developed countries.

About two-thirds of immigrants are settled in rich countries. This still leaves a substantial number who are moving elsewhere. Indeed, China, India, and the Philippines are major sources of migrants to other developing countries. Some of this migration is within Asia but also involves increasingly important flows to the Middle East. The Gulf States depend heavily on Asian immigrants to fuel their economic growth. In Kuwait and Dubai, for example, the native-born are now a minority. Within Africa there are also large flows of migrants, primarily from West and Central Africa to South Africa. In Latin America international migrants tend to move to Venezuela or Argentina. Australia and New Zealand now gain more immigrants from Asia than from Europe (see figure 4.3).

Although most immigrants are economic migrants in the sense that they are responding to incentives to move in order to better their material condition, some immigrants are primarily refugees or political migrants. Economic migration tends to closely follow the business cycle with bursts of immigration followed by contractions as demand for immigrants shifts in response to changing economic conditions. As a result, economic migration does not follow a single upward trajectory but is markedly cyclical. Thus in 2008 flows of economic migrants began to slow and, in some cases, reverse as the world economy entered recession. For example, around half of the 600,000 East European migrants to Britain in the early 2000s had left by summer 2008.[74] But political migrants are something else again. These are people whose homelands are either in the throes of civil war or whose governments persecute religious and ethnic minorities. Refugees are officially classified as those who have crossed a border to escape persecution. Asylum seekers are a subset of this population who have applied for permanent residence because of the threat of persecution if they return to their country of origin. A repatriated population is one that has returned to its country of origin. Displaced people are those uprooted from

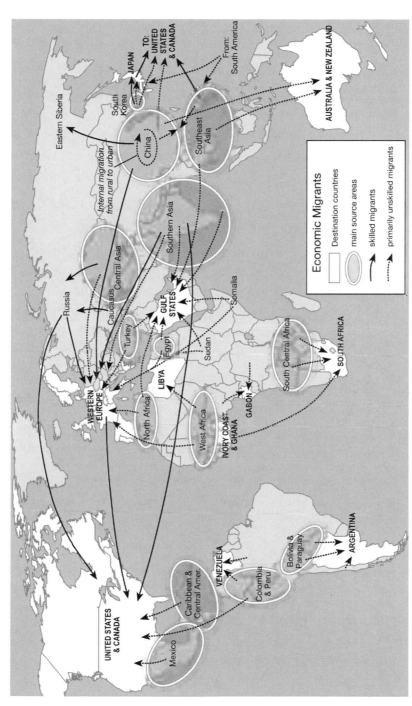

Figure 4.3. Flows of economic migrants around the world, 2008, showing main source and destination regions for skilled and unskilled migrants.

Source: Author from UN published sources.

their homes but still resident within the borders of their state. Of course, not all refugees and displaced people are simply victims of political discrimination. Many are also mired in poverty. Thus, they are also economic migrants but ones whose calculus is based more on being pushed out of where they lived than identifying and responding to the pull of more prosperous places.

At the present, the bulk of the world's refugees are located in the Middle East, South Asia, and Africa, but some have also relocated elsewhere as a result of conflicts and political instability in these regions. For example, there is a large and long-standing Palestinian refugee population scattered around the Middle East, the wars in Iraq and Afghanistan have created large refugee populations in adjacent countries and around the world, and various conflicts in Central and Eastern Africa have produced large numbers of refugees. The trend toward civil wars and ethnic conflict noted in chapter 3 as a manifestation of the breakdown of some states seems likely to increase the numbers of people entering into the refugee and analogous categories. This type of migration, therefore, is more structural and probably likely to continue an upward trajectory than is the admittedly more numerically significant but essentially cyclical economic migration. It also produces migrants who are both more embittered about their experience and less interested in economic returns. They are much more likely to engage in politics oriented to their homelands and to resent their situation as immigrants.[75]

One particularly important category is composed of those defined as officially "stateless." These are refugees and displaced people who have no official nationality and are without the documents needed to travel, such as passports and visas. As stateless people are not recognized by any country, they are largely invisible. Until the 1961 UN Convention no attempt had been made to estimate their number. Since then efforts have been made to identify them. Even so they mainly continue to live outside the structure of "international society" as defined by states. The UNHCR (UN High Commissioner for Refugees) estimates that as of 2006 the number of stateless people worldwide was between 5.8 and 15 million.[76] Most of the world's stateless live in Asia and Africa (figure 4.4). The largest concentrations are associated with the brutal civil war in Sri Lanka (largely Tamils), civil wars and oppressive governments in Southeast Asia, and the breakup of the former Soviet Union. Civil wars and despotic governments in Ivory Coast, Zimbabwe, and the Democratic Republic of the Congo have also produced recent explosions in the numbers of stateless people. Many

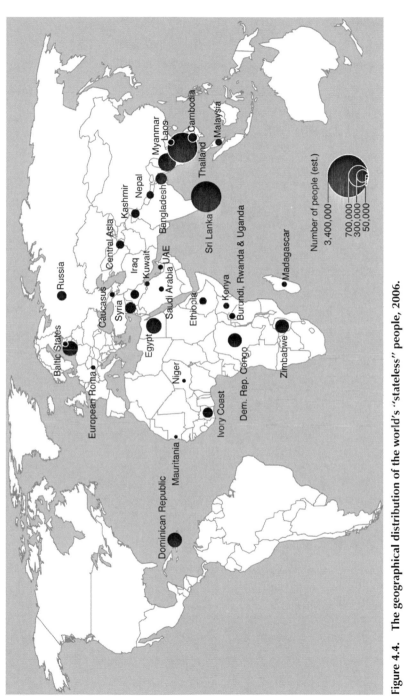

Figure 4.4. The geographical distribution of the world's "stateless" people, 2006.

Source: Author from UN High Commissioner for Refugees (UNHCR).

countries refuse to give nationality to the children of stateless people (e.g., the Dominican Republic will not give citizenship to the children of Haitian farm workers; Lithuania will not recognize 400,000 ethnic Russians as Lithuanian, etc.).

Immigrants tend to go where the jobs are and where their co-nationals (or, more accurately, co-locals) live. Thus, in Britain London is the destination of the vast majority of foreign immigrants. In the U.S. it is cities like Los Angeles, Chicago, San Francisco, Houston, and New York that are the main migrant destinations. Between them, for example, the Los Angeles and New York metropolitan areas account for fully one-third of the foreign-born in the entire United States; 70 percent live in only six states, the highest number (8.9 million) in California. In the 1990s this did diversify somewhat as the poorest immigrants, typically from Mexico and Central America, found their way to Midwestern and southern states to work in agribusiness and meatpacking. When they move, then, immigrants tend to follow well-worn paths. Migration is only statistically actually between countries, as they are the entities that regulate it. Migrants are actually moving from place to place rather than from territory to territory in the sense that I have used these terms in chapter 1. The history of social, economic, and political connections between places is much more important than geographical distance or even average relative affluence in the destination country in driving the process of international migration.[77]

The clustering of immigrants in particular places is by no means new. Indeed, it is a long-standing feature of immigration to the U.S. and elsewhere. It is both reassuring to the immigrants and anxiety producing among the native-born. In the former respect, clustering means that some of the familiar features of home (food shops, language, churches, etc.) are available at the destination. Yet it also suggests, not the least to the native-born, that immigrants are more comfortable with their "own" and are resisting not just assimilation but also even nominal integration into the host society. Such resistance can be given its own justification, as in reference by immigrant political activists to "diasporas" of people who presumably have fixed identities that they bring with them and that are perpetuated by co-residence.[78] But, more often than not, it serves to generate local political hostility. Indeed, immigration has become a major political issue all over the world, from the U.S. to Italy, South Africa, and Australia. Yet even though of significantly greater magnitude than in the recent past, the recent increase in immigration often seems to have generated a disproportionate political response. Some of this can be put down to the unfamiliar-ity of immigration on a large scale in some places (such as Italy), but it also seems to have something to do with the general increase in economic uncertainty, the questioning of established national identities due to globalization, and the rise of ethnic separatisms and religious fundamentalism. The problematic outcome is increased suspicion between immigrant groups, on the one hand, and host populations, on the other.[79] The historic record suggests, however, that similar reactions to immigration were characteristic of previous waves of migration. In the U.S., at least, "fear" of small numbers—of Catholics, Jews, Freemasons, and plain old foreigners—is simply not news. It is as American as . . . apple pie.[80]

Yet, whether or not they form true diasporas, immigrants frequently do maintain strong ties to their home places and homelands. Some source countries depend heavily on remittances from their migrants. Fully 36 percent of the GDP of Tajikistan and Moldova comes from remittances from abroad (table 4.2). Even some wealthy countries benefit from remittances. France, for example, received US$12.5 billion in 2007. Germany and Britain were not far behind with US$7 billion apiece. Beyond economic effects, however, emigrant communities can have significant political and social impacts on where they come from. One impact is when political entrepreneurs use migrants as the basis for political campaigns to establish homelands that currently do not exist, such as for Kurds, Sikhs, and Tibetans, or to further the interests of particular states from which migrants come or to which they are emotionally attached, such as Cuban, Irish, and Jewish groups in the U.S. By way of example, the Israeli lobby has become notorious in the U.S. for using the presumed political clout of the Jewish population to curry favor with U.S. governments. Another less frequently noted impact is the linkage migrants provide for both licit and illicit activities back home. Some of this can involve major investments in public infrastructure in home communities (e.g., sewers, piped water, and schools). Some of it can also involve more traditional private investment.[81] But some

Table 4.2. Top Ten Remittance-Receiving Countries (as Percent of GDP, 2006)

1. Tajikistan	36%	6. Lesotho	24%
2. Moldova	36%	7. Guyana	24%
3. Tonga	32%	8. Lebanon	23%
4. Kyrgyzstan	27%	9. Haiti	22%
5. Honduras	26%	10. Jordan	20%

Source: World Bank, Development Prospects Group, 2008.

of it also involves organized crime and rackets such as human trafficking for purposes of prostitution, drug export, and the re-export of gangsters. Migrants from desperately poor countries such as Kosovo, Honduras, and Moldova, to name just three, are deeply implicated in such criminal activities both as organizers and as victims. A good example of the complex geographical circumstances under which migration connects to transnational criminal activities is the *Mara Salvatrucha* gang, formed in southern California by Salvadoran refugees from the vicious 1980s civil wars in Central America, which has provided not only an important channel for drug smuggling into the U.S. from Mexico and Colombia but also, as a result of the U.S. policy of deporting its members back to Central America, has turned a localized Los Angeles gang into a transnational criminal organization.[82]

In their turn, some states also try to represent, cultivate, and organize their emigrants. During the peak time of Italian emigration to the U.S. in the early twentieth century, Italian governments provided passports and medical certificates to facilitate the emigration of its nationals even when they were not required, supported banks to channel migrant remittances to relatives back home, promoted Italian foreign policies among emigrants, and supported Italian chambers of commerce to benefit Italian businesses in destination countries. More recently, in 2001, the Italian parliament extended voting rights to all Italian citizens resident abroad. The goal has been to encourage a sense of Italian national identity among those who have left the country behind and use them to mobilize those still at home. If the former did once meet with some success, the latter seems entirely unrealized.[83] Mexican governments have recently begun to follow the same model after decades of trying but failing to control migrant outflow. They have emphasized voluntary ties, dual nationality, and migrant rights over citizen obligations. Politically, emigrants have become the most privileged of Mexicans.[84]

CHOOSING IMMIGRANTS, MAKING CITIZENS

Immigrants must run the gauntlet of different citizenship systems that sort potential immigrants into different categories, only some of which qualify one for either permanent residence or citizenship. This is where immigration engages most closely with state sovereignty. Modern citizenship is closely connected to the rise of the state. Conventional views of statehood see control over membership in its territory as a crucial requirement. Exclusive loyalty to a specific state is likewise seen as a sine qua non of citizenship. Statehood has been conjoined to nationhood by means of citizenship. Issuance of passports is a major type of infrastructural power that states have grasped with enthusiasm since the time of the First World War.[85] Political participation is also an essential component of democratic citizenship. Struggles to extend and deepen political representation have always focused on democratic control of state institutions and have served to give states one of their most important sources of legitimation. Consequently, as I have argued earlier, most democratic theory and practice assumes a territorial political community with citizenship as a means of delineating who does and who does not belong to the "people." Today, only states still have the authority under international law to grant or deny the status of citizen. Thus, citizenship is strongly linked to the idea of political community, which in turn in seen as synonymous with the territorial exclusivity of the sovereign nation-state.

But the historic tie between states and citizenship is under increasing pressure from immigration and the development of multinational and global conventions governing human rights (such as those established by the European Union). First of all, rights of residence as opposed to birthright are increasingly driving definitions of citizenship. In Europe and North America a case can be made for a "paradigm (and scale) shift" in understandings of citizenship, a shift that relocates citizenship from nation-state sovereignty to the international human rights regime. This reflects both pressure from the absolute numbers of immigrants and the fears of labor unions and other interests that without some rights of political membership for immigrants the rights of all will be undermined. Yet at the same time political rights that extend across borders from one state to others are also growing. Citizens of a country resident abroad now can have voting and pension rights hitherto restricted to those resident within the country in question. This is now the case, for example, with Mexican citizens resident in the United States. Within the European Union the issue of dual or even multiple citizenship has been transcended by the possibility of a European citizenship that allows for continuing allegiances at not only the state but also at sub-national scales of identity. Plural citizenship, therefore, is an emerging reality.

Recent international migration is distinctive from that in the past in two ways that are particularly threatening to traditional conceptions of citizenship. One is in the long-term concentration of migrant communities in certain cities and localities that rather than assimilating into a national "mainstream" maintain their cultural particularity. This is a result of both greater cultural pluralism and tolerance in host countries and greater cultural differences between the new immigrants and their host societies. Many immigrants remain attached to their "homelands" and see themselves as temporary absentees more than permanent migrants. Another distinctive feature of contemporary global migration is the ease of movement of people and ideas between source and destination areas. With the new transport and telecommunications technologies, it is relatively easy today to keep ties across state boundaries and to develop political and economic attachments without a "final commitment" to one state or the other.

As definitions of citizenship are disrupted by the novel character of contemporary global migration, there are countervailing pressures to reestablish "normalcy." "Invasion panics" based on exaggerated fears about the scope and impact of immigration have afflicted such disparate destinations as California, France, and Italy over the past ten years. Often these are cultural in inspiration, given the increase in flows of migrants from poorer, underdeveloped countries to richer, developed ones who are more visibly different from native populations than previous generations of immigrants. But they also reflect economic concerns about job competition or burdens on public-sector spending for welfare or social security. Political parties play the "immigrant card" in certain areas and constituencies when they use the "threat" of immigration to mobilize native voters. At a certain point in time, however, this strategy can backfire, as it has for the Republican Party in California, when sufficient numbers of immigrants have acquired citizenship and demonstrate their electoral strength by voting en masse against those who would demonize immigrants as the dominant source of local social and fiscal woes.

Citizenship is a core feature of state sovereignty. Whether democratic or not, states rely on a high degree of exclusivity of identity drawn by their citizens to maintain power within their jurisdictions. Historically, some civil and social rights have been granted to non-citizens. Increasingly, however, even political rights have become relatively mobile. Non-resident citizens, immigrant citizens, residents of encompassing jurisdictions (such as the European Union), and multiple citizens are categories of people who experience citizenship in ways that violate the one-to-one correspondence of state and citizenship upon which state licensing of political power has long rested. One of the great advantages of states, to speak and act on behalf of nations, is undermined when the key link between the two, an affective and singular citizenship, is eroded by movements of people that transgress rather than reinforce the boundaries of states.

There are three dimensions to how states can manage immigrants in relation to the process of establishing citizenship. One is whether permanent immigrants are clearly distinguished from temporary immigrants and screened in terms of their credentials for citizenship before or after moving. Many immigrants, for example, South Asians, in the Gulf States are never likely to be offered citizenship there under any circumstances. Many of them are resident without any official status. This makes them vulnerable to exploitation and subject to immediate deportation when they complain about working conditions or go on strike.[86] In the U.S., conventionally a country with a long history of welcoming immigrants, there has been a shift, parallel to the increase in illegal immigration since the 1980s, towards ex-post screening through deportation or adjustment of legal status and away from ex-ante screening and management based on converting legal immigrant status into citizenship. Between 1998 and 2004 the share of permanent residents in the U.S. (the first step to citizenship) arriving on immigrant visas declined from 66 to 38 percent. This represents a recent shift in U.S. practice toward the German system of conferring citizenship on people admitted initially for a period of residence as temporary residents rather than as immigrants from the outset on the path to citizenship. Perhaps the biggest problem with ex-post screening is that it undermines rational expectations of a predictable route to citizenship for budding immigrants and reduces the incentives to learn a new language and settle into the new society. It raises the specter of social exclusion. It discourages social integration.[87]

The second dimension is the extent to which the reception of immigrants is a real issue in relation to citizenship for a state. For some states simply keeping their citizens may be the priority; it is exit not entry that concerns them. For others the priority is more on preventing the fragmentation of their state into parts rather than on integrating immigrants. As described earlier, only some states are the destinations of most of the world's migrants. Figure 4.3 shows the main destination regions and countries: North America, Western Europe, Australia and New Zealand, Japan, Libya, the Gulf States, South Africa, Gabon, Ivory Coast and Ghana, Argentina, and Venezuela. For many of the states in question, immigration is partly about restriction but also about charting a path to national membership and legal citizenship. For others, such as the Gulf States and Libya, the interest is in anything but. Here the goal is to exploit labor and once used up to deport the people whose labor has been exploited back to where they come from.[88] Elsewhere, the concerns are completely different. In China, for example, the interest of the government is with managing the massive internal migration from interior to coastal China and from rural areas to cities. Whether migrants in situations such as those of the Gulf States or China will ever manage to establish a full range of social and political rights is moot (figure 4.5). Citizenship itself is often something of a hollow promise rather than signifying a demonstrable shift in material and symbolic condition.

The third dimension is the particular model of citizenship on which a country has come to rely. Most broadly, these range from a civic or open model to an ethnic or closed model. If the first relies on the idea of cultural affinity and choice, the second is based on a clearly kinship and tribal conception of citizenship. The U.S. and France are often identified with the first, reflecting their respective revolutionary traditions, whereas Germany is classically associated with the second, even though in recent years, and as part of the European Union, Germany has moved toward the more open model. Under the ethnic model, evidence of family ties or "blood" connections to the nation-state trumps residence as the primary factor in establishing qualification for citizenship. At the same time significant barriers are put in the way of qualifying by means of what is often called "naturalization" or a path to citizenship based on residence rather than on familial or ethnic inheritance criteria. Israel, with its "Right of Return" for all Jews anywhere, is an extreme example of this model, one somewhat ironically associated in the citizenship literature more often with Germany than with the Jewish State. Under the civic model, citizenship is about territorial presence and presumed education in the norms of a particular national identity. Consequently, naturalization is about acquiring at least a primitive familiarity with the history and political premises of the state in question. The dilemma for both models is that with globalization citizenship is becoming increasingly divorced from a singular national identity. Many countries have relaxed naturalization procedures (including language requirements), allow dual citizenship, and have embraced territorial birthright citizenship. Following the terrorist attacks of 11 September 2001 the distinction between aliens and citizens was itself drawn into question by the passage of the USA Patriot Act, which allowed for no such differential in applying police powers, and residence not citizenship now seems to be the governing principle in relation to obligations such as paying taxes. It is not surprising, therefore, that citizenship is becoming more by way of a

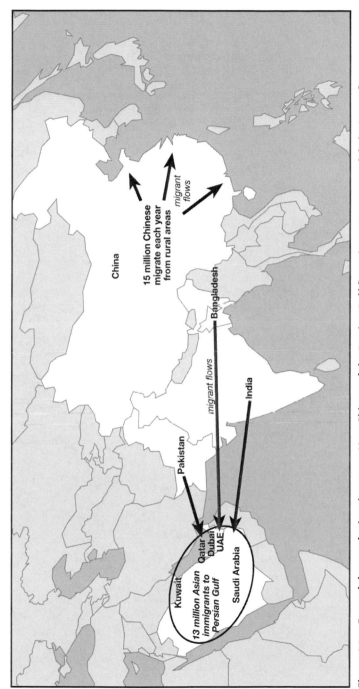

Figure 4.5. Beyond the usual migration story. How China and the Persian Gulf figure in contemporary global migrant flows.

Source: Author.

port in a storm (and a way of acquiring a passport) than a declaration of a primary identity for increasing numbers of people.[89]

If the three dimensions are combined, four categories of immigration regulation/citizenship can be identified:

1. *Immigrant state*: immigration recognized as important to state, a net destination state, historical emphasis on ex-ante regulation, civic model of citizenship;
2. *Reticent immigrant state*: immigration relatively less accepted, a net destination state, historical emphasis on ex-post regulation, ethnic model of citizenship;
3. *Source state*: immigration not important, a net source state, little explicit regulation, mixed or unclear model of citizenship;
4. *Territorial state*: immigration not usually important to state (except for co-ethnics), source and destination of immigrants, emphasis on ex-post regulation, an ethnic model of citizenship.

If countries such as the U.S. and Australia are good examples of category (1), then the countries of the European Union (with, perhaps, the historical exception of France) and the Gulf States (although they largely block the path to citizenship) fit into number (2); most African and Latin American states (except Brazil, Argentina, and Venezuela which are closer to number 1) could be allocated to number (3); and Japan, South Korea, China, Russia, India, and most countries of Southeast Asia (and, in a sense, Israel) fit into number (4). They match the four sovereignty regimes as indicated in table 4.3 with case studies listed down the diagonal.

The combinations are again ideal types. They simplify more complex situations for purposes of exposition and understanding. The norms and

Table 4.3. Sovereignty Regimes and Immigrant/Citizenship Processes (examples along the diagonal)

		SOVEREIGNTY REGIME			
		Classic	*Globalist*	*Integrative*	*Imperialist*
DOMINANT	*Territorial state*	S. Korea			
IMMIGRATION/	*Immigrant state*		U.S.		
CITIZENSHIP	*Reticent state*			Italy (EU)	
PROCESS	*Source state*				Mexico

practices involved parallel those associated with exchange-rate arrangements except that these are much more complex in covering a number of aspects of how immigration rules and citizenship paths, on the one hand, correlate with sovereignty regimes, on the other. Similarly, as with the exchange rates, there is no assumption that these immigration/citizenship arrangements are set for all time. Indeed, as mentioned previously, the U.S., classified here as an "Immigrant State," seems to be moving in recent years toward a more reticent relationship to its immigrants on the path to citizenship. But historic experiences and perceptions of immigration and its relationship to citizenship strongly inform the categorization.

Relative to effective state sovereignty, the *territorial state* process is closest to that of the mythic Westphalian state. The presumption is of limited or no immigration and a high degree of national-ethnic homogeneity. Citizenship is strongly based on an ethnic model. The others, to one degree or another, represent more hierarchical and de-territorialized processes. The *immigrant state* process comes close to the image of open borders. For all the hype about the re-bordering of the United States in recent years, for example, it is relatively easy for immigrants to arrive and settle in the U.S. Acquiring citizenship is undoubtedly more difficult but it is also not always necessary to live a reasonably satisfactory life, particularly in immigrant enclaves where even knowledge of English is not required. The *reticent state* process is more difficult on immigrants. An ethnic or national model of citizenship co-exists uneasily with an official commitment to some cross-border immigrant flow. Many reticent states have a history of emigration and have difficulty dealing with large-scale immigration. They also often have had long imperial histories that complicate the reception of immigrants, particularly from places they formerly ruled. Old stereotypes of superiority and subordination die hard. For example, when it ruled Algeria, France had various categories of citizenship for settlers and natives in the colony that, while no longer in force today, nevertheless still literally color popular understandings of who is and who is not "really" French. France is by no means alone in this regard. In addition, in the EU case a hard external border is also built around the member states while between member states movement is relatively easy. Nevertheless, immigrants from both inside and outside often receive differential treatment in access to legal status and the various services and opportunities that are de rigueur for "native" citizens (as with the way Romanians are treated in Italy, even though they are from another member state of the EU). Finally, the *source state* process is akin to the provision of a labor pool for the other states in a form of hierarchical subordination within the world of states. States in this category can at best adjust what they do to the practices of the more powerful states in the other categories. They have a fundamentally unequal relationship with destination states in their ability to manage migration and regulate citizenship.

CASE STUDIES IN IMMIGRATION/CITIZENSHIP AND EFFECTIVE SOVEREIGNTY

SOUTH KOREA

Founded in the aftermath of the Korean War in 1953, the Republic of Korea was the U.S.-allied twin of a North Korea that modeled itself after the historic Hermit Kingdom of Korea and a Stalinist command economy. Over the course of the 1970s and 1980s and in counterpoint South Korea became a developmental state in which military-led authoritarianism, pro-Americanism, and state-business corporatism led to a dramatic increase in the level of economic growth. Today South Korea has a relatively high per capita income (GNI per capita of US$17,690 in 2006), a low poverty rate, and heavily urbanized population (81 percent of the population). It has also, after a series of popular struggles, acquired a more democratic politics. Since 1987 the country has had a succession of popularly elected presidents and parliaments. This is undoubtedly a "conservative democratization" in that the big business–dominated economy has remained in place with overwhelming political influence (the latest president elected in February 2008 is the former head of Hyundai Construction) and the country remains on a war footing notwithstanding opening up to the North throughout the 1990s. The Asian financial crisis of 1997 brought the developmental state model into open question. Since that time successive governments have adopted more liberal economic policies (including the controversial opening of trade with the U.S.) and allowed some of the previously favored big businesses (such as Daewoo) to fail.[90]

The development state model relied on a relatively closed economy and geopolitical subordination to the U.S. More recent and hesitant steps to liberalization have produced greater openness to inward foreign investment and a desire, at least until very recently, to emphasize both the "neutrality" of South Korea between China and Japan in Northeast Asia and the declining fear of North Korea either militarily or in the form of a humanitarian catastrophe if the regime there collapsed and millions of people sped southward. There has also been an increase in emigration, particularly to the United States. In 2005 South Korea ranked twenty-eighth in countries surveyed in terms of numbers of emigrants (1.6 million) of whom 0.7 million went to the U.S.[91] Like Japan, however, South Korea has long remained largely hostile to the possibility of recruiting immigrants. The preferred alternative in the face of rising wage bills has been to relocate production to China and elsewhere. In the late 1980s, the only relatively large non-Korean groups were a shrinking ethnic Chinese community and American soldiers. These groups were located in the main cities and, with the latter, in Seoul, the capital, and along the border with North Korea.

This has begun to change. But most immigrants remain either illegal (as in the case of the East European women working as prostitutes in Seoul's notorious Itaewon district) or guest workers, mainly from South Asia and Africa, recruited on labor contracts for fixed periods of time or completely undocumented. Many of the latter immigrants work in a garment industry that would have disappeared but for their recruitment at low wage rates. Estimated at several hundreds of thousands, they are vital for the survival of certain manufacturing industries and in low-level service jobs.[92] The largest immigrant group by far, however, and also largely undocumented, consists of ethnic Koreans from China who occupy many of the most undesirable jobs in the country. A final group is of foreign women recruited as wives for farmers. As a result of urbanization, many rural women have found jobs in cities, leaving fewer marriage prospects for rural men. The solution has been to import women from rural China and Southeast Asia. In 2004 about 25 percent of rural South Korean men were married to foreign wives. Strangely then, the Korean countryside is now more cosmopolitan than the cities, which remain overwhelmingly ethnically Korean. Only the imported wives (and perhaps some of the ethnic Korean immigrants from China) can be expected to ever become Korean citizens. And this will happen only after they have become thoroughly Korean. As one commentator has perceptively argued, however:

> Along with the presence of some one million foreign workers [out of a population of 48 million], this high rate of intermarriage has helped to undermine Korea's long-held self-perception—shared with few other countries other than Japan—as an ethnically homogeneous nation. It remains to be seen how successfully South Korea can adapt to this new multi-cultural environment; the Japanese precedent does not offer a very promising model.[93]

THE UNITED STATES

The United States is the archetypal settler state. Immigration and subsequent citizenship can be thought of as its dominant leitmotif. Everyone more or less ultimately comes from somewhere else. In this respect it is the quintessential "globalist" state: open to all comers as well as for business. It is a country built on displacement of a native population and massive immigration to populate an expanding national territory. It remains to this day by far the most important destination country for migrants (38.4 million immigrants as of 2005) and is the largest source of remittances sent by immigrants, US$42.2 billion in 2006 (Saudi Arabia, the second biggest, was at only US$15.6 billion).[94] Of course, whatever the essential truth to these statements, the real story is somewhat more complicated. Until the late nineteenth century most immigrants came as free or indentured settlers from northwest Europe or as slaves from West Africa. As other groups were recruited or simply arrived, beginning with Irish Catholic immigrants in the 1850s and Chinese workers in the 1860s, immigration was increasingly regulated to exclude some foreigners, primarily on racial grounds. This reached its climax with the National Origins Act of 1924, which for the first time imposed quotas for immigration on the basis of nationality. In force down until 1965, this law was only replaced when it proved incapable of producing the immigrants needed for a growing economy. Under the Nationality Act Amendments of 1965 occupational criteria and family reunification took precedence irrespective of source country. After this shift more than 75 percent of foreign immigrants came from Asia and Latin America. Before, the privileging of Europeans had kept the numbers of immigrants from other parts of the world to a minimum, save for Mexicans recruited as seasonal agricultural workers. The 1965 legislation was designed to facilitate ex-ante screening of immigrants for economic suitability and family unification.

As of the 1980s, the U.S. was the world's wealthiest country, bordered to its south by some much poorer countries. Add to this a series of civil wars in Central America, not without U.S. involvement, which disrupted and drove tens of thousands of people from their homes, and you had a setting primed for migration.[95] Many of the refugees had no time to settle their immigration status and arrived in the U.S. illegally. In 1986 an amnesty awarded permanent residence to undocumented immigrants who had resided in the U.S. for a defined period of time. This undoubtedly encouraged the sense that legal status was ultimately negotiable rather than something to be established prior to moving. In the 1990s the tremendous growth in demand in the U.S. for personal services (typically low-skill and low-pay jobs) gave another stimulus to immigration from Latin America. As a result, some 11 million people entered the U.S. during that decade. Around 4.6 million were Latinos who entered legally but the number of undocumented was probably even larger. By 2001, one out of five residents of the United States was either foreign-born or a child of immigrants. Fully 30 percent of this group were non-citizens.[96]

As in previous periods of growth in immigration, there has been a backlash against immigrants in general and Latino (especially Mexican) immigrants in particular. Of course, not all recent immigrants have been from Latin America but numerically they do dwarf the others from Asia and elsewhere. Immigrants have become scapegoats for a wide range of problems and issues with which they are only contingently related. Crime, particularly drug-related crime, is one. Reliance on the public charge, particularly impact on health care and public services such as schools, is another. Since 2001 the whole issue of illegal immigration and defending the U.S.-Mexican border has become confused with security against terrorism. The folding of the old Immigration and Naturalization Service into the new Department of Homeland Security is a practical sign of how this confusion has become definitional. Immigrants, many toiling away in car washes and restaurants at below minimum wage, are portrayed by right-wing politicians as a "threat" to national security. Not surprisingly, therefore, immigrants, both legal and illegal, must now prove their loyalty ex-post before they can be admitted to citizenship.

Yet the immigrants will probably keep on coming, even with some respite during periods of recession. For one thing, the increased hardening of border controls at U.S. land and airport ports-of-entry will encourage erstwhile temporary immigrants to stay on rather than risk exclusion the next time they decide to cross the border. The sorts of jobs that natives refuse to fill pay well above what can be obtained at home and will exercise a continuing incentive to move northward. Eventually some sort of amnesty will probably be applied to those currently without legal status. It simply makes economic sense. Finally, U.S. citizenship is itself an increasingly diminished asset beyond its ownership of a passport. The effective abandonment of ex-ante screening means that it is no longer a scarce commodity. Come and we might (eventually) give it to you. The real prize now is legal residence, *not* citizenship. The proportion of foreigners who naturalize as citizens has been steadily decreasing, from 63.6 percent in 1970 to 37.4 percent in 2000.[97] The watering down of the civic model in the face of official acceptance of plural citizenship and the greater benefits of some employer identification cards over passports (as some U.S. citizens discovered during the 2006 Israel-Hezbollah war in Lebanon) leads Peter Spiro to the following conclusion:

> Beyond the trope of civic faith, territorial presence and strong norms against dual citizenship played crucial functions in maintaining a coherent citizenry coinciding with community on the ground. Those backstops are no longer available to shore up community now breached by the global diffusion of culture and democratic governance.[98]

ITALY (EU)

Famous as a source of emigrants to other countries, particularly settler states such as the U.S., Argentina, and Brazil, in the late nineteenth and early twentieth centuries, Italy has recently become an importer of migrants from a wide range of source countries but largely from North Africa and Eastern Europe. But the country still manages to lose more people to emigration (a stock of 6 percent of the total population in 2006) than it gains through immigration (4.3 percent also as of 2006).[99] The continuing economic divide between an economically developed northern Italy and a lagging south produces many potential migrants from the south. Rather than going northward within Italy most choose to leave Italy altogether. When the trend toward labor shortages in northern industries (and agriculture everywhere) is added to the extremely low national birth rate and high labor-force dependency ratio (fewer people work relative to those who receive pensions than in any other industrial country), one might in fact expect to see a much higher rate of immigration to Italy than currently prevails. Welcoming as it may be of tourists, Italy has been much less hospitable to working immigrants, documented or otherwise.

As one of the founding member states of what became the European Union, Italy's governments until recently have been fervent supporters of European unification. As part of a larger bloc Italy could benefit both economically and politically. In the 1960s this included exporting Italians northward to work in West Germany (and Switzerland). More recently it has been about building a wider European economy within which Italian businesses could flourish. The idea of the European Union rests on lowering barriers to flows of all sorts between members (including migration under the Schengen and other agreements) while maintaining or enhancing barriers to those beyond, except for those countries waiting to join. Thus, the reticence about immigration has a dual basis beyond the historic status of Italy as a net source of migrants: it is about a nation-state committed to becoming European but with a fear that under the influence of immigration, particularly from beyond the confines of Europe, it is out of the European mainstream, a long-time fear of Italian nationalism. Even if the current Italian government is less enthusiastically "European" than past ones, it still shares the fear of reverting, under the taint of Third World immigration, to a marginalized position within the EU.[100]

Italy has the fifth-largest manufacturing economy in the world. This economy is dominated by small and medium-size businesses that have historically relied heavily on family and off-the-books labor. Declining numbers of family members available to work mandate that labor has to be found somewhere else without the possibility of always substituting technology for people. But the tight profit margins of Italian businesses, relative to foreign competitors in China and elsewhere, has meant that employing people legally is even less enticing than it once was. Hence, there is a high demand for undocumented labor. At the same time, and as in the U.S., there has been an explosion in demand for personal services, particularly in areas such as care for the elderly and domestic service. Immigrants numbering 1.7 million, mainly women from the Philippines, Peru, Ecuador, and Romania, are estimated to work in these capacities. As in the manufacturing sector, payment off the books offers advantages, such as tax evasion and underpayment relative to official pay scales.[101] Italy has also found itself front and center in the expansion of various human trafficking and other criminal networks emanating primarily from the Balkans. Powerful domestic criminal organizations have exploited these to advantage. In the aftermath of the civil wars in the former Yugoslavia and as a result of the enlargement of the European Union to include such poor countries as Romania and Bulgaria, Italy has also become the preferred destination for a number of migrants who in the presence of ex-ante controls would probably be excluded.[102]

There is, therefore, a structural bias in Italy in favor of undocumented or clandestine immigration along with a flow of legal, if often unsuitable, immigrants from other EU countries. Officially, the country also remains wedded to an ethnic model of citizenship or what Giovanna Zincone calls "legal familyism."[103] At the same time, for the purposes of legal residence there has been a long history since the onset of significant immigration in the 1980s of regularizing undocumented immigrants through amnesties.

So, as citizenship remains a rather distant possibility for most immigrants, there is a greater possibility of acquiring legal residence through ex-post screening.[104] In the meantime, lax enforcement of immigration control within the country makes the possibilities of clandestine residence attractive particularly for those who have no plans on living in Italy permanently. That many immigrants are a valuable resource for Italy, given higher than average educational levels, younger ages, and commitment to work because of the need to send remittances back home, has become a commonplace among social scientists. It seems to have little resonance with much of the population at large.[105]

The cultural parochialism of many Italians about the self-evident virtues of an Italian style of life, especially when it is closely identified with local place of residence as it is for many Italians, makes co-existence with strangers (even other Italians) with different habits of living, eating, and worshipping extremely difficult.[106] Thus, there is increasing conflict between natives and immigrants, particularly those who are seen as inherently criminal (such as the Romani or gypsies from Eastern Europe) and those, such as Moslems, who are viewed as culturally incompatible. The Italian national election of April 2008 became in part a referendum about such matters. The center-right coalition led by Silvio Berlusconi campaigned vociferously in favor of a massive crackdown on illegal immigrants following news reports of several fatal stabbings and an increase in robberies tied to immigrants. It is by no means clear that the immigrants in question were actually illegal. So, even though immigrants are a relatively small percentage of the population (4.3 percent) compared to other EU countries, but because immigration has become closely tied to criminality and illegality in Italian political discourse, it serves as a lightning rod that takes attention away from other political issues such as the declining competitiveness of the Italian economy, Berlusconi's own legal troubles, and the woeful condition of Italy's national government deficit.[107]

Italy, however, is not all that different from most other rich EU countries in its general attitudes to immigrants and citizenship. The national insecurity about being "insufficiently" European, trapped between Europe and Africa, serves simply to increase the tension well beyond the level the actual impact of immigration would lead one to expect. Indeed, the EU itself now has a common policy on immigration and citizenship that is little different from that exercised in contemporary Italy. Sovereignty over immigration and citizenship is increasingly pooled within the EU.[108] From this perspective, Italy is a "frontline" state for the EU as a whole because of its location relative to North Africa and southeast Europe from whence many immigrants intent on moving to Europe, but not necessarily settling in Italy, come. The EU's 2008 "return directive" allows member governments to detain unauthorized migrants for up to eighteen months. A proposed EU-wide immigration pact would push ex-ante screening of immigrants (but not between member countries such as Italy and Romania), establish a common refugee and asylum policy, beef up border patrols, and expel more illegal immigrants. Yet none of these proposals would address the central issues of the Italian case: the perverse structural incentives to attract undocumented immigrants, the difficulties facing immigrants who only wish to come temporarily, the fact that Italians actually seem more upset at the European immigrants than with those coming from elsewhere, and the ethnic character of the citizenship models in most European countries, which makes it very difficult for co-residents to become fellow citizens.

MEXICO

Mexico has long co-existed with a more potent and wealthy neighbor to the north: the United States. A large part of what is today the western U.S. and Texas was once part of Mexico. Mexicans have long made the trek northward to seek their fortunes. In the past this was often lightly regulated or as part of joint-government programs to provide seasonal labor on the U.S. west coast. Since about 1960 it has become a veritable flood. Mexico itself is also a way-station for immigrants from further south heading to the U.S. The U.S.-Mexico border is far and away the most important migration corridor in the world. With 10.3 million people having passed through as of 2005, the only ones that come even close are Russia-Ukraine (4.8 million), Ukraine-Russia (3.6 million), and Bangladesh-India (3.5 million). As a result, Mexico has the honor (shared with Russia) of being one of the world's top two emigrant countries. Only 0.6 percent of Mexico's population consists of immigrants. People are perhaps Mexico's most important export.[109]

The absolute level of migration from Mexico to the U.S. is surprising insofar as its initiation coincided with what has been called Mexico's "economic miracle" in the late 1970s and 1980s. But the oil-based expansion and the massive infrastructure investments of the period in roads, communications, and irrigation that it paid for were neutralized by a huge population increase and government corruption and crony capitalism. The slump in world oil prices after 1981 meant that the heyday of economic growth had passed without the structural changes in the Mexican economy that would be needed to keep job growth in line with population growth. In the early 1980s as a result of a huge fiscal crisis wages fell precipitously. Neo-liberal reforms designed to cut the national budget deficit exacerbated both poverty and the gap between rich and poor by cutting food and utility subsidies. Meanwhile the U.S. was beginning a recovery from the early 1980s turndown, and with scant enforcement of sanctions against employing illegal aliens many U.S. employers began recruiting laborers in Mexico. Though one of the goals of the North American Free Trade Agreement of 1992 was to encourage investment in Mexico and thus discourage the northward trek, it had a limited effect on immigration into the U.S. from Mexico. Higher wages and well-established social networks made the difference.[110]

The growth of the U.S. economy through the 1990s kept the stream of migrants on course. By 2000 the recognition of mutual benefits on both sides of the border by influential politicians, not least the two presidents Fox and Bush, suggested that perhaps a more rational policy consensus might be forthcoming. This was dashed in the aftermath of 11 September 2001 when the idea of the border as a security threat took precedence in the U.S. over the border as a migration corridor supplying needed immigrants to the U.S. As border controls tightened, potential migrants were increasingly driven to cross the land border in desert and mountainous areas where they became prey to both unscrupulous smugglers and the elements.[111] Yet the border still beckoned because of the relative income gap between the two countries and the ease of disappearing into deeply rooted enclaves inside the U.S. once the border was crossed.[112]

The governments of Mexico, historically embarrassed by the scale of the cross-border movements, have begun to come to terms with the fact that—given their current political institutions, economic disparities, and political corruption—migration is an escape valve for people who might otherwise insist on political reform. In recent years they have acted to normalize the role of Mexico as a source state for migrants to the United States. They now recognize dual nationality, the right of Mexican citizens resident in the U.S. to vote in Mexican elections, and the importance of remittances from the U.S. for economic development in large parts of central and southern Mexico, the regions from which most migrants come. With US$25 billion in remittances (3.0 percent of GDP) in 2007, Mexico is the third-ranking country in the world in terms of the absolute level of remittances. Only India and China, much larger countries, generate more.[113] The question of citizenship in Mexico, therefore, is much more about what to do about Mexicans outside Mexico, especially in the U.S., than about what to do about immigrants in Mexico.

CONCLUSION

I have provided two detailed examples of how the four sovereignty regimes operate in the contemporary world. Both with respect to exchange-rate arrangements for different currencies and to the regulation of immigration and citizenship, it seems that sovereignty is exercised effectively in quite different ways for different states around the world. In each case some of the difference is due to differential perceptions by governments based on prior experience, but much more seems due to the impact of hierarchy, that not all states are equally sovereign, and to the fact that sovereignty is shared or pooled with other states and a wide range of other actors, many of which are non-territorial in the ways they operate. What I hope is particularly clear is that looking at the world solely in terms of either globalization or classic territorial state sovereignty does little justice to the rich complexity of the world as captured by the idea of sovereignty regimes.

NOTES

1. B. J. Cohen, *The Geography of Money* (Ithaca, NY: Cornell University Press, 1998); B. A. Simmons, "The legalization of monetary affairs," *International Organization* 54 (2000): 573–602.

2. E. Schoenberger, "The origins of the market economy: state power, territorial control, and modes of war fighting," *Comparative Studies in Society and History* 50 (2008): 663–91.

3. E. Helleiner, "The southern side of embedded liberalism: the politics of postwar monetary policy in the Third World," in J. Kirshner (ed.), *Monetary Orders: Ambiguous Economics, Ubiquitous Politics* (Ithaca, NY: Cornell University Press, 2003).

4. G. R. D. Underhill, "Global money and the decline of state power," in T. C. Lawson et al. (eds.), *Strange Power: Shaping the Parameters of International Relations and International Political Economy* (Aldershot, UK: Ashgate, 2000).

5. See, for example, E. Helleiner, "Below the state: micro-level monetary power," in D. M. Andrews (ed.), *International Monetary Power* (Ithaca, NY: Cornell University Press, 2006).

6. E. Helleiner, "Historicizing territorial currencies: monetary space and the nation-state in North America," *Political Geography* 18 (1999): 309.

7. J. Goodwin, *Greenback: The Almighty Dollar and the Invention of America* (New York: Henry Holt, 2003), 4.

8. B. J. Cohen, "The macrofoundations of monetary power," in D. M. Andrews (ed.), *International Monetary Power* (Ithaca, NY: Cornell University Press, 2006), makes a persuasive case for what he calls a worldwide Currency Pyramid in which currencies at the top make others, the majority below, pay for adjustment costs across all exchange-rate arrangements. Even after the collapse of the Bretton Woods Agreement, which had semi-fixed exchange rates against the US$ from 1944 until 1972, there was still an undeniable hierarchy among the world's currencies. Nevertheless, the way the hierarchy works is quite different for different exchange-rate arrangements and cannot be reduced to a single worldwide process.

9. The macroeconomics of open economies with fixed and floating exchange rates are examined in detail in Jeffrey D. Sachs and Felipe Larrain B., *Macroeconomics in the Global Economy* (Englewood Cliffs, NJ: Prentice Hall, 1993), chapters 13 and 14.

10. J. Chung and P. Garnham, "Plummeting dollar a big headache for pegged currencies," *Financial Times* (14 March 2008).

11. D. A. Lake, "Escape from the state of nature: authority and hierarchy in world politics," *International Security* 32 (2007): 65–66.

12. J. C. Shambaugh, "The effect of fixed exchange rates on monetary policy," *Quarterly Journal of Economics* 119 (2004): 301–52.

13. G. A. Calvo and C. M. Reinhart, "Fear of floating," *Quarterly Journal of Economics* 117 (2002): 379–408.

14. C. M. Reinhart and K. S. Rogoff, "The modern history of exchange rate arrangements: A reinterpretation," *Quarterly Journal of Economics* 119 (2004), 1–48. Also see, for example, J. Braga de Macedo, D. Cohen, and H. Reisen (eds.), *Don't Fix, Don't Float* (Paris: OECD, 2001).

15. W. W. Widmaier, "The social construction of the 'impossible trinity': the intersubjective bases of monetary cooperation," *International Studies Quarterly* 48 (2004): 437.

16. The freely floating currencies are the most integrated into the global economy with the most independently powerful financial centers where the US$ serves as the most common metric of transactions. The countries with no independent currency obviously use substitute ones. The soft-pegged rates and, to a lesser extent, the managed floats signify those states in which state monetary authority (and other elements of authority) is relatively territorial. The countries with currency boards (hard pegs) are often either in macroeconomic crisis or in transition toward some other exchange-rate regime. "Network externalities," the snowball effect of surrounding countries operating with other systems, make these "intermediate" exchange-rate regimes inherently unstable with financial globalization and will

push them toward shared currencies (as with central European countries awaiting admission to the Euro after joining the EU in 2004), substitute currencies (no independent currency), or, most likely of all in most cases under present conditions, toward free floating (A. Bubula and I. Otker-Robe, "The evolution of exchange rate regimes since 1990: evidence from de facto policies," *IMF Working Papers*, WP/02/155 [2002]; V. Joshi, "Financial globalization, exchange rates and capital controls in developing countries," Conference on Reinventing Bretton Woods, Madrid, Spain [13–14 May 2003]). In other words, forty-two countries (plus the United States) could claim that they have the main features of "classic" monetary sovereignty. As I later show, the U.S. case is rather more complex than this. In most cases the retreat of central state authority is paralleled by an increasingly complex spatiality of currency flows and regulation. Several recent studies show that a wide range of state economic policy decisions are fundamentally constrained by the type of exchange-rate mechanism and monetary targets that states adopt (e.g., IMF, *Exchange Rate Regimes in an Increasingly Integrated World Economy* [Washington, DC: International Monetary Fund, 2000]; M. Dabrowski, "Is there room for national monetary policy in the era of globalization?" *Eldis* [August 2002]; E. Hochreiter, K. Schmidt-Hebbel, and G. Winckler, *Monetary Union: European Lessons, Latin American Prospects* [Santiago, Chile: Central Bank of Chile Working Papers, number 167, 2002]; Shambaugh, "The effect of fixed exchange rates on monetary policy").

17. Strangely, in some of the macroeconomics literature monetary sovereignty is associated with an independently floating currency (e.g., Dabrowski, "Is there room for national monetary policy in the era of globalization?"). Implicitly, this seems to be the logic also accepted by D. Lake ("Escape from the state of nature"). Why giving up control over a currency to the markets should be seen this way perhaps reflects the classical and neo-classical sensibility that a currency should either "stand and deliver" or go to the wall. It certainly seems to have little or nothing to do with the reality of central state authority as indicated by different exchange-rate mechanisms. Perhaps because since the 1970s the US$ is the floating currency that first comes to mind, all other floaters are assimilated to the one currency for which independently floating is not antithetical to monetary sovereignty. In the contemporary world it is soft-pegged currencies and, perhaps, heavily managed floats, as the closest mechanism to fixed rates, which signify the highest relative degree of central state authority in the monetary realm.

18. Helleiner, "Historicizing territorial currencies"; J. L. Broz, "Origins of the Federal Reserve System: international incentives and the domestic free-rider problem," *International Organization* 53 (1999): 39–70; Goodwin, *Greenback*.

19. R. Martin, "Stateless monies, global financial integration and national economic autonomy: the end of geography?" in S. Corbridge, R. Martin, and N. Thrift (eds.), *Money, Power and Space* (Oxford: Blackwell, 1994); N. Thrift, "On the social and cultural determinants of international financial centres: the case of the City of

London," in S. Corbridge, R. Martin, and N. Thrift (eds.), *Money, Power and Space* (Oxford: Blackwell, 1994).

20. A. M. Taylor, "Global finance: past and present," *Finance and Development* (March 2004), 31.

21. E. Helleiner, "The monetary dimensions of colonialism: why did imperial powers create currency blocs?" *Geopolitics* 7 (2002): 5–30.

22. M. T. Daly, "The road to the twenty-first century: the myths and miracles of Asian manufacturing," in S. Corbridge, R. Martin, and N. Thrift (eds.), *Money, Power, and Space* (Oxford: Blackwell, 1994), 165.

23. P. Marsh, "China reverting to form as the world's workshop," *Financial Times* (11 August 2008): 1; *Economist*, "An old Chinese myth" (5 January 2008): 75; *Economist*, "From Mao to the mall" (16 February 2008): 86.

24. M. Wolf, "Who are the villains and the victims of global capital flows?" *Financial Times* (13 June 2007).

25. A. McSmith, "The dollar's decline: from symbol of hegemony to shunned currency," *Independent* (17 November 2007).

26. F. Bergsten, "A partnership of equals," *Foreign Affairs* (July/August 2008): 62.

27. A fully convertible currency is convertible by any holder for any purpose. Under current account convertibility, as presently operative in China, holders of the renminbi have the right of conversion for purposes such as trade or travel but not for capital account purposes such as making loans or buying foreign assets. Capital account convertibility requires that national monetary authorities monitor the use of funds; under full convertibility, as prevails with fully floating and some types of managed exchange rates, this is not necessary.

28. H. Wang, "China's exchange rate policy in the aftermath of the Asian financial crisis," in J. Kirshner (ed.), *Monetary Orders: Ambiguous Economics, Ubiquitous Politics* (Ithaca, NY: Cornell University Press, 2003).

29. D. Hale and L. H. Hale, "China takes off," *Foreign Affairs* 82 (2003): 36–53.

30. H. Kuroda, "How to help the renminbi find its own level," *Financial Times* (17 October 2003): 15.

31. D. Leblang, "To devalue or defend? The political economy of exchange rate policy," *International Studies Quarterly* 47 (2003): 533–49.

32. *Economist*, "Revaluation by stealth" (12 January 2008): 69.

33. B. Eichengreen, *Globalizing Capital: A History of the International Monetary System* (Princeton, NJ: Princeton University Press, 1996), 99.

34. J. G. Ruggie, "International regimes, transactions, and change: embedded liberalism in the postwar economic order," *International Organization* 36 (1982): 379–415.

35. Eichengreen, *Globalizing Capital*, 116.

36. M. Blyth, "The political power of financial ideas: transparency, risk, and

distribution in global finance," in J. Kirshner (ed.), *Monetary Orders: Ambiguous Economics, Ubiquitous Politics* (Ithaca, NY: Cornell University Press, 2003), 240.

37. E.g., J. Gowa, *Closing the Gold Window: Domestic Politics and the End of Bretton Woods* (Ithaca, NY: Cornell University Press, 1983).

38. Eichengreen, *Globalizing Capital*.

39. Eichengreen, *Globalizing Capital*, 139.

40. S. Strange, "From Bretton Woods to the casino economy," in S. Corbridge, R. Martin, and N. Thrift (eds.), *Money, Power and Space* (Oxford: Blackwell, 1994), 59.

41. R. McKinnon, "The international dollar standard and sustainability of the US current account deficit," *Brookings Panel on Economic Activity: Symposium on the US Current Account* (Washington, DC: Brookings Institution, 2001), 3.

42. McKinnon, "The international dollar standard," 3.

43. R. D. Porter and R. A. Judson, "The location of US currency: how much is abroad?" *Federal Reserve Bulletin*, 82/10 (1996), 883–903; P. Davidson, *Financial Markets, Money, and the Real World* (Cheltenham, UK: Elgar, 2002).

44. McKinnon, "The international dollar standard;" Davidson, *Financial Markets, Money, and the Real World*.

45. IMF, *Exchange Rate Arrangements and Currency Convertibility: Developments and Issues* (Washington, DC: International Monetary Fund, 1997); Hochreiter et al., *Monetary Union*.

46. IMF, *Classification of Exchange Rate Arrangements and Monetary Policy Frameworks* (Washington, DC: International Monetary Fund, 2004).

47. McKinnon, "The international dollar standard," 8.

48. E. Cohen, "The Euro, economic federalism, and the question of national sovereignty," in A. Pagden (ed.), *The Idea of Europe: From Antiquity to the European Union* (New York: Cambridge University Press, 2002).

49. Eichengreen, *Globalizing Capital*, 167.

50. Eichengreen, *Globalizing Capital*, 171–81.

51. M. Chang, "Franco-German interests in European monetary integration: the search for autonomy and acceptance," in J. Kirshner (ed.), *Monetary Orders: Ambiguous Economics, Ubiquitous Politics* (Ithaca, NY: Cornell University Press, 2003).

52. M. Artis, "The Maastricht road to monetary union," *Journal of Common Market Studies* 33 (1992): 299–309.

53. T. Plümper and V. E. Troeger, "Fear of floating and the external effects of currency unions," *American Journal of Political Science* 52 (2008): 656–76.

54. A. Walter, "Domestic sources of international monetary leadership," in D. M. Andrews (ed.), *International Monetary Power* (Ithaca, NY: Cornell University Press, 2006).

55. E. Rosenberg, "Foundations of US international financial power: gold standard diplomacy, 1900–1905," *Business History Review* 59 (1985): 169–202.

56. E. Rosenberg, *Financial Missionaries to the World: The Politics and Culture of Dollar Diplomacy, 1900–1930* (Cambridge, MA: Harvard University Press, 1999), 24.

57. E. Helleiner, *The Making of National Money: Territorial Currencies in Historical Perspective* (Ithaca, NY: Cornell University Press, 2003)

58. S. Maxfield and J. H. Nolt, "Protectionism and the internationalization of capital: US sponsorship of import substitution policies in the Philippines, Turkey, and Argentina," *International Studies Quarterly* 34 (1990): 49–81.

59. Helleiner, *The Making of National Money*, 419.

60. E. Helleiner, "Dollarization diplomacy: US policy towards Latin America coming full circle?" *Review of International Political Economy* 10 (2003): 406–29.

61. Helleiner, *The Making of National Money*, 421.

62. B. J. Cohen, "US policy on dollarization: a political analysis," *Geopolitics* 7 (2002): 63–84.

63. K. P. Jameson, "Dollar bloc dependency in Latin America: beyond Bretton Woods," *International Studies Quarterly* 34 (1990): 519–41.

64. B. M. Doyle, *"Here, Dollars, Dollars . . ." Estimating Currency Demand and Worldwide Currency Substitution* (Washington, DC: Federal Reserve Board of Governors, International Finance Paper Number 657, 2000).

65. S. B. Kamin and N. R. Ericsson, *Dollarization in Latin America* (Washington, DC: Federal Reserve Bank of Governors International Finance Paper Number 460, 1993).

66. G. A. Calvo and C. A. Vegh, "Currency substitution in high inflation countries," *Finance and Development* 30 (1993): 34–37.

67. Cohen, *The Geography of Money*, 112–13.

68. A. Berg, E. Borensztein, and P. Mauro, "Monetary regime options for Latin America," *Finance and Development* (September 2003): 24–27.

69. S. Castles and M. J. Miller, *The Age of Migration: International Population Movements in the Modern World* (New York: St. Martin's Press, 1993); N. Harris, *The New Untouchables: Immigration and the New World Worker* (London: Penguin, 1996); W. M. Spellman, *Uncertain Identity: International Migration since 1945* (London: Reaktion Books, 2008). For a salutary debunking of overclaims about the novelty of contemporary international migration and its character, see A. Favell, "Migration, mobility, and globaloney: metaphors and rhetoric in the sociology of globalization," *Global Networks* 1 (2001): 389–98.

70. *Economist*, "Open up: A special report on migration" (5 January 2008).

71. A. Taylor, "OECD states host 75m migrants," *Financial Times*, 21 February 2008.

72. R. Freeman, "People flows in globalization," *NBER Working Paper 12315* (February 2007), www.nber.org/digest/feb07/w12315.html. In Italy, for example, contrary to popular imagination, only 10 percent of illegal immigrants arrive by

sea. Sixty-three percent come into Italy's airports legally and then "disappear" (*Corriere della Sera*, "I clandestini? Il 63% arriva in aereo," 26 July 2008).

73. The figures in this paragraph are all from Taylor, "OECD states host 75m migrants."

74. *Economist*, "A turning tide?" (26 June 2008).

75. P. Rekacewicz, "The world on the move," *Le Monde Diplomatique*, April 2008, 8–9.

76. Rekacewicz, "The world on the move."

77. C. A. Brewer and T. A. Suchan, *Mapping Census 2000: The Geography of US Diversity* (Redlands, CA: ESRI Press, 2001); C. Hirschman et al. (eds.), *Handbook of International Migration: The American Experience* (New York: Russell Sage Foundation, 2001); R. Hernández-Leon, *Metropolitan Migrants: The Migration of Urban Mexicans to the United States* (Berkeley: University of California Press, 2008).

78. As Rogers Brubaker points out, this is to confuse the notion of diaspora as a conceptual tool with the use of the term as a political one. Diasporas are not just any old immigrant group but precisely those who have no homeland as such and thus must always live on the edge of the world of states. The "classic" ones were the Jewish, Armenian, and Greek diasporas (R. Brubaker, "The 'diaspora' diaspora," *Ethnic and Racial Studies* 28 [2005], 1–19).

79. See, for example, A. Appadurai, *Fear of Small Numbers: An Essay on the Geography of Anger* (Durham, NC: Duke University Press, 2006).

80. D. H. Bennett, *The Party of Fear: The American Far Right from Nativism to the Militia Movement* (New York: Vintage, 1995).

81. So-called Hometown Associations formed by international migrants are an important way in which contacts are maintained. See, for example, D. Fitzgerald, "Colonies of the little motherland: membership, space and time in Mexican migrant Hometown Associations," *Comparative Studies in Society and History* 50 (2008): 145–69. Also see, for some examples of the overstatement of the "in-betweenness" of immigrants criticized by Fitzgerald, P. Ehrkamp and H. Leitner, "Rethinking immigration and citizenship: new spaces of migrant transnationalism and belonging," *Environment and Planning A* 38 (2006): 1591–97.

82. L. Napoleoni, *Rogue Economics: Capitalism's New Reality* (New York: Seven Stories Press, 2008), 218–23; M. Glenny, *McMafia: Crime without Frontiers* (London: Bodley Head, 2008). For an evocative story of attempts by a Moldovan woman to fight the criminal networks involved in trafficking women between Eastern Europe and Central Asia, on the one hand, and the Middle East, on the other, see W. Finnegan, "The countertraffickers: rescuing the victims of the global sex trade," *The New Yorker* (5 May 2008): 44–59.

83. M. I. Choate, "Sending states' transnational interventions in politics, culture, and economics: the historical example of Italy," *International Migration Review* 41 (2007): 728–68; M. I. Choate, *Emigrant Nation: The Making of Italy Abroad*

(Cambridge, MA: Harvard University Press, 2008); J. Torpey, *The Invention of the Passport: Surveillance, Citizenship and the State* (New York: Cambridge University Press, 2000).

84. D. Fitzgerald, *A Nation of Emigrants: How Mexico Manages Its Migration* (Berkeley: University of California Press, 2008). More generally, see F. B. Adamson and M. Demetriou, "Remapping the boundaries of 'state' and 'national identity': incorporating diasporas into IR theorizing," *European Journal of International Relations* 13 (2007): 489–526.

85. Torpey, *The Invention of the Passport.*

86. F. Rampini, "La rivolta. dalla Cina al Golfo Persico. Le lotte dei nuovi clandestini," *La Repubblica* (2 June 2008): 31.

87. H. Motomura, *Americans in Waiting: The Lost Story of Immigration and Citizenship in the United States* (New York: Oxford University Press, 2006). More generally on the issue of undocumented immigration in the U.S. and understandings of citizenship, see L. Bosniak, "Universal citizenship and the problem of alienage," *Northwestern University Law Review* 94 (2000): 963–82; and M. Varsanyi, "Interrogating 'urban citizenship' vis-à-vis undocumented migration," *Citizenship Studies* 10 (2006): 229–49. Ex-post screening also leads to an emphasis on nationwide policing and deportation and away from the bureaucratic rationality of an ex-ante emphasis on matching skills to potential jobs and facilitating family reunion; on this, see, for example, M. Coleman, "Immigration geopolitics beyond the Mexico-US border," *Antipode* 39 (2007): 54–76.

88. Entrepreneurial expatriates, however, find that not having citizenship need be no barrier to their activities. Market position and potential economic performance more than national citizenship thus define the rights and entitlements of various groups (A. Ong, "Mutations in citizenship," *Theory, Culture and Society* 23 [2006]: 499–531).

89. P. J. Spiro, *Beyond Citizenship: American Identity after Globalization* (New York: Oxford University Press, 2008).

90. C. Armstrong, "Contesting the peninsula," *New Left Review* 51 (2008): 115–35.

91. World Bank, Development Prospects Group, 2007. www.worldbank.org/prospects/migrations.

92. One measure of their role, if indirect, is the amount of remittances they generate. At US\$4.2 billion in 2006 this ranks thirteenth in absolute levels of remittances across all countries surveyed (World Bank, Development Prospects Group, 2007, www.worldbank.org/prospects/migrations).

93. Armstrong, "Contesting the peninsula," 134.

94. World Bank, Development Prospects Group, 2007. www.worldbank.org/prospects/migrations.

95. In a recapitulation of the infamous domino metaphor, President Reagan announced that the communist Sandinistas from Nicaragua, if not opposed by the

U.S.-supported Contras, would soon arrive in pick-up trucks at Harlingen on the U.S.-Texas border. Presumably the pick-up trucks would be Japanese to make the metaphor completely "foreign." Instead, as we now know, huge numbers of undocumented immigrants and refugees from El Salvador, Nicaragua, and Guatemala showed up, but usually not in their own pick-up trucks.

96. Spellman, *Uncertain Identity*, 65–67.

97. Spiro, *Beyond Citizenship*, 58.

98. Spiro, *Beyond Citizenship*, 162.

99. World Bank, Development Prospects Group, 2007. www.worldbank.org/prospects/migrations.

100. J. Agnew, "The myth of backward Italy in modern Europe," in B. Allen and M. Russo (eds.), *Revisioning Italy: National Identity and Global Culture* (Minneapolis: University of Minnesota Press, 1997).

101. L. Ricolfi, *Le tre società. E ancora possible salvare l'unità dell'Italia* (Milan: Guerini, 2007); *Economist,* "Addio, dolce vita: A survey of Italy" (26 November 2005); I. Diamanti, "Innocenti evasioni in un clima di complicità," *La Repubblica* (15 October 2006).

102. F. Pastore, P. Monzini, and G. Sciortino, "Schengen's soft underbelly? Irregular migration and human smuggling across land and sea borders to Italy," *International Migration* 44 (2006): 95–119.

103. G. Zincone (ed.), *Familismo legale. Come (non) diventare italiani* (Rome/Bari: Laterza, 2006).

104. A. Colombo and G. Sciortino (eds.), *Stranieri in Italia. Assimilati e esclusi* (Bologna: Il Mulino, 2002).

105. M. C. Chiuri, N. Coniglio, and G. Ferri (eds.), *L'esercito degli invisibili. Aspetti economici dell'immigrazione clandestina* (Bologna: Il Mulino, 2007).

106. I. Diamanti, "La società semichiusa che ha paura del futuro," *La Repubblica* (4 June 2006).

107. S. Brown, "Italy thinks again on immigrants," *International Herald Tribune* (28 May 2008); M. Kimmelman, "Italy gives cultural diversity a lukewarm embrace," *New York Times* (25 June 2008); "Immigrati fra paura e rabbia. L'intolleranza sta crescendo," Sunday Supplement: Metropoli, *La Repubblica* (1 June 2008).

108. D. Bigo and E. Guild (eds.), *Controlling Frontiers: Free Movement into and within Europe* (Aldershot, UK: Ashgate, 2005).

109. World Bank, Development Prospects Group, 2007. www.worldbank.org/prospects/migrations.

110. J. W. Sherman, "The Mexican Miracle and its collapse," in M. C. Meyer and W. H. Beazley (eds.), *The Oxford History of Mexico* (New York: Oxford University Press, 2000); C. Yoshida and A. D. Woodland, *The Economics of Illegal Immigration* (New York: Palgrave Macmillan, 2005).

111. M. Serrano, "Bordering on the impossible: US-Mexico security relations after 9/11," in P. Andreas and T. Biersteker (eds.), *The Rebordering of North*

America: Integration and Exclusion in a New Security Context (New York: Routledge, 2003).

    112. Spellman, *Uncertain Identity*, 67–71.

    113. World Bank, Development Prospects Group, 2007. www.worldbank.org/prospects/migrations.

CHAPTER 5

CONCLUSION

The political world we live in is complicated. That much seems clear. But as co-residents in Plato's famous intellectual cave we can only dimly discern from the shadows on the walls what is going on outside. Making sense of complexity leads us to either oversimplify in terms of some inherited nostrum or to give up entirely and retreat into "case studies"—cases of what we can never be quite sure. Telling the story of sovereignty and globalization is replete with examples of both. The dominant oversimplification today is "the state versus globalization" and the two competing views it engenders as described at some length in chapter 1. Other favorites are such nostrums as "it's all about imperialism" or the operations of a "flat ontology" of networks that are said to have totally eclipsed all types of territorial formations, state-based and otherwise. The only problem is that in being about everything, such approaches say nothing very much about anything. On the other side we have every particular case you might care to name, each totally unique in its specifics and described in exhausting detail. I have tried to provide an alternative approach to both of these viewpoints by providing a set of ideal-type sovereignty regimes, as I dub them, which, while offering a degree of explanatory purchase on the contemporary complexity of state sovereignty under globalization, also tries to provide a better vehicle than the typical single- or two-factor explanation in accounting for the wide range of actual sovereignty situations on the ground.

This approach matters for two main reasons, both of which I wish to say something about by way of conclusion to the overarching argument of the book. One is the tendency in conventional approaches to territorialize politics to the extent that the social sciences as a whole have totally neglected the roles of spatial interaction (plus the so-called networks on which this is based) and of place-making in everyday politics. The globalization versus the state mantra in particular tends to simply reproduce the territorialized view of politics (as I have defined it), if politics matters at all: if in one case by giving "the state" a transcendental significance, in the other seeing the future of politics as lying in a scaling-up of the state to the global level. The only novelty is seen to lie in the fact that globalization is a new process that will make this latter a real possibility. Of course, to some of globalization's proponents, globalization is simply replacing states with markets and thus exchanging politics for the magic of the marketplace. This apparently is a really good thing. Politics will be history.

The other reason why understanding states and globalization in terms of sovereignty regimes matters is that globalization seems to be more geographically differentiating than homogenizing in its effects. In other words, around the world today there is a wide variety of relationships between states, on the one hand, and the different processes of global "shrinkage" and "stretching" that have been labeled as "globalization," on the other. Most of these involve flows through networks and the mobilizing of people in places rather than state-based processes or inter-state relationships. Many places are in fact much less interdependent today—indeed they have become more *isolated* with globalization—than they often were in the past. Yet much conventional wisdom insists on squeezing the vast array of human experiential variety into a one-size-fits-all theorizing that is resolutely state-centric in its vision of how globalization works and that, though it may be satisfying in intra-academic scrimmaging, is not always very much use in understanding how the world actually works in specific places.

POLITICS AND TERRITORY

Much of the privilege accorded state territories as the exclusive settings for politics comes from the coupling of nation (and people) with state discussed at length in chapter 2. This typically rests on an oppositional model of identity (and interests) in which being one of "us" can be established only against "them." Indeed, a case could be made that it is a dominant element in a wide range of types of contemporary social science and political theory that rely theoretically on "othering" as their main socio-geographical mechanism.[1] From this viewpoint, territorial social formations are seen as the root of all identities and interests.[2] The borders between territories are then viewed as defined by opposing and exclusionary identities that *pre-exist* the coming of the actual borders themselves. That this is all something of a social construction was the thrust of part of the argument in chapter 2.

Territories undoubtedly have had and have a number of things going for them from a political perspective. One is straightforwardly instrumental: their spatial extent provides clear borders for institutional and public-goods-based externality fields. If much spending on infrastructure projects (education, highways, etc.), for example, must necessarily be defined territorially and the revenues raised concomitantly, as Michael Mann has argued, then territorial membership is necessary to define who is eligible and who is not to share in the benefits of the projects in question.[3] Thus without territorial restrictions on eligibility, cross-border movements of people would undermine the essentially contractual obligations that underpin both state infrastructural power and the autonomous role of the state that depends on it. As argued in chapter 3, however, the tight correlation between territory and state power (both despotic and infrastructural) need not be so close. Indeed, there is much evidence to the contrary, as I have tried to suggest. Infrastructural power in particular can be extended over space at a distance, as some of the examples of monetary power in chapter 4 imply.

Less liberal or instrumental in their underlying nature are the ways in which territory helps focus the question of political identity and authority. This has four aspects to it. The first and most traditional, as discussed in chapter 2, is the claim to sovereignty and its realization since the eighteenth century as a territorial ideal for a people endowed with self-rule. Typically, all struggles to extend and deepen popular rule, associated usually with such terms as *democracy*, have been bound up with the sovereignty ideal pursued with respect to a given territory. Who shall rule around *here*? has been the rallying cry across all political revolutions, from the English to the American, French, Russian, and Chinese. Thus, as a result, Jeremy Rabkin has defined sovereignty as the "authority to establish what law is binding . . . in a given territory."[4] From this viewpoint, laws can only be enforced when the institutional basis to that law is widely accepted. It depends on popular acceptance and agreement to allow coercion in the absence of compliance. Intuitively, the reach of institutions must begin and it must end somewhere. This is a fairly conservative understanding of both political identity and sovereignty. Beyond it lie several other versions of how political identity and politics are served by territory.

One is that identities themselves, our self-definitions, and the interests that follow from them, are inherently state-territorial, irrespective of whether they rely on definition against others. It is enough that we are for us. Contrary to a liberal sense of the isolated self, from this perspective all identities are based on kinship and extra-kinship ties that bind people together overwhelmingly through the social power of adjacency. From clan and tribe to nation, group membership has been the lever of cultural survival. Rather than merely incidental, territories are intrinsic to group formation and perpetuation. Thus a self-defined political progressive such as Tom Nairn can speak openly of a "social nature" that requires "belonging" and "can be chosen and self-conscious" and that can result in people coming to feel "more strongly—and less ambivalently—about their clan, football team or nation, than about parents, siblings and cousins who directly helped to form them."[5] Many nations today are still actively in pursuit of their very own state with its very own borders.[6] Kurds rioting in Turkey, Ossetians revolting against the government of Georgia, and Tibetans protesting Chinese rule are only three of a myriad of recent examples. Elsewhere, however, there is a revival of spatially complex forms of citizenship, as in Spain and the United Kingdom, where people can simultaneously belong to several polities differentially embedded within existing states.[7] Of course, this was once quite common all over Europe.[8] It is becoming so increasingly again because places other than state territories have become more vital in everyday life as globalization has undermined state borders and opened up national economies to increased competition in which local and regional rather than national conditions are often more important.

In this context, three trends are seen as militating against territories as the solely relevant social facts defining politics. One is that economic organization is increasingly working at odds with a singularly territorialized world. In this construction we are living in a world that is in fact increasingly global and local and decreasingly national. Thus, to Manuel Castells, a world of "flows" is rapidly replacing a world of "places."[9] To others it is more that states are losing their regulatory grip and capital is increasingly footloose. This is sometimes posed as if territorial and networked forms of spatial organization are mutually exclusive with one, typically, the latter, replacing the other. This interpretation is unfortunate insofar as it misses the degree to which territory and spatial interaction have always co-existed as modes of spatiality, as claimed in chapter 3.[10] Nevertheless, it is undeniable that territorial limits to exchange are less effective than they once were because of both technological and geopolitical changes that have enabled more globalized types of social, economic, and political organization.

A second trend is the growth of various international and global regimes concerning human rights and governmental behavior that are spreading into political and judicial practice across a wide range of countries. The universality of claims to equal freedom and the inherent rights attached to one's status as a human rather than a specific nationality strongly suggest that territories should be in question if they pose a barrier to movement of people searching for a better life or seeking to escape from persecution or hide behind them unspeakable crimes of one sort or another (as discussed in chapter 4). As a result, some commentators point out how modes of judicial reasoning increasingly move across international borders.[11]

Finally, a trend noted in chapter 4 is that citizenship is seen by more and more scholars as increasingly labile as regards both its presumed association with a singular political identity and its mutual exclusivity, notwithstanding the many difficulties facing international migrants in establishing residency, never mind citizenship. Thus, Melissa Williams suggests that loyalty is increasingly given to religion, social groups, and political communities other than the nation-state.[12] Other writers, such as Peter Spiro, referred to in chapter 4, make the case for how many people now have multiple citizenships and of how "thin" national citizenship can now be in terms of personal affect. He points out, for example, how few people, once they have a green card in the U.S. guaranteeing them a right of residence, ever actually apply for naturalization to citizenship.[13] Riva Kastoryano makes an ancillary point that increasingly "nations" can be global in character as their members scatter around the world but remain more attached to their putative homeland than to where they actually reside.[14] Examples such as Kurds and Armenians come readily to mind.

A second theme about how territory serves political identity and interests is a broadly social democratic emphasis on how social solidarity within national borders furthers goals such as diminished poverty, increased equality of opportunity, and, given the absence of effective global-level institutions, macroeconomic regulation and stabilization. To Paul Hirst, for example, as sources of power are increasingly "pluralistic," the state becomes even more important in providing a locus for political solidarity. In particular, he writes, "Macroeconomic policy continues to be crucial in promoting prosperity, at the international level by ensuring stability, and at the national and regional levels by balancing co-operation and competition. Governments are not just municipalities in a global market-place."[15] Yet, of course, governments in some respects (particularly, perhaps, for the member states of the EU) are like municipalities in a global arena. They have never been the powerful, autonomous actors that writers such as Hirst allege them to have been. That is perhaps one of the most important conclusions of this book as a whole. The idealized state is precisely that. The fields of control and authority associated with sovereignty have never been either monopolized by states or entirely territorial in their application.

A third connection between territory and politics is made by those who emphasize the idea of "the exception" in relation to state territory. From this viewpoint, associated most closely with the conservative argument of Carl Schmitt about the suspension of law to protect the essence of the state and the radical argument of Giorgio Agamben to the effect that the sovereignty of the state puts the very life of people in doubt depending on their biopolitical classification, territory is absolutely central to the definition of the state.[16] It functions to decide who is inside and who is outside in an essential opposition between the "friends" and "enemies" (or Romans and barbarians) into whom the world is divided for these theorists (see chapter 3).

The "idiom" of the exception has recently become extremely popular in trying to understand various facets of the so-called War on Terror, such as the U.S. prison at Guantánamo Bay, Cuba, and the "rendition" of terrorist suspects between states to avoid writs of habeas corpus and to facilitate the use of torture to extract information and exact confessions.[17] But to Agamben, for example, this signals the onset of something much more dramatic: the exception is everywhere becoming the rule. Citizens are now also inmates or detainees in giant "camps" rather than purposeful agents.

The analogy of the camp (most notably, Auschwitz) can be made to territorial containment the world over. Unfortunately, in departing from much by way of any empirical analysis, this approach neither explains the specific political structures associated with a Guantánamo Bay nor how much the notion of the extra-legal exception adds to the understanding of military interventions, international law, or border controls.[18] Nevertheless, in this perspective, the state is still associated closely with a generic territorialized political imagination. The problem, assuming that the idea itself is necessary when states can do all sorts of things without declaring a state of exception, is that the capacity to enforce one is at best true for a few very powerful states, such as the U.S., Russia, and China, and much less true for all others (chapter 3).

With the rise of a so-called world of flows replacing a world of places, however, the prospect is, at least for those who think politically, to look for a territorial solution. For critics of globalization, such as Hirst, for example, this requires the reinstatement of what I would regard, at least for most of the world's states anyway, as a typically mythic effective sovereignty. Those who lean more positively toward the prospect of a more globalized future see the anarchy around states provoking a popular backlash as some sort of "supranational we-feeling" develops as "norm entrepreneurs" push for institutional processes (such as, e.g., the International Criminal Court) that will inevitably lead to a world state.[19] Paying no attention to the complex spatiality of globalization, this sort of argument simply scales up the political future to the world as a single territory.

In my book, a rather more productive way to think normatively about the consequences for politics of globalization is in terms suggested by those who write of an increasingly "transnational" public sphere in which "for any given problem . . . the relevant public should match the reach of those life-conditioning structures whose effects are at issue."[20] In other words, political reach should match the geographical scope of whatever it is that needs regulating or monitoring beyond not only the borders but also the territorial grasp of any individual state, however powerful and well meaning. Yet at the end of the day we are still ill-equipped to think normatively beyond the bounds of territory. The two primary principles of defining political community, the all-inclusive principle (popular self-determination) and the all-affected principle (all those who have a stake in an issue), have been developed almost entirely in territorial terms. If globalization is to be the midwife of a new global politics, it will need, as Sofia Näsström has forcefully argued, not to reaffirm the nation-state or propose a vacuous cosmopolitan democracy as its totalizing ideals but instead accept "a de-territorialized understanding of legitimacy."[21]

SOVEREIGNTY REGIMES IN A WORLD OF PERSISTING SPATIAL VARIATION

Rather than a trend toward just one sovereignty regime, we can expect continuing pluralization because globalization is not working to produce a singular world but rather a much more differentiated one. Just as some places are becoming more interconnected, others are becoming geographically estranged or continue in subordinate roles with the global division of labor. European (and, later, American) cultural hegemony has thus "written the script" for the growth and consolidation of a global nation-state system. The model of statehood has had as its central geographical moment the imposition of sharp borders between one state unit (imagined as a *nation*-state, however implausible that usually may be) and its neighbors. Previously in world history a wide range of types of polity co-existed without any one—empire, city-state, nomadic network, dynastic state, or religious polity—serving as the singular model of "best political practice." It is only with the rise of Europe to global predominance that an idealized European territorial state became the global archetype. Part of the political tragedy of the contemporary Middle East and Africa, for example, lies in the attempted reconciliation of the Euro-American-style territorial state of sharp borders with ethnic and religious identities distributed geographically in ways that do not lend themselves to it.[22] So-called state- and nation-building (the one rarely clearly distinguished from the other), as in contemporary Iraq and Afghanistan, to name just two examples, is from this viewpoint a futile task. If outsiders have to do it, it will never happen. Beyond this, the idea that there are natural territorial "sovereignties" awaiting awakening or liberation from foreign domination is one of the longest-lasting follies of the intellectual influence of the nationalist movements that "liberated" their peoples from European imperialism in the post–Second World War period.

More fundamentally, perhaps, and important to the overall argument of this book, the range of political arrangements around the world and the distinctive relationships different places have to globalization mandate against seeing state sovereignty in a singular mode. In writing about globalization and sovereignty there has been little commentary on how globalization has been accompanied by a seemingly countervailing process of

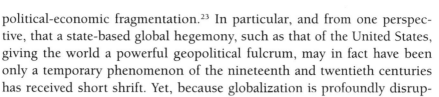

political-economic fragmentation.[23] In particular, and from one perspective, that a state-based global hegemony, such as that of the United States, giving the world a powerful geopolitical fulcrum, may in fact have been only a temporary phenomenon of the nineteenth and twentieth centuries has received short shrift. Yet, because globalization is profoundly disruptive, although hardly destructive, of state territorial identities and interests, a future without a singular hegemonic directorate may well be in the offing.[24] From another perspective, most images of general world order still retain a focus on territorial states and an assumption of "dead space" around them and within them that prevents the possibility of even contemplating alternative geographies of power. A rare writer who does grasp the current moment in much of its complexity, Richard Rosecrance, offers an argument why this is so rare:

> One of the difficulties of most international theory is that it has been analytical rather than historical in character: it has been deterministic rather than contingent. Models have been offered that described one historical age in theoretical terms but failed to account for others. The dynamics of historical development has in this way defeated any purely monistic approach.[25]

On the other side of the debate about globalization from those who remain resolutely state-centric are those who make sweeping claims about the "death of distance," the hypermobility of goods and messages, and postmodern nomads who live permanently on the move. In this frame of reference, economies and cultures are no longer rooted in places. There is no geography at all. But this image of the world depends on two fallacious assumptions. The first is that there once was a totalizing Age of Fixed Territories, based on a "norm of sedentarism," that has now been transcended by technologies of time-space compression.[26] In fact, people and things have been in motion, albeit at slower speeds, for much of human history. What is new about contemporary globalization is the increasingly global dominance of images and practices intimately related to the marketplace society and the speed at which transactions traverse the world. The second is that the global is still intricately interwoven with the local. In one sense there is no such thing as the "global." It exists only as an emergent property; the global is made up of webs of interaction, movement, surveillance, and regulation between people and institutions with discrete locations in particular places. What is new is the density and geographical scope of the weave.

Much of the sociological hype about globalization sees it as synonymous with homogenization, as if the whole world were becoming alike culturally and economically. The literature on time-space compression might also suggest such a prospect, if only on the distant horizon. In fact, there is considerable evidence that globalization is polarizing the world as a whole between geographical haves and have-nots: between regions and localities tied into the globalizing world economy and those outside it (Internet and all) and between those who have received a "leg up" into this economy, on the one hand, and those who may have to remain outside it, on the other.

The first point of note is that the globalizing world economy is not an economy of national territories that trade with one another, notwithstanding the tendency of the World Bank and other international organizations to portray it this way. Rather, it is a complex mosaic of inter-linked global city-regions, prosperous rural areas, resource sites, and "dead lands" increasingly cut off from the technologies of time-space compression that fuel globalization. All of these are widely scattered across the globe, even if there is a basic global north-south structure to the world economy as a whole. Some of the prosperous areas, for example, can be found within even the poorest countries, so it is important to bear the mosaic nature of the emerging world economy in mind throughout the following discussion.[27] The word *mosaic* is used advisedly here, not in the sense that, for example, Peter Taylor associates with a world metageography of territorial states, but as a metaphor for the networked links across places and fractured territoriality that characterizes the new global economy.[28]

In the second place, the major geographical anchors of the new global economy are overwhelmingly located in North America, Europe, and East Asia. For example, during the period 1998–2000, the United States, the EU, and Japan accounted for 75 percent of the inflows of foreign direct investment (FDI) and 85 percent of the outflows, and for almost 60 percent of inward and nearly 80 percent of outward FDI stocks.[29] Trends suggest, however, that since 1985 the U.S. has become relatively less important as both a source and a destination for FDI whereas certain poorer countries have become relatively more important as both destinations and as sources; China, Brazil, South Korea, Mexico, and Malaysia are the outstanding cases.

In this context, therefore, the improved economic performance by some formerly poor countries, predominantly in East and Southeast Asia, is worthy of comment. Since 1987 China has become a major destination for FDI and a major exporter of manufactured goods to the U.S. and elsewhere. Much of this is due to the low wages paid to Chinese factory workers who are as skilled as any in the world. U.S.-headquartered and other multinational companies are thus attracted to China if they have particularly labor-intensive processes of production. But it is also because China has become tightly connected into East Asian business networks anchored to Hong Kong (since 1995 officially part of China but still with a separate administration), Taiwan, and the Chinese diaspora in Southeast Asia and in North America. China's government opened up its economy in the 1980s at precisely the time when wages had begun to increase for workers in such countries as South Korea and Mexico. Not surprisingly, some of China's growth has been at their expense. But the Chinese government has also helped protect and enhance recent national economic growth by freeing local governments and individuals to partner with foreign industries while keeping capital controls and managing the rate of exchange of the currency, the renminbi, against the US$ (see chapter 4). This case illustrates the mix of branch-plant industrialization for export markets, large domestic market, skilled but relatively low-paid labor force, and interventionist government that has lain behind much of the economic success of East Asia since the 1970s.

At the same time, other world regions are on the edge of or are actually falling out of the world economy because they are not attractive to outside investors and, having borrowed heavily in international financial markets to finance national development projects (and elite lifestyles) in the 1970s and 1980s, have become subject to internationally mandated programs of economic restructuring that reflect the dominant neo-liberal ideology of the IMF and global business policy groups more than appropriateness to local circumstances. Large parts of Africa are exemplary. Characteristically, in these cases the economic attributes are more or less the reverse of the ones exhibited by China. In many such countries, however, economic difficulties with declining terms of trade have been exacerbated by disastrous inter-ethnic rivalries, the AIDS epidemic, and a general weakness of state institutions.

States that find themselves in these vastly different situations obviously have very different capacities to establish authority within and beyond the territories that they claim. But the range of possibilities is not just one- or two-fold, a classic territorial state versus a globalized one or a classic one versus an imperialist relationship, for example. As chapter 3 argued, a schema of four sovereignty regimes currently offers much better theoretical purchase on the complexities of a highly differentiated global economy.

The world of spatial variation in economic potentials and political identities is simply too complex for the binary thinking—globalization versus states, markets versus states, etc.—that characterizes so much discussion of sovereignty under contemporary political-economic conditions. Globalization and sovereignty are tied together in a wide variety of ways across the world. We can expect such pluralism to continue.

NOTES

1. For example, in various modalities, A. P. Cohen (ed.), *Symbolizing Boundaries: Identity and Diversity in British Cultures* (Manchester: Manchester University Press, 1986); D. Gregory, *The Colonial Present: Afghanistan, Palestine, Iraq* (Oxford: Blackwell, 2004); D. Bahry et al., "Ethnicity and trust: evidence from Russia," *American Political Science Review* 99 (2005): 521–32.

2. J. Crowley, "Where does the state actually start? The contemporary governance of work and migration," in D. Bigo and E. Guild (eds.), *Controlling Frontiers: Free Movement into and within Europe* (Aldershot, UK: Ashgate, 2005).

3. M. Mann, "The autonomous power of the state: its origins, mechanisms and results," *European Journal of Sociology* 25 (1984): 185–213.

4. J. A. Rabkin, *The Case for Sovereignty: Why the World Should Welcome American Independence* (Washington, DC: AEI Press, 2004), 23.

5. T. Nairn, "The enabling boundary," *London Review of Books* (18 October 2007): 5–7.

6. See, for example, T. Bahcheli et al. (eds.), *De Facto States: The Quest for Sovereignty* (London: Routledge, 2004).

7. M. Berezin and M. Schain (eds.), *Europe without Borders: Remapping Territory, Citizenship and Identity in a Transnational Age* (Baltimore, MD: Johns Hopkins University Press, 2003).

8. D. Ziblatt, *Structuring the State: The Formation of Italy and Germany and the Puzzle of Federalism* (Princeton, NJ: Princeton University Press, 2006); M. Umbach, "Introduction," *European Review of History* 15 (2008): 235–42.

9. M. Castells, *The Rise of Network Society* (Oxford: Blackwell, 1996).

10. J. Agnew, *Hegemony: The New Shape of Global Power* (Philadelphia: Temple University Press, 2005), chapter 3; P. Musso, *Critique des réseaux* (Paris: Presses Universitaires de France, 2003).

11. D. Jacobson, *Rights Across Borders: Immigration and the Decline of Citizenship* (Baltimore, MD: Johns Hopkins University Press, 1996); A-M. Slaughter, "Disaggregated sovereignty: towards the public accountability of global government networks," *Government and Opposition* 39 (2004): 159–90.

12. M. S. Williams, "Nonterritorial boundaries of citizenship," in S. Benhabib

et al. (eds.), *Identities, Affiliations, and Allegiances* (New York: Cambridge University Press, 2007).

13. P. J. Spiro, *Beyond Citizenship: American Identity after Globalization* (New York: Oxford University Press, 2008).

14. R. Kastoryano, "Transnational nationalism: redefining nation and territory," in S. Benhabib et al. (eds.), *Identities, Affiliations, and Allegiances* (New York: Cambridge University Press, 2007).

15. P. Hirst, *From Statism to Pluralism* (London: UCL Press, 1997), 240–41.

16. C. Schmitt, *Political Theology: Four Chapters on the Concept of Sovereignty* (Chicago: University of Chicago Press, 2005 [1922]); G. Agamben, *State of Exception* (Chicago: University of Chicago Press, 2005).

17. See, for example, R. Ek, "Giorgio Agamben and the spatialities of the camp: an introduction," *Geografiska Annaler B* 88 (2006): 363–86.

18. J. Huysmans, "The jargon of exception—on Schmitt, Agamben and the absence of political society," *International Political Sociology* 2 (2008): 165–83.

19. A. Wendt, "Why a world state is inevitable," *European Journal of International Relations* 9 (2003): 491–542.

20. N. Fraser, "Transnationalizing the public sphere: on the legitimacy and efficacy of public opinion in a post-Westphalian world," in S. Benhabib et al. (eds.), *Identities, Affiliations, and Allegiances* (New York: Cambridge University Press, 2007), 63; also see J. Agnew, "The limits of federalism in transnational democracy: beyond the hegemony of the US model," in J. Anderson (ed.), *Transnational Democracy: Political Spaces and Border Crossings* (London: Routledge, 2002).

21. S. Näsström, "What globalization overshadows," *Political Theory* 31 (2003): 829.

22. B. Davidson, *The Black Man's Burden: Africa and the Curse of the Nation-State* (New York: Times Books, 1992).

23. Though see, for example, J. N. Rosenau, *Distant Proximities: Dynamics Beyond Globalization* (Princeton, NJ: Princeton University Press, 2003). Rosenau, unfortunately, cannot envisage any place for regions and localities because his view of geography reduces to a two-sided either/or of presumably territorial states or placeless networks. This polarity plagues much writing about globalization as if it were synonymous with de-territorialization and together both represent the "end of geography," as if territory was all there was to it.

24. Agnew, *Hegemony: The New Shape of Global Power*.

25. R. Rosecrance, *The Rise of the Trading State: Commerce and Conquest in the Modern World* (New York: Basic Books, 1986), 67.

26. D. Morley, *Home Territories: Media, Mobility and Identity* (London: Routledge, 2000).

27. J. Agnew and S. Corbridge, *Mastering Space: Hegemony, Territory, and International Political Economy* (London: Routledge, 1995), 167–68.

28. P. J. Taylor, *World City Network* (London: Routledge, 2004).

29. UNCTAD, *World Investment Report* (New York: United Nations, 2001), 13.

INDEX